PHONICS for the
TEACHER OF READING
Programmed for Self-Instruction

Ninth Edition

Barbara J. Fox
North Carolina State University

PEARSON
Merrill
Prentice Hall

Upper Saddle River, New Jersey
Columbus, Ohio

Library of Congress Cataloging-in-Publication Data

Fox, Barbara J.
    Phonics for the teacher of reading: programmed for self-instruction / Barbara J. Fox.—
9th ed.
        p. cm.
    Includes bibliographical references.
    ISBN 0-13-117799-0
    1. Reading—Phonetic method—Programmed instruction. 2. Teaching—Aids and devices.
I. Title.

LB1573.3.F69 2006
372.46'5—dc22

2004061099

Vice President and Publisher: Jeffery W. Johnston
Editor: Linda Ashe Montgomery
Production Editor: Mary M. Irvin
Design Coordinator: Diane C. Lorenzo
Project Coordination and Text Design: Amy Gehl, Carlisle Publishers Services
Cover Design: Linda Sorrells-Smith
Cover Photo: Images.com
Production Manager: Pamela D. Bennett
Director of Marketing: Ann Castel Davis
Marketing Manager: Darcy Betts Prybella
Marketing Coordinator: Brian Mounts

This book was set in New Baskerville by Carlisle Communications, Ltd., and was printed and bound by
Courier Stoughton. The cover was printed by Courier Stoughton.

Pearson Education Ltd.
Pearson Education Singapore Pte. Ltd.
Pearson Education Canada, Ltd.
Pearson Education—Japan

Pearson Education Australia Pty. Limited
Pearson Education North Asia, Ltd
Pearson Educatión de Mexico, S.A. de C.V.
Pearson Education Malaysia Pte. Ltd

10 9 8 7 6 5 4 3 2
ISBN: 0-13-117799-0

Preface

This text presents the content of phonics as one strategy for identifying and learning new words. A knowledge of phonics is important because the English language writing system is based on the alphabetic principle—the principle that letters represent speech sounds. For classroom teachers, reading teachers, and special education teachers who will soon be entering teaching for the first time, learning the content of phonics will help you better understand the teaching methods and materials you will be using in your classroom. For practicing classroom, reading, and special education teachers, studying the content of this book will sharpen your knowledge of phonics, onsets and rimes, and how syllables affect pronunciation. I hope the information in the chapters, study guides, and appendices in this book will not only help you learn how the alphabetic principle works in English but also give you a resource you can turn to in future years as you make decisions about the teaching of phonics.

How Is This Text Organized?

Phonics for the Teacher of Reading is a self-paced program of instruction that has proven to be a useful technique for presenting phonics background knowledge to future and practicing teachers. The text will guide you through a series of small steps to help you learn the terminology associated with phonics, and clinch your understanding of letter and sound relationships, onsets and rimes, and how syllables affect pronunciation.

Thirteen study guides are interspersed throughout the text to help you review and to provide you with a quick source of information. To assist you in applying your knowledge while teaching, appendices list all the letter and sound relationships of phonics, and the key English sounds (phonemes) and words that represent these sounds. Scattered throughout the book are 10 boxed features that explain some of the more intriguing aspects of the history of our alphabet. These selections take a closer look at a few of the sounds of language and explain the reasons we use certain letters and letter combinations in our language today. These brief accounts will enhance your insight into, and appreciation for, our American-English spelling system.

New to This Revision

To further assist you in your study, this latest revision of *Phonics for the Teacher of Reading* includes more detailed explanations of how words are divided into syllables and how we determine which syllable in a multisyllable word receives the strongest stress, or accent. The revision also provides an explanation of the distinction between phonological awareness and phonemic awareness, and makes more explicit the various activities teachers might use to develop phonemic awareness. To help you solidify your understanding of letter and sound relationships, you will find a comprehensive Review of Phonemes in Part IV with page numbers telling you where information is located in the text. A brief history of the events that shaped English spelling will give you insight into how our English spelling system evolved and why spelling is not always a perfect match for sound. You will read a concise overview of the research foundation for teaching phonics just before you begin your study of the content of phonics. I hope this brief review will help you think about the letter and sound relationships of phonics, as explained in this book, within the context of effective phonics teaching practices, and the contribution phonics makes to reading achievement.

Acknowledgments

I would like to thank the reviewers of this text. I appreciate their insightful guidance: Phyllis Y. Coulter, Eastern Mennonite University; Patricia P. Fritchie, Troy State University, Dothan; Cindy Hendricks, Bowling Green State University; Ginny Muller, Saginaw Valley State University; Mahmoud Suleiman, California State University, Bakersfield; and Ann A. Wolf, Gonzaga University.

Educator Learning Center:
An Invaluable Online Resource

Merrill Education and the Association for Supervision and Curriculum Development (ASCD) invite you to take advantage of a new online resource, one that provides access to the top research and proven strategies associated with ASCD and Merrill—the Educator Learning Center. At **www.educatorlearningcenter.com**, you will find resources that will enhance your students' understanding of course topics and of current issues, in addition to being invaluable for further research.

How the Educator Learning Center Will Help Your Students Become Better Teachers

With the combined resources of Merrill Education and ASCD, you and your students will find a wealth of tools and materials to better prepare them for the classroom.

Research
- More than 600 articles from the ASCD journal *Educational Leadership* discuss everyday issues faced by practicing teachers.
- A direct link on the site to Research Navigator™ gives students access to many of the leading education journals, as well as extensive content detailing the research process.
- Excerpts from Merrill Education texts give your students insights on important topics of instructional methods, diverse populations, assessment, classroom management, technology, and refining classroom practice.

Classroom practice
- Hundreds of lesson plans and teaching strategies are categorized by content area and age range.
- Case studies and classroom video footage provide virtual field experience for student reflection.
- Computer simulations and other electronic tools keep your students abreast of today's classrooms and current technologies.

Look into the Value of the Educator Learning Center Yourself

A 4-month subscription to Educator Learning Center is $25 but is **FREE** when packaged with any Merrill Education text. In order for your students to have access to this site, you must use this special value-pack ISBN number **WHEN** placing your textbook order with the bookstore: 0-13-186208-1. Your students will then receive a copy of the text packaged with a free ASCD pincode. To preview the value of this website to you and your students, please go to **www.educatorlearningcenter.com** and click on "Demo."

Contents

Part III   Vowels   101

Part IV   A Review of the Phonemes   157

Part V   Onset and Rime   175

Part VI   Syllabication and Accent   187

Self-Evaluation I:

A Pretest

This is a test designed to give an indication of your present knowledge in the field of phonics. Read each item, including <u>all</u> the choices. Indicate the answer you consider best by circling the appropriate letter (a, b, c, d, or e) or marking the appropriate letter on an answer sheet. Be sure to respond to every item. Time: 30 minutes.

I. Multiple Choice. Select the best answer.

1. A requirement of a syllable is that

   a. it contain at least one consonant letter.
   b. it contain no more than one vowel letter.
   c. it contain no more than one vowel phoneme.
   d. it contain no more than one phoneme.
   e. All of the above

2. Which of the following most adequately completes the sentence? The consonant speech sounds in the American-English language are represented by

   a. the distinctive speech sounds we associate with the 21 consonant letters of the alphabet.
   b. 18 of the consonant letters of the alphabet plus certain digraphs.
   c. the single-letter consonants plus their two- and three-letter blends.
   d. The American-English language is too irregular to represent the consonant speech sounds with any degree of accuracy.

3. The letter *y* is most likely to be a consonant when

   a. it is the first letter in a word or syllable.
   b. it is the final letter in a word or syllable.
   c. it follows *o* in a syllable.
   d. it has the sound of *i* as in *might*.
   e. None of the above

4. Generally, when two like-consonants appear together in a word,
    a. only one is sounded.
    b. one is sounded with the first syllable and the other with the second.
    c. both are sounded when the preceding vowel is *i.*
    d. both are sounded when the following vowel is *e.*
    e. neither is sounded.

5. The second syllable of the nonsense word *alithpic* would be expected to rhyme with
    a. aright.
    b. brick.
    c. kith.
    d. pyth (as in python).
    e. hit.

6. The open syllable in the nonsense word *botem* would most likely rhyme with
    a. coat.
    b. hot.
    c. rah.
    d. low.
    e. gem.

7. A diphthong is best illustrated by the vowels representing the sound of
    a. *ow* in *snow.*
    b. *ou* in *mouse.*
    c. *oo* in *foot.*
    d. *ai* in *said.*
    e. a and b

8. The sound of the schwa is represented by
    a. the *a* in *baited.*
    b. the *e* in *early.*
    c. the *e* in *happen.*
    d. the *w* in *show.*
    e. All of these

9. How many phonemes are represented in *knight?*
    a. one   b. two   c. three   d. four   e. six

10. An example of a closed syllable is
    a. desk.
    b. hot.
    c. tight.
    d. All of these
    e. None of these

11. The consonant cluster is illustrated by
    a. the *sh* in *shirt.*
    b. the *ng* in *thing.*
    c. the *ph* in *graph.*
    d. the *br* in *brought.*
    e. a, c, and d

12. Which of the following has an incorrect diacritical mark?
    a. căll   **b.** sĕll   **c.** ĭll   **d.** hŏt   **e.** ŭp

13. Which of the following has an incorrect diacritical mark?
    a. māde   **b.** sēe   **c.** tīme   **d.** lōve   **e.** ūse

14. When the single vowel *i* in an accented syllable is followed by a single consonant and a final *e,* the *i* would most likely have the sound of
    a. the *i* in *active.*
    b. the *y* in *my.*
    c. the *i* in *easily.*
    d. the first *e* in *bee.*
    e. None of the above

15. If *o* were the only and final vowel in an accented syllable, that *o* would most likely represent the same sound as
    a. the *o* in *nothing.*
    b. the *a* in *wanted.*
    c. the *o* in *do.*
    d. the *ew* in *sew.*
    e. None of these

16. The letter *q* could be removed from the alphabet because it could adequately and without conflict be represented by
    a. the "soft sound of *c.*"
    b. *ch* as in *chair.*
    c. *k* as in *keep.*
    d. All of the above
    e. The idea is foolish; *qu* represents a distinctive consonant sound.

17. If *a* were the single vowel in an accented syllable ending with one or more consonants, that *a* would most likely represent the same sound as
    a. the *ai* in *plaid.*
    b. the *ay* in *ray.*
    c. the *a* in *all.*
    d. the *a* in *any.*
    e. None of these

18. When *oa* appear together in a syllable, they usually represent the same sound as
    a. the *o* in *bottle.*
    b. the *o* in *labor.*
    c. the *o* in *toil.*
    d. the *o* in *come.*
    e. None of these

19. The symbol *s* is used in the dictionary to show the pronunciation of the sound heard in
    a. shall.   **b.** his.   **c.** sugar.   **d.** seem.   **e.** Both b and d

20. If *e* were the only vowel in an open syllable; the *e* would most likely represent the same sound as
    a. the *e* in *pine.*
    b. the *ea* in *meat.*
    c. the *y* in *my.*
    d. the *e* in *set.*
    e. None of these

21. The word *if* ends with the same sound as
    a. the *ph* in *graph.*
    b. the *f* in *of.*
    c. the *gh* in *taught.*
    d. the *gh* in *ghetto.*
    e. a and b

22. The letter *c* followed by *i* is most likely to represent the same sound as
    a. the *s* in *sent.*
    b. the *c* in *cello.*
    c. *c* followed by *o.*
    d. *c* followed by *e.*
    e. Both a and d

23. The letter *g* followed by *o* is most likely to represent the same sound as
    a. the *j* in *joke.*
    b. the *g* in *ghost.*
    c. the *g* in *swing.*
    d. *g* followed by *e.*
    e. Both a and d

II. Multiple Choice. Where does the accent fall in the words or nonsense words given at the left? Indicate your answer by selecting the last two letters of the accented syllable found in the same row as the word.

Look at the example: *showboat.* The first "word" in a compound word is generally accented: *show' boat.* Look for the last two letters of *show, ow,* in the row to the right. You would circle b or mark b on your answer sheet.

Example:

showboat   **a.** ho   (**b.**) ow   **c.** bo   **d.** at

24. contract (noun)   **a.** co   **b.** on   **c.** nt   **d.** ra   **e.** ct
25. frottomly   **a.** ro   **b.** ot   **c.** to   **d.** om   **e.** ly
26. plargain   **a.** la   **b.** ar   **c.** rg   **d.** ga   **e.** in
27. desridly   **a.** de   **b.** es   **c.** ri   **d.** id   **e.** ly
28. cidaltion   **a.** ci   **b.** id   **c.** da   **d.** al   **e.** on
29. phight   **a.** hi   **b.** ig   **c.** gh   **d.** ht

III. Multiple Choice. There are three "words" in each item (a, b, c). Select the word in which you would hear the same sound as that represented by the underlined part of the word at the left. You may find that the sound is heard in all three words; if so, mark d. If none of the words contain the sound, mark e.

30. men<u>ti</u>on   **a.** special   **b.** sugar   **c.** machine   **d.** All   **e.** None
31. <u>th</u>e   **a.** thistle   **b.** mother   **c.** think   **d.** All   **e.** None
32. <u>j</u>et   **a.** gnome   **b.** gentle   **c.** sang   **d.** All   **e.** None
33. in<u>t</u>o   **a.** thick   **b.** watch   **c.** hoped   **d.** All   **e.** None
34. su<u>cc</u>ess   **a.** cheese   **b.** knee   **c.** queer   **d.** All   **e.** None
35. <u>h</u>ome   **a.** honor   **b.** night   **c.** who   **d.** All   **e.** None
36. t<u>a</u>ll   **a.** talk   **b.** fault   **c.** gnaw   **d.** All   **e.** None
37. f<u>oo</u>d   **a.** look   **b.** blood   **c.** bought   **d.** All   **e.** None
38. b<u>oi</u>l   **a.** mouse   **b.** employ   **c.** riot   **d.** All   **e.** None
39. w<u>ou</u>ld   **a.** whom   **b.** once   **c.** cow   **d.** All   **e.** None
40. sa<u>ng</u>   **a.** ranger   **b.** ponder   **c.** thinker   **d.** All   **e.** None

IV. Multiple Choice. Select the letter(s) at the right that represents the onset in each one-syllable word.

41. splurge   **a.** sp   **b.** ge   **c.** lur   **d.** spl   **e.** urge
42. cherry   **a.** ch   **b.** erry   **c.** her   **d.** cher   **e.** erry
43. throw   **a.** thr   **b.** ro   **c.** ow   **d.** th   **e.** row
44. fluid   **a.** uid   **b.** id   **c.** lui   **d.** fl   **e.** flu
45. roast   **a.** roa   **b.** oa   **c.** st   **d.** oast   **e.** r

V. Multiple Choice. Select the letter(s) at the right that represents the rime in each one-syllable word.

46. steam	**a.** ea	**b.** eam	**c.** st	**d.** team	**e.** ste
47. rhyme	**a.** rh	**b.** yme	**c.** rhy	**d.** hyme	**e.** rhy
48. catch	**a.** atch	**b.** tch	**c.** cat	**d.** ch	**e.** at
49. school	**a.** ch	**b.** choo	**c.** ool	**d.** hool	**e.** sch
50. dress	**a.** ess	**b.** dr	**c.** dre	**d.** ress	**e.** re

VI. Multiple Choice. Select the word in each row that is <u>incorrectly</u> syllabicated.

51. **a.** ro bot	**b.** ro bin	**c.** ro bust	**d.** ro tor	**e.** rouge
52. **a.** let hal	**b.** rab bit	**c.** re cov er	**d.** mer cy	**e.** con nect
53. **a.** un der line	**b.** un e qual	**c.** un ite	**d.** pre dic a ment	**e.** re mit
54. **a.** home work	**b.** book man	**c.** eye ball	**d.** now here	**e.** egg nog

VII. Complete each sentence by selecting the word for which the correct pronunciation is indicated.

55. I went to the park for a

a. pĭc′nĭc   **b.** wôk   **c.** rəst   **d.** păr′tē   **e.** rĭde

56. When I picked my vegetables, I dropped a

a. lĕt′ĭs lēv   **b.** kūk′ŭm bər   **c.** kăr′ŏt   **d.** kăb′ĭg   **e.** bēt

57. The tree we planted was a

a. pälm   **b.** wĭl′ou   **c.** māp′le   **d.** kŏt′ ən wŭd   **e.** sĭk′ə môr

58. I went to the men's store to get (a)

a. sŏgz   **b.** sho͞oz   **c.** trou′sərs   **d.** chərt   **e.** nək′ tī′

59. The wall is

a. krăkt   **b.** smo͞oth   **c.** rôf   **d.** pānt əd′   **e.** t͡hĭk

60. The comittee was composed of

a. klûr′ gĭ mĕn   **b.** bo͞ok mĭn′   **c.** băngk′ ərz   **e.** tē zhərs   **e.** jŭd′jĭs

(See p. 227 for answers to Self-Evaluation I.)

Number correct _____

Part I

General Knowledge and Terminology

What kind of background do you have in phonics? To help determine the depth of your present knowledge or lack of knowledge, and to aid in evaluating your growth, this text includes a pretest and a posttest. Do not examine the posttest now. You may wish to remove the posttest and file it away, awaiting the completion of your study of this programmed text.

Turn to page 1 and take the pretest now. Correct it. At your next sitting, turn back to this section and continue reading.

Now that you have completed the pretest, you are ready to continue with this program.

Events That Shaped English Spelling

The English language did not exist in the middle of the fifth century when three Germanic tribes, the Angles, the Saxons, and the Jutes, sailed across the North Sea and marched onto the shores of the British Isles. There they found the Celts, a peace-loving people who were overwhelmed by the invaders. The Saxons became the dominant tribe and, eventually, distinctions among the tribes disappeared. As the Anglo-Saxons settled down to life in their new homeland, their Germanic-based language began to change. These naturally occurring changes marked the beginning of the English language.

The early Anglo-Saxons were relatively illiterate (Bryson, 1990). Their meager use of the runic alphabet left few records, save for inscriptions on stones used in religious ceremonies. All this changed at the end of the sixth century when monks made their way into Great Britain, bringing with them the Christian religion, the Roman alphabet, and literacy (Burnley, 2000). As literacy spread across Great Britain, scribes used the Roman alphabet (with some modifications) to create a written record of regional dialects.

The imported Roman alphabet had only 26 letters to represent approximately 44 English sounds (phonemes). The problem of too few letters could have been solved by inventing new letters or using diacritical marks to indicate pronunciation.

Rather than add letters or use diacritical marks, English made up for the shortfall by combining letters (*oi* and *oo*, for instance), forming letter patterns (the final, silent *e* indicating that the preceding single vowel is long), and using one letter to represent more than one sound (the *o* in *hot, doll,* and *for,* for example).

The spelling of many English words had not yet been established when the French-speaking Normans conquered Great Britain in 1066, and legions of French-speaking scribes poured into England. When asked to spell English words, a language they did not know, the scribes turned to letter combinations related to French spelling, introducing into the English spelling system combinations such as *qu, ou,* and *ch.* The Normans more or less ignored English, a second-class language spoken only by the working classes. The Norman French indifference created a fertile climate in which many different English dialects developed. Dialectical variation is significant because it affected English spelling when the speakers of one dialect adopted the spellings of another (Bryson, 1990).

Wholesale borrowing from classical languages also affected English spelling. In the 17th century zealous scholars borrowed words from the Latin and Greek languages, perhaps in the belief that these two respected languages would raise the stature of English. Not only did the scholars borrow from Latin and Greek, but they also changed the spelling of some existing English words to suggest a Latin influence, even though the spellings were not particularly consistent with English pronunciation.

By the mid-17th century, the English language spelling system was more or less standardized. Unfortunately, this standardization was quickly followed by a shift in pronunciation (Burnley, 2000). For example, the initial k (knight), g (gnat), some instances of initial w (write), and the l in some positions (chalk) were no longer pronounced. As a consequence, some contemporary spellings represent 17th century pronunciation (Bryson, 1990).

English spelling continues to change and evolve in the 21st century (Burnley, 2000). Pronunciation is changing, and foreign words (*peso*) are finding their way into English. Yet in spite of military intervention and social change, the use of only 26 letters to represent 44 sounds, and a plethora of foreign words entering the English language, phonics still gives readers insight into pronunciation. This brings us to a discussion of research on the teaching of phonics.

What Does the Research Say About Teaching Phonics?

Phonics is the relationship among the letters of our alphabetic writing system and the sounds in spoken words, as well as approaches for teaching these relationships. Phonics, reading comprehension, and listening comprehension are highly interdependent (Hagtvet, 2003). The better the phonics skills the greater the likelihood that students will understand what they read and hear (Carver, 2003).

Learning phonics has substantial, long-lasting effects on reading ability (Torgesen, Alexander, Wagner, Rashotte, Voeller, & Conway, 2001). Phonics contributes to developing skill in word identification, a large vocabulary of instantly recognized words (Aaron et al., 1999; Connelly, Johnston, & Thompson, 2001), the ability to spell, and the ability to read independently (National Reading Panel, 2000), regardless of the students' social or economic backgrounds (Armbruster, Lehr, & Osborn, 2001). Furthermore, beginning readers who use phonics have more positive concepts of themselves as readers than students who only use picture clues, meaning clues, and word order (syntactic) clues (Tunmer & Chapman, 2002).

Research shows that learning phonics increases the achievement of struggling readers who have an incomplete understanding of letter and sound relationships (Torgesen, 2004). Phonics instruction helps to prevent reading problems in students at risk of reading difficulties (Ehri, Nunes, Stahl, & Willows, 2001), and to close the achievement gap between struggling and average readers (Foorman, Chen, Carlson, Moats, Francis, & Fletcher, 2003; Hatcher, Hulme, & Snowling, 2004; National Reading Panel, 2000; Torgesen, Alexander, Wagner, Rashotte, Voeller, & Conway, 2001).

Phonics instruction is most effective when it is early, intense, direct, and systematic (National Reading Panel, 2000), combined with instruction in reading comprehension (Berninger, et al., 2003), taught throughout the day, and integrated into ongoing classroom instruction in spelling (Ehri, 2004). Even so, the same amount and intensity of phonics instruction is not equally beneficial for all of the students whom we teach. Students who begin school with good letter knowledge require less intense instruction than their classmates with relatively limited knowledge (Juel & Minden-Cupp, 2004; Torgesen, 2004).

An extensive body of research evidence shows that phonemic awareness—the understanding that words consist of sounds and the ability to act on this understanding (explained in the next portion of this section)—is necessary for using phonics and for success in reading (National Reading Panel, 2000). Researchers agree that teaching phonics along with phonemic awareness is more effective than teaching either of these skills separately (Foorman, Chen, Carlson, Moats, Francis, & Fletcher, 2003; Hatcher, Hulme, & Snowling, 2004; Qudeans, 2003).

Effective phonics instruction also includes the teacher modeling how and when to use phonics (Goswami, 2001; Nation, Allen, & Hulme, 2001; Schunk, 2003), and opportunities for students to apply phonics as they read and write (Juel & Roper-Schneider, 1985). In order for you, the teacher, to be effective in the teaching of phonics you need to understand how written English uses the 26 letters of the alphabet to represent as many as 44 different speech sounds.

spoken	**1.** The language of any people is the <u>sound</u> system by which the individuals communicate with one another. The written language is merely a system of <u>symbols</u>, a code, used to represent the _____ language. (written, spoken)
code (or symbols)	**2.** Therefore, one of the basic steps in the reading process is **decoding:** translating the _____ into the sounds of the spoken language.
symbols (or code)	**3.** We study phonics to learn the code so that we can translate the written _____ into the spoken sounds. But, to our regret, the code is not perfect; part of our study involves its inconsistencies. We shall begin our study by examining the basic elements of the code, the **phoneme** and the **grapheme.**
phoneme	**phoneme grapheme** **4.** The suffix *eme* denotes a basic structural element of a language. *Phon* (tele<u>phone</u>, <u>phon</u>ograph, etc.) refers to voice or sound. One speech sound is called a _____ (*phon + eme*).
sound	**5.** These word-pairs illustrate the definition of a phoneme. As you pronounce each pair, notice the sound that makes the top word different from the one beneath it. *p<u>i</u>n* *p<u>i</u>n* *p<u>i</u>n* *p<u>i</u>n* <u>t</u>in p<u>e</u>n pi<u>t</u> <u>ch</u>in **A phoneme is the smallest unit of _____ that distinguishes one word from another.**
t	**6.** To attain a better understanding of a phoneme, let us examine these words more closely. How does *pin* differ from *tin*? *pin* *tin* The sounds <u>represented</u> by the *p* and the _____ are the smallest units of sound that distinguish *pin* from *tin*.

sound i, e	**7.** Compare the phonemes represented by the underlined letters *pin* in the set of words at the right. *pen* Remember that the phoneme is a _____ , so say the words aloud. The sounds that are represented by the _____ and the _____ are the smallest units that distinguish *pin* from *pen*.
n, t	**8.** Pronounce the words at the right. The sounds that are *pin* represented by the _____ and the _____ *pit* are the smallest units that distinguish *pin* from *pit*.
/r/ /p/	**9.** We can hear sounds, but we cannot write sounds. For example, we cannot write the sound of I. We can say, "the sound represented by I," or "the phoneme recorded by I." There is also a symbol, / /, which indicates that we are referring to the phoneme of the specific letter or letters enclosed with slashes: /I/: How will we write symbolically the phoneme we associate with the letter *r?* _____ The phoneme represented by the key symbol *p?* _____ **The symbol /b/ refers to the phoneme represented by the key symbol b.**

BOX 1.1

Green Glass or Green Grass?

Two English Phonemes

Use your knowledge of the phonemes in the English language to answer the three questions below. Read each question aloud, and write the answer on the line.

   1. The second phoneme in *glass* and the second phoneme in *grass* are _____.
                                                                (the same, different)

   2. The first phoneme in *late* is _____ the first phoneme in *rate*.
                          (the same as, different from)

   3. *Fire* and *file* are _____ English words.
                   (the same, different)

   The /r/ and /l/ phonemes (here presented between two slashes) are distinctly different in the English language. Therefore, you hear two separate phonemes and, by extension, two different words when you pronounce *glass* and *grass*. These phonemes, which are entirely distinct to you, a fluent speaker of the English language, are not so distinct and so simple to differentiate for native speakers of the Japanese language.

   The Japanese language does not have an equivalent phoneme for the English /r/. Because the Japanese r is a combination of the English /r/ and /l/, speakers of Japanese may perceive the /l/ and the /r/ as variations (allophones) of the same phoneme. Not only do speakers of the Japanese language have difficulty in distinguishing the English language /r/ from the /l/, but they may well confuse these two phonemes when pronouncing English words, perhaps saying "grass" when the intended word is "glass."

   We listen for and perceive those phonemic differences and similarities that are particular to the language that we speak. Not all languages share exactly the same phonemes, however. Children bring to your classroom, and to the speaking, reading, and writing of the English language, an awareness of the phonemes in their home, or native, languages. You can, therefore, anticipate that some children who speak Japanese as their first language may occasionally confuse the /r/ and /l/ when pronouncing, reading, and spelling English words. When children who learn to speak English as a second language have opportunities to hear, speak, read, and write English in your classroom, they develop greater sensitivity to the English language sound structure and, in so doing, create mental categories for those English phonemes that differ from the phonemes in their native language.

allophone	**allophone** **10.** *Allo*(*o*) denotes a variant form (allegory, parallel). We have learned that *phon* refers to the voice or sound (phoneme, telephone). A variant form of the same phoneme is called an _____ (*allo* + *phone*).
no allophones /b/	**11.** Pronounce the words at the right. Listen carefully to the sound represented by the underlined letter. Do you hear precisely the same sound in each word? _____ The (yes, no) slight variations in pronunciation are called _____. How would you symbolically represent the phoneme? _____
phoneme	**12.** The first sound in *pin,* the second sound in *spin,* and the last sound in *stop* are allophones. Even though we pronounce the allophones differently, we treat them as the same _____.
allophones phonemes	**13.** Let us review what we have learned about allophones and phonemes. Allophones are variant forms of a single phoneme. The sounds represented by the underlined letters in the first set of words are _____. The underlined letters in the second set of words represent two different _____. It is the phonemes that are important for learning phonics.
grapheme	**14.** Sounds cannot be written! Letters do not speak! We use a letter or letters to <u>represent</u> a phoneme. *Graph* means "drawn, written, recorded." The _____ (*graph* + *eme*) is the written representation of the phoneme. It is the unit in the written code.
p i n *p i n*	**15.** When you say the word *pin,* you hear three phonemes. We represent these three phonemes with the letters _____ _____ _____. Put another way, the three graphemes in *pin* are _____ _____ _____. **The grapheme is the written representation of the phoneme. As the phoneme is the unit in the sound system, the grapheme is the unit in the written code.**

Words at right of item 11:
bee
brown
lab
blue
tub

Words at right of item 13:
bag
brag

bat
pat

BOX 1.2   ✕◇✕◇✕

An Allophone Adventure

You have learned that allophones are naturally occurring variations in the phonemes of the English language. You know that, if you listen carefully, you can hear these slight variations. For example, you can identify variations in /b/ as it is pronounced in the words *brick, crab,* and *blank.* But can you also feel the difference when you pronounce some allophones? Try this to find out.

1. Put your hand in front of your mouth, palm toward your face and fingers near your lips.

2. Say "pin." Notice that you feel a puff of air when pronouncing the /p/ in *pin.* Phonemes that produce a puff of air are called aspirated.

3. Say "spin." Notice that you do not feel a puff of air when pronouncing the /p/ in *spin.* Phonemes that do not produce a puff of air are called unaspirated. When /p/ follows /s/ in English words, /p/ is unaspirated (*spoon, speed*).

Although the /p/ in *pin* is aspirated and the /p/ in *spin* is unaspirated, we treat them as the same sound because each is an allophone of the same English phoneme, the /p/.
     You have now demonstrated, through this experiment, that the aspirated and unaspirated allophones of /p/ can, indeed, be both heard and felt.

phonemes one	**16.** Reread frame 5. We used word-pairs to illustrate the *pin* definition of a phoneme. When you said the word *chin*, you *chin* heard three _____. *Ch* represents <u>one</u> unit of sound; you cannot divide it. Since the grapheme is the written representation of the phoneme, *ch* is _____ grapheme(s). (How many?)
ch i n *ch*	**17.** We represent the three phonemes in *chin* with the graphemes _____ _____ _____. The sounds represented by the *p* and the _____ are the smallest units of sound that distinguish *pin* from *chin.*
ch	**18.** We represent the first phoneme in the word *chart* with the grapheme _____.
phoneme	**19.** A grapheme is the written symbol of the _____. It may be composed of one or more letters.

grapheme phoneme graphemes k, c, q	**20.** The phoneme is a speech sound. The _____ is composed of the symbols we use to picture the sound on paper. Say the words at the right. In each one you will hear the _____ that *keep* we commonly associate with the underlined grapheme. *come* *quit* Three different _____ are used to represent this phoneme. They are _____, _____, and _____.
three, three w, a, sh sh	**21.** Grapheme and letter are not synonymous. A grapheme never consists of less than a letter, but it may consist of more than one letter. The grapheme represents the phoneme. Examine the word *wash. w a sh* Say it aloud. Wash consists of _____ phonemes. Therefore, it consists of _____ graphemes—one grapheme to represent each phoneme. The graphemes are _____, _____, and _____. What letters comprise the final grapheme of the word *wash*? _____
phonemes **(or speech sounds)**	**22.** Although there are hundreds of different speech sounds (consider the variations due to dialect, individual speech patterns, change in stress, etc.), for all practical purposes in the task of teaching reading, **we can consider the American-English language to** **contain 44 separate _____.**
phoneme, grapheme	**23.** If the code were consistent (that is, if we had one grapheme for each _____ and one phoneme for each _____), the task of teaching children to read would be much simpler than it now is.
26 phonemes	**24.** The truth is that we have only _____ letters in our alphabet, only 26 symbols to represent 44 _____.
phonemes	**25.** We add symbols to our system by using combinations of letters (such as *ch, th*) to represent the _____ not represented by the 26 letters of the alphabet.

phoneme, *a*	**26.** We also add symbols by using one letter to represent more than one _____. (The letter _____ , for example, represents three different phonemes in the three words *ate, pan, all*.)
k, g, h	**27.** Another of the many complications is the use of symbols that do not represent any sound: *knight* has three letters that do not represent sound; the _____ , _____ , and _____ .
gh, ph phoneme	**28.** Besides lacking a one-to-one correspondence between the letters of the alphabet and the phonemes needed, the spelling of the English language is further complicated by its many inconsistencies. One of the greatest of these is the use of different symbols to represent the same phoneme. For example, the sound we associate with *f* is represented by *f* in *fine*, by _____ in *cough*, and by _____ in *elephant*. This is an example of three graphemes representing one _____ .
letter (or symbol or grapheme)	**29.** Sometimes when a grapheme represents more than one phoneme, there are clues within the word to indicate which sound the _____ represents. A teacher of reading should be able to recognize these clues.
phoneme phonemes, graphemes	**30.** Our alphabet represents speech at the level of the _____ . Therefore, learning the code requires that readers separate (segment) spoken words into _____ and associate _____ with these phonemes.
rhyme	**31. Phonological awareness** is the understanding that spoken language consists of words, syllables, rhymes, and phonemes. Readers who are phonologically aware know that the words /man/, /pan/, and /van/ _____ .
phonemes	**32. Phonemic awareness** refers only to the understanding that spoken words are composed of _____ and the understanding that individual phonemes, when blended together, form meaningful words.

phonemes words	**33.** Reread the definition in the previous frame. You will see that phonemic awareness consists of two understandings: 1. The understanding that spoken words are composed of _____. 2. The understanding that phonemes, when blended together, form recognizable _____.
three four segment (or separate)	**34.** Let us consider the first understanding. Readers who are aware of the individual phonemes in spoken words can segment, or separate, words into sounds. Pronounce the word *tip* aloud. *Tip* is composed of _____ phonemes. (How many?) Say the word *trip*. *Trip* is composed of _____ phonemes. (How many?) When you count the phonemes in a word, you _____ the word into individual sounds.
four three, five	**35.** Now try *meadow, cough,* and *admit.* (Do not be misled by the number of letters in a word's spelling!) The word *meadow* consists of _____ phonemes, *cough* of (How many?) _____ phonemes, and *admit* of _____ phonemes. (How many?) (How many?)
/p/ /i/ /n/ segment	**36.** Say the word *pin* aloud. *Pin* begins with the phoneme _____. The phoneme in the middle of *pin* is _____. *Pin* ends with the phoneme _____. You have demonstrated the ability to _____ the word *pin* into phonemes. (segment, blend)
/p/, /a/, /n/ /m/, /i/, /l/, /k/ /s/, /e/, /n/, /s/	**37.** Segment the following words by saying them aloud and then writing each phoneme enclosed with a slash. The word *pan* consists of the phonemes _____, _____, and _____. *Milk* consists of the phonemes _____, _____, _____, and _____. *Sense* consists of the phonemes _____, _____, _____, and _____.

phoneme	**38.** Our alphabet represents speech at the level of the _____. Therefore, readers of our English language must be able to segment
phonemes	or separate spoken words into _____.
count	**39.** Review frames 34 through 37. In frames 34 and 35, you were asked to _____ the phonemes in a word. (count, note the position of)
note the position of	Frame 36 required that you _____ the (count, note the position of) phonemes by identifying the beginning, middle, and last phonemes in a word. Frame 37 asked you to pronounce the phonemes one-by-one.
	40. We will now consider three other activities that the teacher of reading may use to develop and demonstrate phonemic awareness in the beginning reader. Let us begin with phoneme addition. In phoneme addition, the reader attaches one or more phonemes to a word or word part. Use your awareness of the phonemes of the English language to complete the phoneme addition activities below. Combine the phonemes to pronounce a word. Write the new word on the line beside each activity.
table	**A.** Add /t/ to /able/. The new word is _____.
bikes	**B.** Add /s/ to the end of /bike/. The new word is _____.
mall	**C.** Add /m/ to /all/. The new word is _____.
bit	**D.** Add /b/ to /it/. The new word is _____.
	41. Phoneme deletion, the next activity we will examine, is defined as removing one or more phonemes from a word. Complete the phoneme deletion activities below. Write the new word on the line beside each activity.
at	**A.** Say /flat/. Delete the /fl/ from /flat/. The new word is _____.
top	**B.** Say /stop/. Delete the /s/ from /stop/. The new word is _____.
car	**C.** Say /card/. Delete the /d/ from /card/. The new word is _____.
bee	**D.** Say /beet/. Delete the /t/ from /beet/. The new word is _____.

	42. Phoneme substitution, the last activity we will consider, requires that the reader delete one or more phonemes from a word (or word part) and replace them with one or more different phonemes. Complete the phoneme substitution activities below. Write the new word on the line beside each activity.
sad	**A.** Say /sat/. Substitute /d/ for /t/ in /sat/. The new word is _____.
send	**B.** Say /mend/. Substitute /s/ for /m/ in /mend/. The new word is ____.
ship	**C.** Say /shop/. Substitute /i/ for /o/ in /shop/. The new word is _____.
pig	**D.** Say /big/. Substitute /p/ for /b/ in /big/. The new word is _____.
	43. We have studied activities that the teacher of reading may use to develop or demonstrate phonemic awareness in the beginning reader. These activities ask the reader to consciously and intentionally count phonemes, note the position of phonemes in words, fully segment a word by pronouncing its phonemes one-by-one, add, delete, and substitute phonemes. Write the name of the activity on the line beside the description. Read all the descriptions before answering!
deletion	**A.** Removing the /s/ from /sat/ to form the new word /at/ is an example of phoneme _____.
noting the position of phonemes in words	**B.** Pronouncing the middle phoneme in a three-phoneme word is an example of _____.
substitution	**C.** Exchanging /h/ for /f/ in /fat/ to pronounce the new word /hat/ is an example of phoneme _____.
counting phonemes	**D.** Telling how many phonemes are in a spoken word is an example of _____.
addition	**E.** Attaching /b/ to /at/ to pronounce the new word /bat/ is an example of phoneme _____.
segmenting (or separating)	**F.** Saying each phoneme in /mat/ one-by-one (/m/ /a/ /t/) is an example of fully _____ a spoken word into phonemes.
blend	**44.** We will now turn our attention to the second aspect of phonemic awareness: the ability to _____ individual phonemes into meaningful spoken words.

	45. Use your knowledge of phonics to say the phoneme represented by each grapheme in the word **laf.**
/l/	The grapheme **l** represents the phoneme _____.
/a/	The grapheme **a** represents the phoneme _____.
/f/	The grapheme **f** represents the phoneme _____.
	You have now pronounced each phoneme in isolation. Have you
no	pronounced a word? _____
	46. To identify the spoken word that the graphemes in the word **laf** represent, you must associate a phoneme with each grapheme, and
blend	then you must _____ the phonemes together.
	47. Now blend the phonemes together. Say the phonemes aloud as you blend. The phonemes /l/ + /a/ + /f/ form a word you recognize in speech. Write the word the way that you would
laugh	normally spell it. _____
	48. Sometimes blending is described as "folding sounds together." The reader blends, or folds, the phonemes together so that they form a whole spoken word. Blending is an essential aspect of
decoding	_____.
	Try blending the phonemes below. Write the word the way that it is normally spelled.
cat	/k/ + /a/ + /t/ = _____
lamp	/l/ + /a/ + /m/ + /p/ = _____
tent	/t/ + /e/ + /n/ + /t/ = _____
gem	/j/ + /e/ + /m/ = _____
	49. We have learned that readers who are successful at using phonics
phonemic awareness	to decode words have developed _____. These readers can
phonemes,	segment words into their individual _____, and can
blend	_____ individual phonemes to pronounce the words we use in everyday conversation.

BOX 1.3

Spanish Phonemes

Different languages use different phonemes and different graphemes. Let us consider four Spanish phonemes that do not have an exact English language equivalent, and the graphemes that represent them.

1. The Spanish *ñ* is pronounced like the *ny* in the English word *canyon*, and is represented by the grapheme *ñ*. We hear this phoneme in the Spanish loan words *El Niño* and *La Niña*.

2. The Spanish trilled *r* is pronounced by rolling the *r* on the upper palate. A single *r* is the grapheme that indicates a slightly trilled pronunciation; a double *rr* represents a strongly trilled pronunciation. The Spanish word for dog, *perro*, is pronounced with a strongly trilled *rr*.

3. In Latin America, the *ll* is the grapheme that represents the sound of the *y* in *yellow*. In Spain, the *ll* is pronounced like the *lli* in *mi**lli**on*. *Tortilla*, a cornmeal, flat bread used in tacos and other dishes, is an example of a Spanish loan word in which the *ll* is pronounced like the *y* in *yellow* or the *lli* in *million*.

4. The Spanish *j* is pronounced like the English /*h*/ in *happy*, only farther back in the throat and with more emphasis. *Javelina*, the wild pig of the southwestern United States, is an example of a Spanish loan word in which the letter *j* represents /*h*/.

The native speaker of English who wishes to speak the Spanish language must learn to pronounce the four Spanish phonemes that are not among the 44 American-English phonemes. The best way to do this is to speak Spanish, and to listen to Spanish as it is being spoken. Similarly, Spanish-speaking children who learn English as a second language benefit from many and varied opportunities to speak and listen to English, to participate in English conversations, and to hear English books read aloud.

graphophonic	**50. Graphophonic cues** consist of the 26 letters and combinations of these letters (graphemes), the 44 sounds (phonemes), and the system of relationships among the letters and the sounds (phonics). Readers use _____ (*grapho* + *phonic*) cues to translate the written code into the sounds that form the words of spoken language.
cot *coat*	**51.** Pronounce the words at the right. Graphophonic cues indicate that the *o* in *rod* represents the same sound as the *o* in _____, and that the <div align="center">(*cot, coat*)</div> *oa* in *road* represents the same sound as the *oa* in _____. <div align="right">(*cot, coat*)</div> *hot boat* *rod road* *top coal*

syntactic	**52.** Besides graphophonic cues, readers use **syntactic cues** and **semantic cues** to determine the identity of words. Syntax is the manner in which words are ordered to form phrases, clauses, and sentences. Therefore, readers who use _____ clues recognize the manner in which word order and grammatical function are clues to the identity of a word.
hit syntactic	**53.** Consider the word order and grammatical function to determine the missing word in this sentence: The batter _____ the ball to the right fielder. You know to choose a word that is a verb because English syntax requires the use of an action word in the structure of this sentence. When you decide that the missing word is a verb, you use _____ cues. (graphophonic, syntactic)
semantic	**54. Semantic** refers to the meaning of language. Therefore, the meaning of a passage provides readers with _____ cues.
semantic	**55.** Consider once again the word omitted from the sentence in frame 53. To determine that the missing word is *hit,* you must combine a background knowledge of baseball with an understanding of the meaning of this sentence. This is an example of the use of _____ cues. (syntactic, semantic)
truck Semantic *truck*	**56.** Now read the following sentence: The dog barked at the red and blue _____. (*truck, tree*) _____ cues within the sentence indicate that the missing (Syntactic, Semantic) word is _____.
graphophonic cues syntactic cues semantic cues	**57.** The three types of cues used to identify unfamiliar words are: _____, which consist of letter and sound relationships. _____, which consist of grammatical relationships. _____, which consist of meaningful relationships.

graphophonic	**58.** Readers frequently combine the information from graphophonic, syntactic, and semantic cues to determine the identity of words. Readers use _____ cues to translate the written code into (graphophonic, semantic) speech sounds.
syntactic	Readers use _____ cues to identify words that are consistent (syntactic, semantic) with grammatical order and function.
semantic sense	Readers use _____ cues to identify words that make (semantic, graphophonic) _____ in a sentence.
graphophonic syntactic semantic	**59.** You have learned that readers use _____ cues to determine the pronunciation of words they do not recognize. However, the process of word identification is strengthened when graphophonic cues are used in combination with _____ cues and _____ cues.
phonemes sound (or phoneme)	**60.** We have noted that the alphabet is a symbolic representation of our speech sounds (or _____), that there is not a one-to-one correspondence between the symbol and the _____, and that there are many inconsistencies in the symbolic system. The code is far from perfect.
	61. However, there are certain symbols that are reliable and there are patterns of reliability within the inconsistencies. The teacher of reading must be aware of these. It is the purpose of this program to aid you in your understanding of one set of word recognition skills, that of phonics. We shall begin our study with the most reliable of the 26
letters	_____ of the alphabet, the consonants. (letters, phonemes)

The reviews should give you some indication of the effectiveness of your study and provide means for additional reviewing. Write the answers to the reviews on another sheet of paper. Correct them and analyze the results. Then recheck yourself after a few days by answering the review questions again. Keep track of your scores so that you will know where additional study and review are needed.

�֍◇֍ Review 1

Close your eyes and summarize the information contained in the first section. On another piece of paper, write the answers to this review without looking back. Complete the entire review before you check the answers.

1. In order to read, we must be able to _____, that is, to translate the written symbols into the correct speech sounds.

2. The smallest unit of sound that distinguishes one word from another is called a _____.

3. For all practical purposes, the American-English language contains _____ phonemes.
   (26, 44)

4. Phonemic awareness consists of the ability to (1) _____ words into their individual phonemes, and (2) _____ individual phonemes together to form meaningful spoken words.

5. Separating the word *sat* into its individual phonemes /s/, /a/, and /t/ is an example of _____.

6. Combining the three phonemes /s/ + /a/ + /t/ to pronounce the word *sat* is an example of _____.

7. A _____ is the written representation of a phoneme.

8. Clues within words that indicate which phoneme a letter represents are called _____ cues.

9. The way that words are ordered and function in sentences provides _____ cues to word identification.

10. The meaning of a passage provides readers with _____ cues to the identity of words.

Turn to the Answers section for Part I, page 97, and check your answers. You should have answered all the questions correctly. If you did not succeed, analyze your study procedure. Is your mind active? Are you writing all the answers? Do you complete a frame before you move the mask down? Did you summarize your learnings before you started the review? Study the appropriate parts of the Introduction again. Congratulations to those who had a perfect score! Your learning should be very profitable.

References

Aaron, P. G., Joshi, R. M., Ayotollah, M., Ellsberry, A., Henderson, J., & Lindsey, K. (1999). Decoding and sight-word naming: Are they independent components of word recognition skill? *Reading and Writing: An Interdisciplinary Journal, 11,* 89–127.

Armbruster, B. B., Lehr, F., & Osborn, J. (2001). *Put reading first: The research building blocks for teaching children to read kindergarten through grade 3.* Washington, DC: National Institute for Literacy.

Berninger, V. W., Vermeulen, K., Abbott, R. D., McCutchen, D., Cotton, S., Cude, J., Dorn, S., & Sharon, T. (2003). Comparison of three approaches to supplementary reading instruction for low-achieving second-grade readers. *Language, Speech, and Hearing Services in Schools, 34,* 101–116.

Bryson, B. (1990). *Mother tongue: English and how it got that way.* New York: William Morrow and Company.

Burnley, D. (2000). *The history of the English language: A source book* (2nd ed.). Edinburg Gate, England: Pearson Education Limited.

Carver, R. P. (2003). The highly lawful relationships among pseudoword decoding, word identification, spelling, listening, and reading. *Scientific Studies of Reading, 7,* 127–154.

Connelly, V., Johnston, R., & Thompson, G. B. (2001). The effect of phonics instruction on the reading comprehension of beginning readers. *Reading and Writing: An Interdisciplinary Journal, 14,* 423–457.

Ehri, L. C. (2004). Teaching phonemic awareness and phonics: An explanation of the national reading panel meta-analysis. In P. McCardle & V. Chhabra (Eds.), *The voice of evidence in reading research* (pp. 153–186). Baltimore, MD: Paul H. Brookes Publishing.

Ehri, L. C., Nunes, S. R., Stahl, S. A., & Willows, D. M. (2001). Systematic phonics instruction helps students learn to read: Evidence from the National Reading Panel's meta-analysis. *Review of Educational Research, 71*(3), 393–447.

Foorman, B. R., Chen, D. T., Carlson, C., Moats, L., Francis, D. J., & Fletcher, J. M. (2003). The necessity of the alphabetic principle to phonemic awareness instruction. *Reading and Writing: Interdisciplinary Journal, 16,* 289–324.

Goswami, U. (2001). Early phonological development and the acquisition of literacy. In S. B. Neuman & D. K. Dickinson (Eds.), *Handbook of early literacy research* (pp. 111–125). New York: Guilford Press.

Hagtvet, B. E. (2003). Listening comprehension and reading comprehension in poor decoders: Evidence for the importance of syntactic and semantic skills as well as phonological skills. *Reading and Writing: An Interdisciplinary Journal, 16,* 505–539.

Hatcher, P. J., Hulme, C., & Snowling, M. J. (2004). Explicit phoneme training combined with phonic reading instruction helps children at risk of reading failure. *Journal of Child Psychology and Psychiatry and Allied Disciplines, 45,* 338–350.

Juel, C., & Minden-Cupp, C. (2004). Learning to read words: Linguistic units and instructional strategies. In R. B. Ruddell & N. J. Unrau (Eds.), *Theoretical models and processes of reading* (5th ed., pp. 313–364). Newark, DE: International Reading Association.

Juel, C., & Roper-Schneider, D. (1985). The influence of basal readers on first grade reading. *Reading Research Quarterly, 20,* 134–152.

Nation, K., Allen, R., & Hulme, C. (2001). The limitations of orthographic analogy in early reading development: Performance on the clue-word task depends on phonological priming and elementary decoding skills, not the use of orthographic analogy, *Child Psychology, 89,* 75–94.

National Reading Panel (2000). *Report of the national reading panel. Teaching children to read: An evidence-based assessment of the scientific research literature on reading and its implications for reading instruction: Reports of the subgroups* (NIH Publication No. 00–4754). Washington, DC: U.S. Government Printing Office.

Qudeans, M. K. (2003). Implication of letter-sound concepts and phonological awareness skills of blending and segmenting: A pilot study examining the effects of instructional sequence in word reading for kindergarten children with low phonological awareness. *Learning Disabilities Quarterly, 26,* 258–280.

Schunk, D. H. (2003). Self-efficacy for reading and writing: Influence of modeling, goal setting, and self-evaluation. *Reading & Writing Quarterly, 19,* 159–172.

Torgesen, J. K. (2004). Lessons learned from research on interventions for students who have difficulty learning to read. In P. McCardle & V. Chhabra (Eds.), *The voice of evidence in reading research* (pp. 355–382). Baltimore, MD: Paul H. Brookes Publishing.

Torgesen, J. K., Alexander, A. W., Wagner, R. K., Rashotte, C. A., Voeller, K. K. S., & Conway, T. (2001). Intensive remedial instruction for children with severe reading disabilities: Immediate and long-term outcomes from two instructional approaches. *Journal of Learning Disabilities, 34,* 33–58, 78.

Tunmer, W. E., & Chapman, J. W. (2002). The relation of beginning readers' reported word identification strategies to reading achievement, reading-related skills, and academic self-perceptions. *Reading and Writing: An Interdisciplinary Journal, 15,* 341–358.

Part II

Consonants

Place the mask over the left-hand column. As you work through these sections, it will be necessary for you to make sounds out loud. Be sure that you are seated where this is possible. Now work out the first frame, move the mask down to check, and proceed as you did in the first section. Keep an active mind! You may need to study the entire frame before you make your response.

vowels	**1.** The 26 letters of the alphabet can be divided into two major categories: consonants and _____.
consonants	**2.** There is, however, a degree of overlapping between these categories. Certain letters, notably the *w* and *y,* sometimes function as vowels and at other times as _____.
consonants, 21	**3.** Recognizing the fact that we are oversimplifying the situation, we shall, in this part of the program, consider all letters except *a, e, i, o, u* to be _____. There are then _____ consonant (How many?) letters.
is not	**4.** We have noted previously that in the American-English language there _____ a consistent one-to-one correspondence (is, is not) between letter and phoneme. Let us now see how this applies to consonants.

21, 25	**5.** There are (for our purposes in the teaching of reading) 44 phonemes, 25 of these being consonant phonemes. There are _____ consonant letters; _____ (How many?) (How many?) consonant phonemes.
is not	There _____ one letter for each phoneme. (is, is not)
grapheme	**6.** There are more phonemes than letters. We gain seven additional phonemes through the use of the two-letter _____ . (grapheme, phoneme)
digraph	**7.** We call these two-letter combinations **digraphs.** Note the spelling—<u>di</u> for two; <u>graph</u> referring to writing. The two-letter combination *ch* as in *chair* is called a _____.
not	**8.** Pronounce the word *chair* as though <u>each</u> consonant were sounded. You said either "*s-hair*" or "*k-hair.*" Now pronounce *chair* as it should be pronounced. Note that you hear neither the sound represented by the *c* nor by the *h*. The combination *ch* represents a phoneme _____ (already, not) represented by a single consonant letter. It functions like another letter of the alphabet.
c h	**9.** **A digraph is a two-letter combination** **that represents a single speech sound.** The **digraph** *ch* does not represent the sound of the _____ and the _____ with which it is spelled.
not	**10.** The phonemes of our language are very familiar to us, but to prepare ourselves to teach others to read, it is necessary to identify <u>each</u> of the 44 phonemes. Since there is _____ a one-to-one correspondence between sound and letter, it will be helpful to designate a key symbol for <u>each</u> phoneme. In this way we will know the sound to which we are referring no matter how it is represented in the word (that is, no matter how it is spelled).

	11. When possible, the key symbol will be the same as the letter we ordinarily associate with the sound. For example, *b* will serve as the key symbol for the sound we hear at the beginning of the word *box*. Would you expect *d* to serve as the key symbol for the sound heard at
yes	the beginning of the word *dog*? _____
44	**12.** There are 44 phonemes; 25 of these are consonant phonemes. We will, therefore, identify _____ key symbols altogether, of (How many?)
25	which _____ will be consonants. (How many?)
	There will be one key symbol for each phoneme. **Each phoneme will have one key symbol.**
phonemes	There will be a one-to-one correspondence between key symbols and _____.
symbol	**13.** Most of the consonants are reliable with respect to sound. Therefore, in most cases, the key _____ that designates a certain phoneme heard in a word will be the same as the consonant
letter	_____ seen in that word. For example, *b* will serve as the
bomb	key symbol for the initial sound we hear in the word _____ . (*bomb, mob*)
no (The final *b* represents no phoneme: It is a silent letter.)	**14.** Will *b* serve as the key symbol for the final sound we hear in the word *bomb*? _____
4	**15.** The word *graph* has _____ phonemes and therefore (How many?)
4, *g*	_____ graphemes. They are _____ , (How many?)
r, a, ph	_____ , _____ , and _____ . So that we have a clue to its pronunciation, the logical key symbol to assign to
f	the final phoneme in *graph* is the letter _____ .

ph *f*	**16.** Pronounce *photo.* The initial grapheme is _____. The key symbol to represent this sound is _____.
     key symbols digraphs	**17.** We can divide the 25 consonant phonemes into two major groups: (1) Eighteen consonant phonemes identified by key symbols composed of **single letters;** and (2) Seven consonant phonemes identified by _____ _____ composed of **two-letter combinations** called _____.

 Review 2

Summarize your learnings. What new words have you learned thus far? Define them.

1. Is there a one-to-one correspondence between the consonant letters and the consonant phonemes?

2. We shall learn to identify a key symbol for each of the consonant _____ of the American-English language.
(letters, phonemes)

3. The *m* is a very dependable letter; it is the key symbol for the initial sound heard in *man.* We would expect the key symbol representing the sound heard at the end of the word *jam* to be _____.

4. Dictionaries also use _____ as the key symbol to represent the sound heard at the beginning of the word *man.*

5. Most of the key symbols will be single letters; however, seven of the consonant symbols will be composed of _____ letters called _____.

6. We can divide the consonant phonemes into two groups according to whether the key symbol representing the phoneme is composed of one or of two _____.

7. *Ch,* a _____, represents how many phonemes?

(See the Part II Answers Section for the answers to Review 2, page 97.)

◇ Single-Letter Consonants

a̸	**1.** Place the mask firmly over the responses at the left. Do not move it until the entire frame is completed.
b	
c̸	**a.** Write the 26 letters of the alphabet, in order, in the column at the right.
d	
e̸	**b.** Draw a diagonal line through each of the five vowel letters.
f	
g	**c.** Three of the 21 consonant letters do not represent distinctive sounds. Draw a horizontal line through the three unnecessary letters.
h	
i̸	A puzzle? Clue: Say the words below, listening for the sounds that are represented by the underlined consonant letters.
j	
k	<u>c</u>ity and <u>c</u>old
l	anti<u>q</u>ue and <u>q</u>uiet
m	e<u>x</u>am and refle<u>x</u>
n	**As single letters, *c*, *q*, and *x* do not represent distinctive phonemes.**
o̸	
p	When these words are spelled so that each consonant letter represents a distinctive phoneme, the words look like this:
q̶	
r	sity and kold
s	antikue and kuiet
t	egzam and refleks
u̸	Eliminating the three unnecessary letters leaves us with
v	_____ single consonant letters that have distinctive sounds. In other words, our alphabet
w	
x̶	supplies us with _____ single-letter
y	grapheme to represent 18 of the 25 consonant _____ of our language.
z	

18

18

phonemes

		Key Words
phonemes	b	boat
3	d	dog
	f	fish
	g	goat
	h	hat
	j	jeep
	k	kite
	l	lion
	m	moon
	n	nut
	p	pig
	r	ring
	s	sun
	t	table
	v	van
	w	wagon
	y	yo-yo
	z	zipper

2. As you repeat the letters of the alphabet, write the 18 consonant letters (the **key symbols**) that represent 18 distinctive _____.

You will omit the _____ consonant letters that do not represent distinctive phonemes.

How can we know exactly which phoneme has been assigned to each of the key symbols? We use a key word that has that phoneme as its initial sound. The selected key words follow, but they are out of order. Write each key word next to its key symbol.

Key Words

kite	pig	van	boat	goat	dog
ring	moon	wagon	zipper	jeep	yo-yo
sun	lion	table	fish	nut	hat

Key Symbols	Key Words
_____	_____
_____	_____
_____	_____
_____	_____
_____	_____
_____	_____
_____	_____
_____	_____
_____	_____
_____	_____
_____	_____
_____	_____
_____	_____
_____	_____
_____	_____
_____	_____
_____	_____
_____	_____

3. Which key symbol and key word should be used to identify the initial sound heard in each of these words? Refer to frame 2 for the key words.

m moon	g goat
y yo-yo	h hat
s sun	r ring

mat _____ _____   got _____ _____

yellow _____ _____   have _____ _____

city _____ _____   ride _____ _____

4. Which key symbol and key word should be used to identify the initial sound heard in each of the following words? Use frame 2 for the key words.

j jeep *f* fish	
j jeep *k* kite	
k kite *b* boat	
g goat *g* goat	

jelly _____ _____   fat _____ _____

gerbil _____ _____   candy _____ _____

cat _____ _____   book _____ _____

ghost _____ _____   gone _____ _____

Now check with the answers. If you missed any, say aloud the key word you selected while you listen carefully to the first phoneme. Substitute that sound in the specific study word above. Correct it so the initial sound in the study word is the same as that in the key word.

girl

gym

goat

5. Now, when we use a key symbol such as *g*, we will know that we are referring to the sound heard in _____ and not to that
                                                                (*girl, gym*)
heard in _____ .
              (*girl, gym*)

Check yourself. If the phoneme you have selected the same as that heard in the key word _____?

key

6. As we study each consonant letter, we need to ask certain questions:

A. How reliable is it?
    Does it always represent the sound we associate with its

    _____ symbol?
    Are there patterns of reliability?
    Patterns of inconsistencies?

B. Does it have distinctive characteristics?

The consonant letters have been grouped to facilitate our study in answering the above questions.

◇ m, q, r, v

symbol			**1.** Four of the 21 consonant letters are extremely dependable: *m, q, r,* and *v.* When we see *m, r,* or *v* in a word, we can be sure it represents the phoneme we associate with its key _____ and is the initial sound heard in its key word.

Fill in the columns at the right with the key symbols (2), and the key words (3). Select the words from the following:

van   queen   fish   ring   kite   moon

				1	2	3
m	*m*	*moon*		*m*	_____	_____
r	*r*	*ring*		*r*	_____	_____
v	*v*	*van*		*v*	_____	_____
q	*k*	*kite*		*q*	_____	_____

2. Since *q* is an unnecessary letter, how can we call it dependable?
When we see *q,* we know it represents the sound we associate with the key symbol *k.* In other words, /q/ = /k/. We can depend on it! Now write the key symbol and key word for *q* above.

---

3. We did not use *q* for a key symbol because the sound it represents

k

had already been assigned to the letter _____. We have selected one symbol to represent each of the 25 consonant sounds of our language. The key word we have selected to help identify /k/ is

kite

_____.

---

	opak
	unik
	plak
k	antik
k, u, e	

4. Study the words at the right. The *que* combination at the end of a word represents the phoneme we associate with the key symbol

opaque   _____
unique   _____
plaque   _____
antique   _____

_____. Or we might say that the *q* represents the sound we associate with _____ , while the _____ and _____ are silent.

Rewrite these words using the proper key symbol to stand for each of the consonants. Omit the silent "*ue*" combination and the silent consonants. Copy the vowels as they are, pronouncing them as they would sound in the real word.

u	**5.** The letter *q* is almost always followed by the letter _____. In *unique,* the *u* that follows the *q* is silent.
	There are a few words that begin with *q* in which the *u* is also silent as in *quay,* or the *u* is pronounced as *u,* as in *queue.* We may miss this point because we may be mispronouncing these words. *Quay* is pronounced as though it were spelled *key; queue* is pronounced as though it were spelled *cue.*
	The first phoneme in both *key* and *cue* (therefore in *quay* and *queue*) is
k	represented by the key symbol _____. Pronounce *quay* and *queue.* correctly several times (*quay* as key; *queue* as *cue*). Practice reading this: *The people boarding the ship formed a queue on the quay. Three of them wore queues.*
	6. More commonly, the *u* following the letter *q* becomes a consonant and represents the sound we associate with the key symbol *w.*
	Say these words: *quilt, equal, quiet, queen, quill.* In these words the *q*
k	represents the sound we associate with _____ , and the *u*
w	represents the sound we associate with _____.
kwick	**7.** Pronounce the words at the right aloud. Rewrite the words using the proper key symbols to show the pronunciation of the *qu* combination. *quick* _____
kwit	*quit* _____
kwiz	*quiz* _____
kween	*queen* _____
k	In these words, the letter *q* represents the sound we associate with the key symbol _____ , and the
consonant, *w*	letter *u* represents the sound of the _____ letter _____. (consonant, vowel)
	8. Let us summarize:
	The letters *m, q, v,* and *r* are very dependable. The *m, v,* and *r* represent distinctive sounds of their own.
k	**The *q* always represents the same sound as the _____.**
	The letter *q* has a distinctive characteristic: It is almost always
u	followed by the letter _____. This *u* may be silent or
consonant, *w*	represent the sound of the _____ _____. (consonant, vowel)

BOX 2.1

How Would a Duck Quack Without Q?

Without a sound of its own, the letter *Q* is tantamount to an alphabetical orphan in the modern English alphabet. Let us take a look at how we got this extra letter in our alphabet. The letter *Q*, known as *koppa* in the archaic Greek alphabet, fell out of use and did not survive long enough to become part of the classical Greek alphabet. We would not have the letter *Q* in our own alphabet today had not the Etruscans revived the *Q*. They passed it along to the Romans who used *Q* to spell /kw/ words (*quake, question*). Western languages inherited the Latin alphabet, although the Anglo-Saxons did not borrow this letter from Latin. The French language did borrow the Latin *Q*, however, and it was the French who added the *Q* to the English alphabet. After the Norman Conquest in 1066, French scribes began to use *Q* when spelling English words—perhaps because adding the *Q* made English words look more like French words. By sometime around 1500, the letter *Q* had become part of the English alphabet, where it remains today. If the letter *Q* were to disappear from our alphabet as it did from the classical Greek alphabet, we would use the letters *kw* and *k* in its place, depending on the sounds in the words to be spelled, such as *kwest, technik, kwiz, kwilt, opak, kwip,* and *kwit*. Consider this *kwestion:* If you could choose, would you discard the letter *Q* or keep it as the 22nd letter of the English alphabet?

———

Ouaknin, M. C. (1999). *Mysteries of the alphabet: The origins of writing* (J. Bacon, Trans.). New York: Abbeville Press Publishers.

Review 3

1. How many phonemes are there in *panda?* How many graphemes?

2. How many phonemes are there in *chat?* How many graphemes?

3. We do not have a sufficient number of consonant letters in our alphabet to represent all the consonant sounds. Rather, we supplement the single letters with seven _____.

4. Which letters have not been assigned a key symbol of their own? Why?

5. To establish our code, we select key _____ and key _____ to represent each phoneme.

6. What key symbol represents /m/? _____ /q/? _____ /r/? _____ /v/? _____.

7. *Q* is followed by _____ in English words. The *u* may be _____ as in *antique,* or have the sound of the consonant _____ as in *quilt.*

8. Using our code, how would we write the consonants in these words? *mover* _____ *quiver* _____.

9. What do we mean when we say, "The *v* is a very dependable letter"? (See the Part II Answers section for answers to Review 3, page 97.)

◇ *b, h, k, l, p*

b	*b*	*boat*
h	*h*	*hat*
k	*k*	*kite*
l	*l*	*lion*
p	*p*	*pig*

1. The five consonants *b, h, k, l,* and *p* are very dependable except for the fact that on occasion they represent no phonemes. When you see one of these letters in an unknown word, you expect it to represent the sound you hear in its key word. Complete the table at the right with the letter (1), key symbol (2), and key word (3) for each.

1	2	3
——	——	——
——	——	——
——	——	——
——	——	——
——	——	——

Select the key word from the following:

lion   cat   hat   pig   queen   boat   kite

---

boat

2. You will associate *b* with the sound heard at the beginning of the key word _____. Can you say that sound aloud? It is <u>very</u> difficult. Many consonant phonemes cannot be pronounced easily without adding a bit of the vowel sound. Some teachers, trying to pronounce the initial phoneme in *boat,* say "*buh.*" This will not help the child to identify the word *boat: buh-oat* <u>is</u> <u>not</u> *boat!* Some experts advise teachers to say "the first sound we hear in *boat*" or "the last sound we hear in *tub*" rather than to attempt to sound the phoneme in isolation. Keep in mind that it is very difficult to sound most

consonant

_____ phonemes in isolation.
(consonant, vowel)

---

vowel

3. Try pronouncing /m/, /v/, /ll/, and /r/. Listen to the sound you give them in *hum, dove, call,* and *car.* Say them aloud again. These are fairly easy to sound in isolation. Now say /b/, /k/, and /p/ aloud. Listen to them in the words *tub, back,* and *help.* Do not hang on to the sound (as you can in *hummmmmmmmm*); just softly expel your breath. Try to sound them with as little of the _____ phoneme as possible.

---

silent

4. Sometimes these consonant letters have no phonemes. It is common practice to call them "_____ letters." Certain patterns help determine whether these letters represent a phoneme or

silent

are _____ in an unknown word.

5. One pattern is very common to almost all consonants:

Two like-consonants appearing together in a word generally represent one phoneme.

Is this true even of the consonants we called extremely dependable?

yes

_____.

Say these words aloud. How many phonemes do the two like-

one

consonants represent? _____ Make a slash through the second like-consonant to depict the silent letter. Then rewrite the words omitting the silent consonant.

muffin, mufin, letter,
leter, purr, pur
ribbon, ribon,
happen,
hapen, less, les

muffin _____   letter _____   purr _____

ribbon _____   happen _____   less _____

clim

6. Pronounce the words at the right. Rewrite these words omitting the silent letters. (Do not be concerned with the vowel sounds at this point. We will indicate the vowel sounds later.)

lam

bom

number

climb _____

lamb _____

bomb _____

number _____

b, m

The _____ is silent when it follows an _____ in the same syllable.

7. The *b* is not silent in *number,* because it is not in the same

syllable, m

_____ as the _____.

8. Pronounce the two words at the right. The *b* when

is

followed by the *m* in *bomb* _____ silent. The *b* in

(is, is not)

bomb

is not

bombard _____ silent.

(is, is not)

bombard

syllables

The *b* and the *m* in *bombard* are in different _____.

dout	**9.** Pronounce the words at the right. Rewrite the words *doubt* _____
det	omitting the silent consonants.
obtain	*debt* _____
sutle	*obtain* _____
	subtle _____
t	The *b* is silent when it is followed by a _____ in the same syllable.
subtle	Which word does not belong in the set? _____ Then
t	notice that *b* is silent even though the *b* and the _____ are in different syllables.
b	**10.** Let us summarize:
	When *b* follows *m* or precedes *t* in the same syllable, the _____ is usually silent.
/h/ hat	**11.** *H*, as a single letter (phoneme / /, key word _____),
final	has a distinctive characteristic: It is never heard as the _____ sound in a word or syllable. (initial, final)
	12. *H* is silent when it follows the vowel in a word or syllable. Put a slash through the silent *h*s in the following words:
oh̸, hurrah̸, shah̸	oh hurrah shah
	Check carefully. Do you hear the /h/ at the end of these
no	words? _____
	13. The *h* may even be silent when it appears as the initial consonant of a word. There are no clues to tell us whether the initial *h* represents a phoneme. In fact, some people consider the *h* to be silent in *homage, humble, herb*. Circle the words below in which the initial *h* is silent.
heir, hour, honest	here heir hour happy honest
	14. Study the words at the right. The letter *h* is
g, k,	silent when it follows the consonants _____, _____,
r	and _____ .

(14. right column words: ghost   khaki / rhyme   ghastly / khan   rhino)

gost, kaki, ryme, gastly, kan, rino	**15.** Rewrite the words in the preceding frame, omitting the silent consonants: _____ , _____ , _____ , _____ , _____ , _____ .

16. Review by filling in these blanks. Use the words at the right to assist you.

khaki, ghost	**The letter _h_ is silent when it follows the consonants**	hurrah
rhino	_k_ (as in _____), _g_ (as in _____), or	khaki
hurrah	_r_ (as in _____). _H_ is silent when it follows a vowel	hour
hour	(as in _____). **Sometimes _h_ is silent at the**	ghost
	beginning of a word (as in _____).	rhino

17. Aside from the fact that _h_ is often silent, as a <u>single</u> letter grapheme, it is reliable. However, we cannot say that whenever we see an _h_ in a word we know it will either be silent or represent the initial sound heard in _hat_. _H_ is a component of several digraphs (a two-letter combination that represents a single speech sound). Study the words at the right. How many digraphs contain the letter _h_, but not /h/? _____ Underline them.

gh laugh	laugh
sh wi<u>sh</u>	wish
ph <u>ph</u>one	phone
ch <u>ch</u>ange	change
wh <u>wh</u>ite	white
th <u>th</u>orn	thorn
6 (or 5. You would not be incorrect if you omitted _wh_ /hw/.)	

18. Except when silent, the _k_ is a very dependable letter. Let us be sure we understand: There are other graphemes that represent the sound we associate with the key symbol _k_ (_queen_, <u>_ch_</u>_oir_, <u>_c_</u>_oat_), but when we see the letter _k_ in a word, we can be quite sure that when

phoneme	we hear the word, we will hear the same _____ as that
kite	heard at the beginning of its key word, _____.

19. Study the words at the right to discover the "silent _k_" pattern.

The _k_ is silent at the beginning of a word or syllable when followed by _____.

Rewrite these words omitting the silent _k_s. Pronounce aloud the words you have written.

nob	knob _____
unnown	unknown _____
_n_ nit	knit _____
nee	knee _____

nife *buble* *hero*	**20.** Rewrite the following words, omitting silent consonants.
clim *onor* *nee*	*knife* _____ *bubble* _____ *hero* _____ *climb* _____ *honor* _____ *knee* _____

lion /l/	**21.** The consonant *l* is another very reliable letter. To help distinguish its phoneme, we have chosen the key word _____. We can represent its phoneme, thus / /.

baloon *dolar* *jely* *bel*	**22.** However, the *l* may be silent. Study the words at the right to see if this generalization applies. **Two like-consonants appearing together in a word generally represent one phoneme.** Rewrite the words omitting silent consonants.	*balloon* _____ *dollar* _____ *jelly* _____ *bell* _____

cam (kam) *pam* *yok* *chak* *woud* *shoud*	**23.** To discover another pattern, study the words at the right. **The letter *l* is sometimes silent when followed in the same syllable by *m*, *k*, or *d*.** Rewrite these words omitting silent consonants. (Do you hear the /l/ when you say *calm* and *palm?* If so, this is a regional difference in pronunciation, and a natural variation in the way we pronounce words.)	*calm* _____ *palm* _____ *yolk* _____ *chalk* _____ *would* _____ *should* _____

no *gold* *tak* *film* *milk* *caf* *wak*	**24.** Is this a dependable pattern? _____ Rewrite the words below omitting silent consonants. *gold* _____ *talk* _____ *film* _____ *milk* _____ *calf* _____ *walk* _____ (Pronouncing the /l/ in *gold, film,* and *milk* is not a consequence of regional differences. These are true exceptions to the pattern.)

p, help	**25.** Next we turn our attention to the consonant *p*. In this study, we are establishing a key symbol for each phoneme in our language. The logical key symbol to use to identify the first phoneme heard in *pig* is _____. It is the last phoneme heard in _____. *(help, graph)*
p	**26.** We establish a key symbol and a key word to help distinguish this phoneme from any other. *Pig* is the key word we have selected to identify the sound represented by _____.
p	**27.** Next we examine its dependability. *P,* as a <u>single</u> consonant, is very reliable. When we see *p*, we can expect to hear the sound we are associating with the key symbol _____.
no f	**28.** Do we expect to hear the sound we associate with the key symbol *p* in *phone*? _____. The two-letter grapheme *ph* represents the sound we associate with the key symbol _____.
silent *aple hapy* *pupet pupy*	**29.** Sometimes, however, the *p* has no phoneme; it is _____. Rewrite the following words, omitting the consonant letters that represent no phonemes. *apple* _____ *happy* _____ *puppet* _____ *puppy* _____

no
 	
 p
	30. Is *p* sounded in the following words? _____
	 pseudo psychology psalm pterodactyl pneumonic pneumonia
	 We can generalize:
	     When *p* is followed by *s, t,* or *n* at the beginning of a word,
	           the _____ is usually silent.**

silent	**31.** **The consonants *b, h, k, l,* and *p* as single letters** **are very reliable.** However, they are not always sounded; each has "_____ letter" patterns.

STUDY GUIDE
Consonants
b, h, k, l, m, p, q, r, v

Consonant	Key Symbol	Key Word
b	*b*	*boat*
h	*h*	*hat*
k	*k*	*kite*
l	*l*	*lion*
m	*m*	*moon*
p	*p*	*pig*
q	no key symbol	no key word
r	*r*	*ring*
v	*v*	*van*

Bb is usually silent when it follows *m* or precedes *t* in the same syllable (*climb, doubt*).

Hh is silent when it follows the consonants *g* (*ghost*), *k* (*khaki*), or *r* (*rhino*). *H* is also silent when it follows a vowel in a word or syllable (*hurrah*). Sometimes *h* is silent at the beginning of a word (*hour*).

Kk is silent at the beginning of a word or syllable when followed by *n* (*knee*).

Ll is sometimes silent when followed, in the same syllable, by *m* (*calm*), *k* (*chalk*), or *d* (*should*). If you hear an /*l*/ in *calm,* this is a regional difference in pronunciation.

Mm is a very dependable letter. When we see *m* in a word, we can be sure that it represents the phoneme we associate with the key word *moon.*

Pp is usually silent when followed by *s* (*psychology*), *t* (*pterodactyl*), or *n* (*pneumonia*) at the beginning of a word.

Qq has no key symbol. The *q* may represent the /*k*/ (*antique*). *Q* is almost always followed by the letter *u*. The *u* may be silent or represent the sound of the *w*. When the *u* represents the sound of *w*, the *qu* stands for *kw* (kween).

Rr is a dependable letter. When we see *r* in a word, we can be sure that it represents the sound we associate with the key word *ring.*

Vv is a dependable letter. When we see *v* in a word, we can be sure that it represents the sound we associate with the key word *van.*

Silent Consonants

Two like-consonants appearing together in a word generally represent one phoneme (*bubble, puddle, waffle, jelly, summer, dinner, puppet, carrot, buzz*).

✖◇✖ Review 4

1. Phonics is used to decode unknown words. The pronunciation of these nonsense words is unknown to you. Using the generalizations you have studied, decide which key symbol should represent each of the underlined consonants. Rewrite the "words" omitting silent consonants.

   a. _knoh_   **b.** _psaph_   **c.** _mell_   **d.** _plarrah_
   e. _ghaeve_   **f.** _lalm_   **g.** _khaque_   **h.** _ptovom_
   i. _rolk_   **j.** _rhimb_   **k.** _quimmel_ **l.** _kloppem_
   m. _vobter_

2. _Ph_ and _ch_ are examples of _____: each represents _____ phoneme(s).
   (How many?)

3. Why is it difficult to pronounce /b/, /k/, and /p/ aloud?

4. Why did we omit _q_ in our list of key symbols?

   (See the Part II Answers section for the answers to Review 4, page 98.)

◇ d, f, j, n, z

			1. Each of the five consonants, _d, f, j, n,_ and _z_, has minor irregularities. Complete the table at the right with the letter (1), key symbol (2), and key word (3) for these consonants. Select the key words from the following:	**1**	**2**	**3**
_d_	_d_	dog		____	____	____
_f_	_f_	fish		____	____	____
_j_	_j_	jeep		____	____	____
_n_	_n_	nut		____	____	____
_z_	_z_	zipper		____	____	____
				____	____	____
			jeep nut fish gerbil dog zipper moon			

	_f_	2. Say the word _fish_. Now start to say the word again but hold the first sound. This is the sound we represent by the key symbol _____. The _f_ is, in general, a reliable letter. Write the key symbol for the sound represented by _f_ in each of the words at the right. Listen carefully!	fiesta	____
	_f_		fan	____
_f_	_f_		effect	____
	_f_		off	____
	_v_		of	____
	_f_		if	____

v	**3.** The *f* represents the sound we associate with the key symbol _____ in the word *of*. (Try to pronounce *of* using /f/.)
silent off	**4.** One *f* in the word *effect* is not sounded. It is clear then that *f* can be a _____ letter. Another example of an unsounded *f* in the list in frame 2 is in the word _____.
f /v/ gh, ph	**5.** We have noted that *f* is, in general, a reliable letter: When we see *f* in a word, we expect, when the word is spoken, to hear the sound represented by the key symbol _____. (Exception: in *of*, the *f* = / /.) However, there are other letters that are used to stand for the sound represented by the key symbol *f*. We will digress to study them here. What letters represent the /f/ in the word *enough*? _____. In the word *phonics*? _____.
fone, nit, dou enouf, gost, lam graf, dauter, hi	**6.** The *gh* digraph can be silent. Rewrite these words using key symbols for all consonants and omitting silent letters. Copy the vowels as they are, pronouncing them as they would sound in the original word. *phone* _____ *knight* _____ *dough* _____ *enough* _____ *ghost* _____ *lamb* _____ *graph* _____ *daughter* _____ *high* _____
b r t t s t t	**7.** Study the words at the right. The *gh* digraph *bright* _____ is usually silent when followed by _____. *sight* _____ What consonants are sounded in these words? *ought* _____
gh /f/ beginning h	**8.** Study these words: *ghost, high, rough*. The digraph _____ is silent or represents / / when it appears after the vowel in a syllable. When it appears at the _____ of the syllable, the _____ in the two-letter combination is silent.
ph	**9.** Study these words: *dolphin, graph, phrase*. The digraph _____ can be found at the beginning or end of a syllable (that is, both before and after the vowel).

foto	**10.** Rewrite the words at the right to indicate their pronunciation. Use the key symbols for the consonants. Copy the vowels as they appear. *photo* *phoneme* *fork* *alphabet* *foot*
foneme	
fork	
alfabet	
foot	**The digraph *ph* represents the sound we associate with the key symbol _____.**
f	

	11. We have identified three graphemes that represent /f/. Pronounce the words below. Underline the grapheme in each word that represents /f/, and write the key symbol on the line below.
<u>f</u>irst, lau<u>gh</u>, <u>ph</u>one	first laugh phone
a<u>f</u>ter, cou<u>gh</u>, ne<u>ph</u>ew	after cough nephew
li<u>f</u>t, enou<u>gh</u>, gra<u>ph</u>	lift enough graph
f, f, f	_____ _____ _____
silent	**The *gh* may represent /f/ or it may be _____ (*high, through*).**

	12. Say *jeep* out loud. Now pronounce the first phoneme in that word. We will represent the initial sound heard in *jeep* with the key
j	symbol _____. *J* is a <u>very</u> reliable letter. When we see a *j* in
jeep	a word, we will use the same sound as that in its key word _____.

	13. There is one exception! Pronounce "Hallelujah." You see a *j*, but you do not say /j/. Can you determine what key symbol you would
y	use to represent the *j*? _____

	14. It might be well at this time to look at a combination of letters that represents /j/, the *dg*. Rewrite these words to indicate their pronunciation. (Omit each silent *e* and copy the other vowels as they are.)
juj, nowlej, ej	judge _____ knowledge _____ edge _____
	Perhaps you hear the /d/, but try pronouncing the words as though /dg/ = /j/. It comes out the same, does it not?

no	**15.** Study the one-syllable words below. Does the *dg* digraph occur at the beginning of English words? _____ At the end of
	<div align="center">(yes, no)</div>
no	English words? _____
	<div align="center">(yes, no)</div>
	<div align="center">*fudge* *budget*</div>
	<div align="center">*dodge* *pidgin*</div>
	<div align="center">*judge* *gadget*</div>
j	**The *dg* is a very reliable digraph. What key symbol do we use to represent the phoneme?** _____
d	**16.** We shall represent the initial phoneme heard in *dog* with the key symbol _____. Say *dog* aloud. Listen carefully as you say the initial phoneme in *dog*.
	17. The *d* is fairly dependable. It, however, may be silent as in *ladder* and *sudden*. Rewrite these words omitting silent consonants.
lader, suden	*ladder* _____ *sudden* _____
	18. But let us examine more closely the sounds the *d* represents. The key symbol represents the sounds heard in *doll, did, day, led*. Now read these words out loud to discover another sound that the *d* represents: *jumped, clipped, hoped, missed.*
	These *ds*, represent the sound we associate with the key symbol
t	_____.

	19. Study each word at the right.	missed <u>mist</u>
hopt	*Missed,* for example, has four phonemes. Rewrite each word showing the pronunciation of the consonants by using key symbols.	hoped _____
jumpt		jumped _____
slipt	In spite of their appearance, these are	slipped _____
one	all _____ -syllable words.	
	<div align="center">(one, two)</div>	

t *one* *d*	**20.** We have noted that the *d* sometimes is pronounced as though it were _____ (as in *kissed*). Now examine the words below. They are also _____-syllable words. The final consonant represents the sound we associate with the key symbol _____. *played smiled called*
two *ed* *d* *t* *d*	**21.** Notice the sound the *d* represents when *ed* forms a separate syllable. Say each of these words out loud. *seated* *wanted* These are _____-syllable words. In each *waited* the suffix _____ forms a separate syllable. The final *d* represents the sound assigned to the key *needed* symbol _____. Look at the letters preceding *sanded* the suffixes (*sea<u>t</u>ed*). They are either _____ *folded* or _____.
syllable, *d* *d*	**22.** In general, the suffix *ed* forms a separate _____ when it is preceded by *t* or _____. When the *ed* forms a separate syllable, the final *d* represents the sound we associate with the key symbol _____.
d *t*	**23.** To summarize: **When the suffix *ed* forms a separate syllable, the *d* represents the sound associated with the key symbol _____. When the suffix does not form a separate syllable, the *d* may represent the sound associated with the key symbol *d* or with the key symbol _____.**
/j/ soljer fuj	**24.** We have noted that *dg* forms a special combination representing / /. Occasionally a *d* or *di* represents the /j/. Perhaps you hear /j/ when you pronounce *graduation*. Rewrite these words using key symbols to represent the consonant sounds and omitting any silent letters. *soldier* _____ *fudge* _____

sudden *jumped, soldier* *fudge*	**25.** We have seen that *d* can be silent as in _____ . *D* can represent /t/ as in _____ , and /j/ as in _____ , (*jumped, pulled*) (*gem, soldier*) and /j/ as a part of the combination *dg* as in _____ . (*fudge, handgrip*)
nut *colum maner*	**26.** The /n/, identified by the first phoneme in the key word _____ , can be silent as in *running* and when preceded by *m* as in *hymn*. Rewrite these words omitting silent letters. column _____ manner _____
1 yes 2 no	**27.** *N* is very reliable, with one common but confusing exception. First, let us note that *n* is a part of the digraph *ng* as heard in *sing*. The *n* and the *g* represent _____ phoneme(s) in *sing*. (How many?) Is *ng* a digraph in *bring*? _____ The *n* and *g* represent (yes or no) _____ phoneme(s) in *ungrateful*. Is the *ng* a digraph in (How many?) *ungrateful?* _____ (yes or no)
yes *think*	**28.** Say *thing.* Is the *ng* a digraph? _____. Add the phoneme represented by *k* to *thing* (*thing + k*). We do not spell this word *thingk:* We spell it _____. The letter *n* represents /ng/ in *think!*

thang + k	**29.** There are many words in which you hear /ng/ but see only *n*.
	These words follow a pattern: Generally the letter following the *n* is
	either *k* or *g*. Pronounce *thank*. Which of these "keys to
	pronunciation" is correct? _____
	
	          than + k
	
	          thang + k

fing ger	**30.** Pronounce the "words" at the right. This is hard! Which set of key symbols (consonant sounds only) indicates the correct pronunciation of *finger?* _____ *fin ger* *fing ger* *fing er*
ng *g*	**31.** In *finger,* the *n* represents the sound we associate with the key symbol _____. The *g* represents the sound we associate with the key symbol _____. To show pronunciation, we need both the *ng* and the *g.*

kang ga roo *sing gle*	**32.** Which set of symbols below indicates the pronunciation of *kangaroo?* Of *single?*
	
	     kan ga roo *kang ga roo* _____
	
	     sin gle *sing le* *sing gle* _____

ran *bank (bangk)*	**33.** It is clear that the grapheme *n* sometimes represents the phoneme associated with the key symbol *n,* as in _____ , and
	                  (*ran, rang*)
	 sometimes with the digraph *ng,* as in _____ .
	                  (*bank, band*)

engage	**34.** We have also noted that when we see *n* and *g* together in a word, the *ng* may represent the two separate phonemes that we associate with the separate symbols *n* and *g* as in _____ (*engage, clang*)

solemn *banker*	**35.** We have seen that the letter *n* may be silent as in _____
	                (*solemn, rang*)
	 The single letter *n* may also represent the /*ng*/ as in _____
	                (*ingredient, banker*)

zipper *buzz*	**36.** The key symbol *z* represents the phoneme heard at the beginning of its key word _____. In general, it is fairly reliable. It may be silent as, for example, one *z* is silent in _____ . (*zigzag, buzz*)

BOX 2.2

Why Z Comes Last

The letter *Z* has not always been the last letter of the alphabet. Thousands of years ago, *Z* was the seventh letter in the Phoenician (tenth-century B.C.) and the Greek (eighth-century B.C.) alphabets. When the Greeks passed their alphabet to the ancient Romans, the letter *Z* became part of the Latin alphabet as well. Although the *Z* represented a speech sound in the Greek language, it served no real purpose in Latin because the Latin language did not use the sound represented by the letter. The *Z* may have stayed in the Latin alphabet had it not been for the fact that the letter *C* represented two Latin phonemes, the /k/ in *kite* and the voiced /g/ in *goat*. The Romans wanted to give the voiced /g/ its own letter, so they introduced a new letter, the letter *G*. The letters *G* and *C* are visually quite similar, which is not surprising since the Romans created the letter *G* by modifying the letter *C*. To keep the order of the letters in the Latin alphabet intact, the Romans decided to delete the useless letter *Z*, and to replace it with the newly created letter *G*. The letter *G* then became the seventh letter in the Latin alphabet, as it is in our own English alphabet. When later contact with the Greeks made it necessary for the Romans to translate Greek words into Latin, the Romans found that they needed to add the letter *Z* to the Latin alphabet. Putting the letter *Z* into its old slot as the seventh letter would have changed the letter sequence, something the Romans did not want to do. The Romans solved their problem by adding the letter *Z* to the end of the alphabet, where it remains today in our own English alphabet.

———
Ouaknin, M. C. (1999). *Mysteries of the alphabet: The origins of writing* (J. Bacon, Trans.). New York: Abbeville Press Publishers.

s, azure	**37.** The *z* occasionally stands for the sound represented by the key symbol _____ as in *quartz* and the *zh* as in _____. *(seize, azure)*
seize	Pronounce *seize* and *azure* aloud. Which has the phoneme you hear in *zoo?* _____
zero *prize*	**38.** Check the words at the right in which the *z* stands for the phoneme heard at the beginning of the word *zipper*. *zero* *waltz* *prize* *azure*

STUDY GUIDE
Consonants d, f, j, n, z
Digraphs dg, gh, ph
-ed Suffix

Consonant	Key Symbol	Key Word
d	*d*	*dog*
f	*f*	*fish*
j	*j*	*jeep*
n	*n*	*nut*
z	*z*	*zipper*

Digraph	Key Symbol	Key Word
dg	*j*	*jeep*
gh	*f, g,* or silent	*fish, goat,* or no key word when silent
ph	*f*	*fish*

Suffix	Key Symbol	Key Word
-ed	*d*	*dog* (fold*ed*)
-ed	*t*	*table* (hop*ed*)

Dd   may be silent (*ladder*), or may represent /t/ (*jumped*) when part of the *-ed* suffix.

Ff   is, in general, a reliable letter, with a notable exception in the word *of,* in which the letter *f* represents /v/.

Jj   is a very reliable letter (*jelly*).

Nn   may be silent when preceded by *m* (*autumn*). The single *n* may represent /ng/ (*thank*).

Zz   represents the /z/ in the key word *zipper,* and occasionally stands for /s/ (*waltz*) and the /zh/ in *azure.*

gh   The *gh* digraph is usually silent when followed by *t* in a syllable (*night*). The *gh* is silent (*through*), or represents /f/ (*cough*) when it follows the vowel in a syllable. When *gh* occurs at the beginning of a word, the *h* is silent (*ghost*). There are only a handful of English words that begin with *gh.* They include: *ghost, ghetto, ghastly,* and *ghoul.*

dg   The *dg* digraph represents /j/ (*fudge, budget*).

ph   The *ph* digraph represents /f/, and may occur at the beginning (*phone*) or end (*graph*) of a syllable (that is, before or after the vowel).

-ed Suffix   The *-ed* suffix forms a separate syllable when it is preceded by *t* or *d* (*salted, folded*). When the *-ed* forms a separate syllable, the final *d* represents /d/ (*folded*). When the suffix does not form a separate syllable, the *d* may represent the sound associated with /d/ (*played*), or with /t/ (*hoped*).

39. We have noted that the consonants *d, f, j, n,* and *z* have irregularities. In the next two frames, select the word at the right that illustrates the irregularity described.

The consonant may represent a phoneme other than that of its key symbol:

f = /v/	*fish, of*
d = /t/	*missed, list*
n = /ng/	*bank, bone*
z = /s/	*zoo, waltz*
z = /zh/	*his, azure*

of
missed
bank
waltz
azure

40. **The key symbol may be represented by a different letter or digraph:**

ph = /f/	*phone, puff*
gh = /f/	*bough, rough*
dg = /j/	*jug, fudge*

phone
rough
fudge

Review 5

1. Write the key symbols that represent the sounds of the consonant letters in these words:

a. *bough*	**b.** *tough*	**c.** *hedge*	**d.** *of*	**e.** *phone*
f. *tight*	**g.** *ghastly*	**h.** *soldier*	**i.** *gender*	**j.** *huffed*
k. *planted*	**l.** *quilt*	**m.** *zero*	**n.** *sleigh*	**o.** *column*

2. In which words do you hear the same phoneme as that represented by the underlined part of the first word?

a. *dog clapped don't ride soldier moved*
b. *fish fine graph of photo off*
c. *jeep wedge soldier gold hallelujah Roger*
d. *nut sling hymn knot stranger lank*
e. *zipper his puzzle does seizure waltz*

(See the Part II Answers section for the answers to Review 5, page 98)

◇ c, g, w, y

				1	2	3
g	g	goat	**1.** Each of the four consonants *c, g, w,* and *y* is very irregular. However, each has a pattern of consistency within its inconsis- tencies. The *c* and *g* have some patterns in common as do the *w* and *y*. *C* has been omitted in the table at the right because it has no phoneme of its own. Complete the table for each of the other three with the key symbol (2) and key word (3). Select the words from the following:	g	_____	_____
w	w	wagon		w	_____	_____
y	y	yo-yo		y	_____	_____

yo-yo, jeep, wagon, why, goat, kite, van, city

goat	**2.** *G* is the key symbol for the phoneme we hear at the beginning of its key word _____. Check its reliability: Does it always
no	represent the sound we associate with the *g* in *goat*? _____ Pronounce these words using /g/ whenever you see a *g*. Then pronounce them correctly. Check those in which you hear /g/.
guess glass	guess huge page ginger glass
go begin	go enough gnat begin sing

	3. It is clear that *g* is a very unreliable letter. In the words above, *g* represents its hard sound (/g/, as in *goat*) in the words
guess, glass, go	_____ , _____ , _____ , and
begin	_____.
huge	*G* represents the soft phoneme, /j/, in the words _____ ,
page, ginger	_____ , and _____.
gnat	*G* is silent when followed by *n* as in _____.
	G is part of a digraph, representing a different sound from either of its
enough, sing	components in _____ and _____.

4. _G_ is the key symbol for the hard sound we hear at the beginning of _goat._ We have noted that the letter _g_ often represents the <u>soft</u> sound

_j_

we associate with the key symbol _____. Are these used interchangeably or is there a pattern to the words that might give a clue as to whether the _g_ represents the soft sound we associate with

_j_

the key symbol _____ or the hard sound we identify with

_g_

the key symbol _____? Let us examine some known words to see.

5. Study the sets of words below. Add a word from the list at the right to each set. Choose a word in which the _g_ represents the same phoneme as the other underlined letters in the set and has the same vowel following the underlined _g_.

gone
gem
gum
get
gym
gate
giant

1	2	3	4	5	6
gain	_gentle_	_giraffe_	_go_	_gulp_	_gypsy_
a_gain_st	a_ge_	en_gi_ne	wa_go_n	re_gu_lar	ener_gy_
_____	_____	_____	_____	_____	_____

1. _gate_   2. _gem_

3. _giant_   4. _gone_

5. _gum_   6. _gym_

6.   **The letter _g_ usually represents the sound we associate with the key symbol _j_ (the soft sound) when it is followed by the vowels _____ , _____ , or _____ .**

_e, i, y_

Carefully study the sets of words above before you answer.

7. The word _usually_ in the generalization indicates that this is not always true.

get

The word _____ is an exception. When _g_ is followed by
         (gem, get)
the letter _e,_ the _g_ usually represents the sound we associate with the

j, get

key symbol _____. The word _____ does not
                                    (get, gentle)
follow this generalization.

a, o, u	**8.** Make a generalization about the phoneme that we associate with the key symbol *g:* **The letter *g* usually represents the sound we associate with the key symbol *g* when it is followed by the vowels _____ , _____ , or _____ .**
e, i, y hard (or the one associated with *g*)	**9.** What happens when other letters follow *g?* Study the words at the right. The generalization will read: The *g* usually represents the soft sound when followed by _____ , _____ , or _____ . When followed by any other letter or when it appears at the end of a word, the *g* represents the _____ sound. Memorize these sets: /j/—e i y /g/—a o u You may wish to compose a phrase to help you remember, as "*an <u>o</u>rnery <u>u</u>gly <u>g</u>oat.*" *great* *ghost* *pilgrim* *gleam* *egg*
e, i, y *g*	**10.** Do not forget that there are exceptions. The generalization above, however, is a useful one. When you see a word you do not recognize, a word that contains a *g*, try the generalization. Try the phoneme represented by the key symbol *j* when the *g* is followed by _____ , _____ , or _____ ; otherwise, try the hard sound, represented by the key symbol _____ .
j yes	**11.** Many words end in the letters *ge*. Pronounce the words at the right. The key symbol that represents the final sound in each of these words is _____ . Does the generalization apply to words that end in the letters *ge?* _____ *huge* *sponge* *cage* *orange*

	12. Rewrite these words to show the pronunciation of the consonant letters. Omit each silent consonant and the silent *es*. Copy the other vowels as they are.
guard, guilt, ej	guard _____ guilt _____ edge _____
gastly, naw, paj	ghastly _____ gnaw _____ page _____
	(It is interesting to note that an unnecessary *u* has been added to many words that "makes the *g* hard" and so eliminates many
guilt	exceptions, for example, _____ above.)
symbol	**13.** The letter *c* is also very irregular, but on top of that, it has no phoneme of its own, and therefore, no key _____ or key
word	_____. (See Frame 1, page 31.)
c	**14.** Study these words: *cute, city.* Both start with the letter _____. The first phoneme in *cute* represents the sound we
k	associate with the key symbol _____. The first phoneme in *city*
s	represents the sound we associate with the key symbol _____.
	15. As a single-letter grapheme, the *c* not only represents no phoneme of its own, but commonly serves to represent <u>two</u> other
k, s	phonemes, the _____ and the _____.
	There are some clues to guide us to the sounds the *c* represents in words we do not know.

	16. Study the sets of words below.				coat
	For each set, choose a word from the six at the right in which the *c* represents the same phoneme as the other underlined letters in the set and has the same vowel following it.				*bicycle* *city* *curl* *cent* *cat*

	1	2	3	4	5	6
1. *cat* 2. *cent* 3. *city*	c̲ane	c̲enter	c̲ircus	c̲ook	c̲urrent	c̲ymbal
4. *coat* 5. *curl*	bec̲ame	mic̲e	dec̲ide	bac̲on	circ̲us	encyc̲lopedia
6. *bicycle*	_____	_____	_____	_____	_____	_____

BOX 2.3

Why Not *K* for *Cat?*

Alphabetically speaking, the letter C has a rather checkered past. The Greeks called the letter C, *gamma,* and used it to represent the voiced /g/ heard in *goat* (the hard *g*). The Etruscans, who inherited the alphabet from the Greeks, did not use the voiced /g/ in their spoken language. Rather than eliminate the letter C altogether, the Etruscans decided to use it to represent the /k/ heard in *kite.* In changing the sound represented by the gamma from a /g/ to a /k/, the Etruscan alphabet came to represent /k/ with four different letter sequences. In the Etruscan alphabet, the /k/ could be represented with *ka, ce* or *ci,* and *qu!* The Etruscan alphabet subsequently passed to the Latin alphabet, and eventually to our own English alphabet. Today we continue the practice that was passed down from the Etruscans, using the same three letters to represent the /k/ in English words: *k, c,* and *q* (as in *antique*).

Ouaknin, M. C. (1999). *Mysteries of the alphabet: The origins of writing* (J. Bacon, Trans.). New York: Abbeville Press Publishers.

1, 4, 5 *a, o, u*	**17.** Which sets of words in frame 16 have **c**s that represent the hard sound, that of the /*k*/? _____ What vowels follow the *c* in each of these groups? _____
a, o, u	**18.** Complete the generalization: **The letter *c* usually represents the sound we associate with the *k* when it is followed by _____, _____, or _____.**
s, e, i, y	**19.** What about the soft sound? **The letter *c* usually represents the sound we associate with the _____ when it is followed by _____, _____, or _____.**
The letter *g* usually represents the soft sound (*j*) when it is followed by *e, i,* or *y.*	**20.** What is the generalization about the phoneme we associate with the soft sound of *g*?

yes	**21.** Are there similarities between the generalizations concerning the sounds represented by *c* and *g*? _____ The combined generalization might read: The consonants *c* and *g* represent their
a, o, u	hard sounds when followed by _____ , _____ , and _____ .
e	They usually represent their soft sounds when followed by _____ ,
i, y	_____ , and _____ .
	If you remembered the phrase "*an ornery ugly goat,*" you might relate it to "*an ornery ugly kid.*" C generally represents the sound heard in *kid*
a, o, u	when followed by _____ , _____ , or _____ .

22. Study the words at the right. What happens when other letters follow *c* and *g*? The *c* then represents the sound

regret

glad

k	we associate with _____ and the *g* the sound we
	crow
g, hard	associate with _____ . These are the _____ sounds.
	comic
	What happens when *c* or *g* is the last letter in the word?
	climb
hard	In that position they also represent their _____ sounds.
	big

23. Let us summarize the generalizations:

> **The c and g usually represent their soft sounds when followed by e, i, or y. When followed by any other letter or when they appear at the end of the word, the c and the g**

hard	**represent their _____ sounds.**

24. Now apply the generalizations to the words at the right. Place a check mark next to the words that <u>do</u> <u>not</u> follow the generalization.

cube	giant
cello	girl
cotton	guide
cash	gift
receive	give

cello *girl*	
gift	
give	

silent	*siense*
	skool
	sene
	skalp
	skale
	skold
	skreen
	skum

25. There are many words in which *s* is followed by *c*. Examine the first word at the right. Note that *c* can be a _____ letter. Rewrite each word using key symbols for the consonants.

science _____

school _____

scene _____

scalp _____

scale _____

scold _____

screen _____

scum _____

---

ch

k

26. You have learned that *c*, as a single letter, is unnecessary. Examine these words: *chair, child, check*. We have no substitute for the *c* in the digraph _____. We cannot get along without the *c*. We could get along without the *q*, because _____ substitutes perfectly.

---

only one is sounded

27. Complete the generalization:

When two like-consonants appear together in a word, usually _____.

---

k

s

28. Does this hold for the *c?*

This generalization does not hold when the consonants represent different sounds.

In the word *success,* the first *c* represents the sound we associate with the key symbol _____ , the second *c* the sound we associate with the key symbol _____.

---

akses, stoping

skil, aksident

aksept, aksent

29. Examine the following words. Rewrite them using key symbols for the consonants. Omit the silent letters.

access _____   stopping _____

skill _____   accident _____

accept _____   accent _____

c *blok* *duk* *n, k* *blak* *bak*	**30.** In words containing *ck,* the ________ is usually silent. What consonants are sounded in *knock?* ________. Rewrite the words at the right to show pronunciation of the consonants. *block* ________ *duck* ________ *black* ________ *back* ________
a, o, u, end letter (consonant), digraph *ch,* silent	**31.** *C* and *g* generally represent their hard sound when followed by ________ , ________ , ________ , or come at the ________ of a word, or are followed by another ________. Both *c* and *g* are part of a ________ (*c* in ________, *g* in *gh*). Both *c* and *g* can be ________ as in *back* and *gnome.*
y	**32.** Say *yo-yo* aloud. Listen to the first phoneme as you pronounce this key word again. The initial sound heard in *yo-yo* will be identified by the key symbol ________.
yo-yo *yellow young canyon* *consonant*	**33.** The *y* is very unreliable. You cannot assume that, when you see *y* in a word, it will represent the sound you hear in its key word ________. Pronounce these words aloud, use /y/ for each *y* you see: *yellow sky rhyme young sadly play canyon* Underline those in which the *y* represents the phoneme you hear in *yo-yo.* When *y* represents the phoneme heard in *yo-yo,* it is a ________.
beginning	**34.** Now pronounce the above words correctly. Listen to the sound represented by the *y* in each word. You will notice when the *y* is at the ________ of a word or a syllable it has the /y/ phoneme. (beginning, end)
vowel	**35.** You will notice also that each *y* within or at the end of a syllable has a ________ sound. (consonant, vowel)

consonant /y/	**36.** The *y* is unreliable, but there is a distinct pattern to help us select those which are consonants. When the *y* appears at the beginning of a syllable, it is a _____ and has the sound we associate with _____. (Exception: some words in chemistry with a (another vowel, /y/) foreign origin, as in *Ytterbia.*)
consonant *yo-yo*	**37.** As a consonant, *y* is very reliable. When we see a *y* at the beginning of a syllable, we can be sure it is a _____ and represents the sound heard in its key word _____.
w *consonant*	**38.** Say *wagon* aloud. Listen to the first phoneme as you pronounce this key word again. The initial sound heard will be identified by the key symbol _____. The *w* is very unreliable. Like the *y,* it serves as a vowel as well as a _____.

went
 	
always
	39. Use the words at the right for this and the following five frames (40–44) to illustrate the characteristics of the consonant *w. W,* as a consonant, always appears before the vowel in a syllable. (Note: *w* as a vowel always follows another vowel.) *W* is generally an initial consonant in a
	
	word or syllable as in _____
	           (select a one-syllable word)
	
	and in _____.
	   (select a two-syllable word)
		once
		
		quilt
		
		went
		
		write
		
		antique
		
		who
		
		snow
		
		dwell
		
		one
		
		queen
		
		always

dwell (*quilt* and *queen* are okay, too!)	**40.** The phoneme represented by *w* may, however, be part of a blend of two consonants as in _____.
quilt *queen*	**41.** The *u,* when following *q,* often represents the consonant phoneme we associate with the key symbol *w.* We hear this when we say the words _____ and _____.

write	**42.** The *w* is silent before *r* as in _____.
who (hoo)	**43.** Occasionally the letter *w* fools us. It appears to be a part of the digraph *wh* but is actually silent, as in _____. (This is a puzzle. Can you solve it?) Remember to refer to frame 39.
one *once*	**44.** We are familiar with the word *won.* But note the grapheme we use in the word pronounced the same but spelled _____. We use the same grapheme to represent the *w* in _____.

vowel
before
 	
away, wring
	45. The *w* may be a consonant or a _____. As a consonant, it appears _____ the vowel in the syllable and represents the
	        (before, after)
	phoneme heard in _____. It is sometimes silent as in _____ .
	       (away, blow) (wish, wring)

unreliable /g/, /j/ /ng/ /f/, silent	**46.** We have been studying four _____ consonants: *c, g,* (reliable, unreliable) *w, y.* We have found that *g* may have the sound of / /, as in *goat;* or / / as in *genius;* it may be a part of a digraph that has the sound of / / as in *sing* or / / as in *enough.* It may be _____ as in *gnaw.*
It has no key symbol of its own.	**47.** What is the distinctive key symbol for *c?*
/k/, /s/ h, digraph /ch/, silent	**48.** *C* may represent the sound of / / as in *acorn* or of / / as in *nice.* It may, with the letter _____, form a _____ as in *much,* having the sound of / /. It is _____ in *scissors.*
e i, y, /k/ a, o u, consonant end of a word, /j/ e, i, y; /g/ a, o u, consonant end of a word	**49.** *C* usually has its soft sound when followed by _____, _____, _____. It usually has its hard sound, / /, when followed by _____, _____, _____, any other _____, or comes at the _____. *G* usually represents its soft sound / / when followed by _____, _____, _____ ; and its hard sound / / when followed by _____, _____, _____, any other _____, or comes at the _____.

	50.	The consonants *w* and *y* are positioned before the vowel in a syllable. The consonant *y* is never silent. The consonant *w* may be silent
wrote, two, who		as in the words (check those correct). *quit, wrote, wing, two, who.* W
digraph		may be a part of a _____ as in *white*.

�֍◇֍ Review 6

1. What generalization helps you to determine the sound of /g/ in an unknown word?

2. Write the key symbols for the consonants in these words:

   a. *giant*   **b.** *bank*   **c.** *girl*   **d.** *big*   **e.** *circus*
   f. *cook*   **g.** *who*   **h.** *match*   **i.** *yellow*   **j.** *way*
   k. *quick*   **l.** *write*   **m.** *yet*   **n.** *knack*

3. Which of the above contains an exception to the "hard-soft *g*" generalization?

4. What generalization helps you to determine the sound of a *c* in an unknown word?

5. The suffix *-ed* may have the sound of / / as in *quilted*, of / / as in *called*, of / / as in *jumped*.

6. What generalization helps you to determine whether *w* represents /w/ and *y* represents /y/?

7. What key symbol indicates the pronunciation of the last phoneme in each of the following words?

   a. *beg*   **b.** *church*   **c.** *judge*   **d.** *quack*   **e.** *knowledge*
   f. *back*   **g.** *ache*   **h.** *unique*   **i.** *critic*   **j.** *rough*

8. The two-letter key symbols *ch* and *ng* are called _____.

9. Rewrite the following words using key symbols to indicate the pronunciation of the underlined parts. Omit silent consonant letters. Underline the digraphs.

   range _____   *wrinkle* _____   *ransom* _____

   manger _____   *triangle* _____   *links* _____

10. As a single letter, we can expect *g* to represent the hard sound we associate

    with the key symbol *g*, <u>except</u> when followed by _____ ,

    _____ , or _____ .

11. When *g* is part of a _____ as in *enough,* it is not considered a single-letter consonant: The *g* in *enough* does <u>not</u> represent the sound we associate with the key symbol *g* as in _____.

    (go, ginger)

    The *g* in *enough* does <u>not</u> represent the sound we associate with the key symbol _____ as in *gem.*

    Nor is the *g* in *enough* a _____ letter as it is in *knight.*

    (See the Part II Answers section for the answers to Review 6, page 98.)

❖ *s, t, x*

s	*s*	sun	**1.** The three consonants *s, t,* and *x* are unreliable. You cannot assume that when you see one of them in a word, you will hear the same phoneme as that in its key word. Complete the table adding key symbols (2) and key words (3). Select key words from this set: *city, sun, chin, she, table, zipper, ax, thin.*	1 2 3		
t	*t*	table		*s* _____ _____		
				t _____ _____		

	2. Why is there no *x* in the table above? The letter *x* has no key symbol because it has no distinctive sound of its own. It represents sounds we associate with other key symbols. Pronounce *box* aloud.
boks	Try to write *box* using other letters: _____.

	3. Pronounce *exact.* Rewrite it using other key symbols:
egzact (or *egzakt*)	_____. The letter *x* represents the sounds we associate with
box, gz	*ks* in _____ and _____ as in *exact.* And we often
	(box, exam)
Either is correct.	interchange them! How do you pronounce *exit?* _____
	(egzit, eksit)
	We are more apt to use /*gz*/ when *x* appears between two vowel phonemes.

/ks/, /gz/	**4.** We have seen that *x* may represent the phonemes / / or / /. This may sound confusing, but it presents no problem to an English-speaking person, who will automatically use the acceptable phoneme.

5. Then consider the word *xylophone*. At the beginning of a word, *x* consistently represents the sound we associate with the key symbol

z

_____. Of course, at times we use *x* as a letter; such as *X-ray*.

eks

In this instance, _____ could be used as the grapheme to represent the *x*.

siks	**6.** **The *x* could be omitted from our alphabet by using the letters *gz, ks,* or *z*.**	*six* _____
zylofone		*xylophone* _____
egzample		*example* _____
boks	Spell the words at the right, substituting the proper graphemes for the letter *x* in each one.	*box* _____
zeroks		*Xerox* _____
egzist		*exist* _____

7. The phonemes represented by *c, q,* and *x* need no key symbols. In our one-to-one correspondence they are already represented.

k

We could omit the letter *q* entirely by substituting the _____.

gz, ks, z

We could omit the letter *x* by substituting _____, _____, or _____.

ch

We do use the *c* as part of the digraph __ _____ , but as a

s, k

single letter, the _____ (*city*) and _____ (*coat*) could adequately take its place.

8. The phoneme represented by *s* (key symbol _____) is

s

heard in its key word _____. Does it represent the sound

sun

heard in *list?* _____ *has?* _____

yes, no

*she?*_____ *was?* _____ *surely?* _____

no, no, no

The letter *s* _____ very reliable. When you see the letter *s*

is not

                    (is, is not)

in a word you _____ be sure you will hear /s/ when it is

cannot

                    (can, cannot)

pronounced.

9. Say the words at the right aloud. Listen very carefully to the underlined part. Which key symbol represents each part? Write it in the space following the word.

s   *this* _____

s   *history* _____

z   *his* _____

	10. The grapheme *s* is used to represent different phonemes. Study the words at the right. The single consonant *s* represents the sound we usually associate
see, ask	with *s* in the words _____ and _____
rose, his	with *z* in the words _____ and _____
sure, sugar	with *sh* in the words _____ and _____
television, treasure	with *zh* in the words _____ and _____

Words at right for item 10:

see
ask
rose
his
sure
sugar
television
treasure

z *z*	**11.** Pronounce *his* and *has* aloud. The key symbol that represents the final sound in these words is _____. There are many words in which the grapheme *s* represents the / /. Write the key symbol for each of the plural endings of the words below. If you have trouble, try both the /s/ and the /z/. You must say them aloud.
z, z, z, s, s	*toys* *dogs* *beds* *cats* *hops* _____ _____ _____ _____ _____

sizorz	**12.** Rewrite the words at the right using the key symbol that represents the sound of each consonant. Copy the vowels as they are but omit the silent *es*.
zylofon	
fuzy	
us	
uz	
fuz	
miks	

Words at right for item 12:

scissors _____
xylophone _____
fuzzy _____
us _____
use _____
fuse _____
mix _____

13.   **The consonant *s* is unreliable: It often represents the phonemes we associate with *z*, *sh*, and *zh*, as well as its key symbol *s*.**

Rewrite the following words using *s*, *z*, *sh*, or *zh* to indicate the sound the *s* represents. Copy the vowels as they are, pronouncing them as they sound in the real word.

rugz, iz, doez

rugs _____   is _____   does _____

peaz, some, pleazhure

peas _____   some _____   pleasure _____

whoze, so, shurely

whose_____   so _____   surely _____

14. When we see an *s* in an unknown word, we have few clues to tell us which phoneme it represents. We might note the following:

(1) The letter *s* usually represents the sound we associate with the key

s, sun

symbol _____. It is the sound heard in _____.
                                                              (*sun, sure*)

(2) Except for certain foreign names (as *Saar*), the *s* at the beginning

miss

of a word stands for the sound heard in _____.
                                                    (*miss, whose*)

(3) Except when acting as a plural, the *s* at the end of words represents /s/ or /z/ with about equal frequency.

(4) We tend to use the phoneme represented by the *z*, the voiced counterpart of /s/, when the preceding phoneme is voiced. (English-speaking people use the correct ending automatically, thus we have not studied voice-voiceless phonemes in this edition.)

15. The letter *t* as a single consonant (as heard in its key word

table

_____) is fairly reliable. However, we must distinguish between *t* as a single letter and *t* as part of a digraph. Pronounce these words: *this, think, with*. We do not hear /t/ in the two-letter

th

grapheme _____. We will study this grapheme later.

16. But then pronounce these words: *Thomas, thyme*. (Exceptions! Exceptions!) The *th* in each of these words does represent the

/t/, h

phoneme / /. Or we could say that the _____ is silent.

no, *shun*	**17.** One of the common "endings" in our language is found in these words: *motion, convention, station.* Pronounce them. Do you hear /*t*/? _____ This ending could be spelled _____. (*shun, ton*)

/ch/
/ch/
/t/
/ch/
/sh/
	18. Examine these words. Pronounce them, paying special attention to the underlined parts. What phoneme does each part represent? Work carefully. *righteous* / /
	                question / /
	                mountain / /
	                natural / /
	                action / /

beginning	**19.** It is clear there are many word "parts" (never at the _____ of the word) in which the *t,* in combination with a (beginning, ending) vowel, represents a phoneme other than /*t*/.
silent	**20.** Pronounce these words: *bouquet, beret, debut.* There are several common words derived from the French language in which the *t* is _____.

t
 	
often
soften
listen
fasten
moisten
	21. When *t* follows *f* or *s,* the _____ is sometimes silent. These words are written without the silent consonants; write them correctly:
	
	                ofen _____
	                sofen _____
	                lisen _____
	                fasen _____
	                moisen _____

match, watch, hatch	**22.** The *t* is also silent in the *tch* combinations. Pronounce the words below saying the /*ch*/ as in *chair.* Spell them correctly. *mach* _____ *wach* _____ *hach* _____

23. **The *t* is fairly reliable. However, it may be silent and often loses the /t/ phoneme when combined with other letters.**

The words at the right will aid you in filling in the blanks below. We have noted that *t*, as a single letter, is fairly reliable.

It may be silent as when it follows *f* (as in _____)

or _____ (as in _____) and when it

precedes _____ (as in _____). Only

one *t* is sounded in such words as _____.

It may also be silent in words adopted from the French as

_____. In connection with a vowel, the *t* may

represent /ch/ as in _____ or /sh/ as in

_____. It is often a part of a consonant digraph

as in _____ , in which case the /t/ is not heard.

	catch
	father
soften	*soften*
s, listen	*letter*
ch, catch	*listen*
letter	*future*
	lotion
ballet	*ballet*
future	
lotion	
father	

---

24. We have noted that several different graphemes may represent the initial sound heard in *sun* as well as the initial sound heard in *zipper*. To illustrate, write the key symbol that indicates the pronunciation of each of the consonants in the words at the right.

(If you get these, you are really thinking!)

ng z t	*anxiety*	_____
z	*is*	_____
t s	*its*	_____
s n t	*scent*	_____
z n z	*zones*	_____
s r k l	*circle*	_____
z l f n	*xylophone*	_____

---

25. We have also noted that the grapheme *s* may represent sounds other than that heard in *sun*, and that the grapheme *z* occasionally represents sounds other than that heard in *zipper*. Check the words at the right in which the *s* stands for a phoneme other than that heard at the beginning of *sun*.

sugar	*sugar*	_____
	this	_____
pleasure	*pleasure*	_____
	whisp	_____
hose	*hose*	_____

---

26. We called *x* an unnecessary letter because it could be replaced by _____ in *ax*, by _____ in *example*, and by _____ in *xylophone*.

ks, gz, z

STUDY GUIDE
Consonants
c, g, s, t, w, x, y

Consonant	Key Symbol	Key Word
c	no key symbol	no key word
g	*g*	*goat*
s	*s*	*sun*
t	*t*	*table*
w	*w*	*wagon*
x	no key symbol	no key word
y	*y*	*yo-yo*

Cc   does not have a key symbol. *C* usually represents /s/ (the soft sound) when it is followed by *e* (*cent*), *i* (*city*), or *y* (*cycle*). *C* usually represents /k/ (the hard sound) when followed by *a* (*cat*), *o* (*coat*), or *u* (*cut*), when it appears at the end of a word (*comic*), and when followed by any other letter (*cloud*). *C* can be silent when it follows *s* (*scene*).

Gg   may represent /j/ (the soft sound) when it is followed by the vowels *e* (*gerbil*), *i* (*giant*), or *y* (*gypsy*), although with exceptions. *G* usually represents /g/ (the hard sound) when it is followed by *a* (*gate*), *o* (*go*), or *u* (*gum*), when it appears at the end of a word (*leg*), and when followed by any other letter (*glass*).

Ss,   except when acting as a plural at the end of words, represents /s/ (*miss*) or /z/ (*whose*) with about equal frequency. *S* also represents /zh/ (*television*), and occasionally stands for /sh/ (*sugar*).

Tt   may be silent when it follows the letter *s* (*listen*) or *f* (*soften*), and when it precedes *ch* (*catch*). In connection with a vowel, *t* may represent /ch/ (*future*) or /sh/ (*station*). When part of a digraph (*th*), the *t* is not heard (*father*). *T* may also be silent in words adopted from the French language (*ballet*).

Ww   serves as a consonant and a vowel. As a consonant, *w* precedes the vowel (*wagon*). As a vowel, *w* follows the vowel (*snow*). The *w* is silent before *r* (*write*). *W* may also be part of a blend (*dwell*) or a diagraph (*what*). Occasionally, the letter *w* fools us. It appears to be part of the digraph *wh*, but is actually silent (*who*).

Xx   does not have a key symbol. It may represent /ks/ (*six*), /gz/ (*exam*), or /z/ (*xylophone*). We are more apt to use /gz/ when *x* appears between two vowel phonemes (*exempt*).

Yy   serves as a consonant and as a vowel. The *y* at the beginning of a syllable acts as a consonant and represents /y/ (*yellow*). *Y* within a syllable or at the end of a syllable acts as a vowel and may be silent (*play*), or may represent a vowel sound (*rhyme*).

✖◇✖ Review 7

1. There are three consonants which, as single letters, represent no distinctive phonemes:

    a. The *c* usually represents the sound we associate with *s* when followed by

    _____ , _____ , or _____ .

    The *c* usually represents the sound we associate with _____

    when followed by the vowels _____ , _____ , or

    _____ , most other consonants, or when appearing at the end of a word.

    b. The *q* always represents the sound we associate with _____ .

    c. The *x* can adequately be represented by the consonants _____ ,

    _____ , and _____ .

2. There are other letters that represent two or more sounds, one of which is the sound we commonly associate with that particular letter (key symbol).

    a. The *g* represents "its own sound," /g/, (the _____ sound)
    (hard, soft)

    when followed by the vowels _____ , _____ ,

    _____ , or by other consonants, or appears at the end of a word.

    b. The *g* usually represents its _____ sound, that which we
    (hard, soft)

    ordinarily associate with the letter _____ , when followed by

    _____ , _____ , or _____ .

3. The two most common sounds represented by the single letter *s* are:

    a. The sound we ordinarily associate with the letter *s,* as in _____
    (some, sugar).

    b. The sound we ordinarily associate with the letter _____ , as in
    hi s̲.

4. The letter *d* may represent the sound we associate with _____ or

    with _____ when it appears in the suffix *-ed.*

5. *F* occasionally represents the sound we associate with _____ , as in *of.*

6. *T* in combination with a vowel may represent different sounds as _____

    in *question* and _____ in *patient.*

7. Generalizations:

 a. Consonant letters may represent more than one sound.

   The *s* represents the sound of _____ (as the key symbol indicates),

   of _____ (*sure*), of _____ (*has*), and of _____ (*treasure*).

   The *z* represents the sound of _____ (as the key symbol

   indicates), of _____ (*quartz*), and of _____ (*azure*).

 b. Consonant sounds may be represented by more than one letter. The
     sound we hear at the beginning of *say* is often represented by *s*, by

   _____ (*cent*), or by _____ (*chintz*).

   The sound we hear at the beginning of the word *zipper* is sometimes

   represented by the letters _____ and _____.

 c. Consonant letters may represent no sound. The three consonant letters

   that represent no sound in *knight* are _____ , _____ ,

   and _____. We call them _____ letters. The letter

   _____ is _____ in *soften, ballet,* and *latch.*

8. Reread the generalizations in question 7. Be sure you determine the
   difference between them. These generalizations would carry more precise
   meanings if the words *phoneme* and *grapheme* were used. Then they would
   read:

 a. Consonant _____ may represent more than one _____.

 b. Consonant _____ may be represented by more than one

   _____.

 c. Consonant letters may represent no _____.

   (See the Part II Answers section for the answers to Review 7, page 99.)

◈ Consonant Digraphs

	1. We have been relating each of the consonant phonemes to its respective consonant letter.
26	There are _____ letters in the alphabet.
vowels, 21	Five are _____ , so there are _____ consonant letters.
Three	_____ of these have no distinctive phoneme of their own.
18	This leaves _____ single-letter consonant graphemes, each of which has been assigned a key symbol so as to build up a one-to-one correspondence between symbol and phoneme.

7	**2.** Eighteen symbols, but 25 consonant sounds! Where do we find the _____ remaining symbols?
	We use two-letter combinations called digraphs to stand for the seven phonemes not represented by single-letter graphemes.

	3. The *ch* is one of the two-letter digraphs we will study. Pronounce *chair*. Does the *ch* in *chair* represent the sound we usually associate
no	with the *c* in *cat*? _____ Does the *h* represent the sound
	(yes, no)
no	we usually associate with the *h* in *hat*? _____ The digraphs
	(yes, no)
	represent unique phonemes. The phonemes do not represent the sound usually associated with either letter when it occurs alone.

4. The key symbols that represent the seven missing phonemes are listed at the right. Fill in the missing items in the table: digraphs (1), key words (3). Select the key words from these: *ship, whale, king, thumb, chair, treasure*. Pronounce aloud the word and phoneme each represents. Notice that each is a distinctive consonant sound not represented by any single letter in our alphabet.

				1	2	3
<u>ch</u>	ch	chair		_____	ch	_____
<u>sh</u>	sh	ship		_____	sh	_____
<u>th</u>	th	thumb		_____	th	_____
<u>th</u>	th̸	that		_____	th̸	<u>that</u>
<u>wh</u>	wh	whale		_____	wh	_____
	zh	treasure			zh	_____
<u>ng</u>	ng	king		_____	ng	_____

BOX 2.4

Too Many English Sounds, Too Few English Letters: The French Solution

History books tell us that the French-speaking Normans ruled England from 1066 to roughly 1500 A.D. French became the language of the government, and hordes of French-speaking scribes were moved to England to keep the official records. The Norman French scribes were relatively unfamiliar with the English language. When the scribes realized that there were not enough English letters to represent the sounds in English words, they turned to the French writing system for a solution, introducing the *ch, sh, wh,* and *th* digraphs to represent the /ch/, /sh/, /wh/, voiced /tⱨ/, and unvoiced /th/. Let us consider why the Norman French scribes chose these particular two-letter combinations.

In Old French, the letter *h* was occasionally used to signal when the preceding consonant had an atypical pronunciation. When the French-speaking scribes wanted to represent the English /ch/, they used the *h* in English just as it had been used in Old French—to mark the unexpected pronunciation of the consonant letter. This is the reason why the *ch* digraph is spelled with a *c+h.* Following the same line of reasoning, the scribes used the letter *h* to alert the reader to the unexpected pronunciation of *s* when the /sh/ phoneme occurs in English words. The *sh* digraph reliably represents /sh/, except in French loan words in which the Norman scribes used the *ch* digraph to represent /sh/ (*machine, chivalry, chef, sachet*).

In Old English spelling, the *wh* in <u>when</u> was written as *hw.* The French-speaking scribes reversed the letters, thereby introducing the *wh* digraph. Say *when.* Do you hear /hw/? The Old English *hw* letter sequence is a more accurate description of English pronunciation. Modern dictionaries use the Old English letter sequence—hw—to record the pronunciation of the *wh* digraph in words such as *hwen, hwite,* and *hwisper.*

Old English used two letters, the *thorn* and the *edh,* to record the voiced *tⱨ* (*this*) and the unvoiced *th* (*thumb*). These two Old English letters were used interchangeably, so the reader did not know whether to use the voiced or unvoiced pronunciation. The Norman French scribes preferred the *th* digraph, and used it to represent both the voiced and unvoiced phonemes. Eventually, both the *thorn* and the *edh* disappeared from the English alphabet. In the Middle English period, after the Old English *thorn* had dropped from the alphabet, the letter *y* was occasionally used to represent /th/ in the initial position. How would you pronounce, "Ye Olde Malt Shoppe," in modern English? (If you said, "The Old Malt Shop," you are right! In the word *ye,* the letter *y* represents the /th/!)

---

ng

5. Some dictionaries use key symbols other than those shown in column 2 of the previous frame to indicate pronunciation. Some join each set of letters to show one sound, as <u>ch</u>, <u>sh</u>, $\widehat{ng}$. Some use č to represent the initial phoneme heard in *chair.* ŋ is often used to

represent _____ as heard in *king.* Look up *chair, ship,* and *king* in your dictionary to see how the pronunciation is indicated.

---

f

6. There are other consonant digraphs as *ph* and *gh*. However, they are not listed in frame 3 because they are already represented. The

key symbol _____ indicates the sound of the *ph* and the *gh*.

✖◇✖ Review 8

Check yourself: Are you writing every answer and finishing each frame before moving the mask down? Are you getting almost every answer correct? Do you study more carefully when you miss one? Do you analyze your errors? Can you give yourself 100 on each review?

1. A grapheme composed of two letters that represent a single sound is called

a _____.

2. Indicate the pronunciation of the underlined parts of the following words by using key symbols:

q*u*ick   *wh*o   mea*s*ure   *wh*y   *wh*ich   bo*th*

*th*is   no*ti*on   *s*ugar   wi*sh*   vi*si*on   stron*g*

3. In the following words, underline all the consonant digraphs that serve as key symbols and cannot be replaced by a single letter from our alphabet:

weather   enough   whom   which   bring

wrist   wish   both   through   condemn

4. There are 25 consonant sounds in the American-English language. We

identify 18 of them with single _____ symbols. We should have

_____ more consonant letters in the alphabet. Since we do not, we

use two-letter combinations called _____ to serve as key symbols

for these phonemes. Write the seven two-letter symbols. _____

5. Our sound-symbol system is complicated by the use of other consonant digraphs standing for phonemes already represented in the system. Select three examples of such digraphs from these words:

   tough,   chalk,   sheath,   short-sighted,   chloroform,   phoneme

6. These three digraphs are already represented by (use key symbols) _____,

_____, _____.

7. Rewrite these words using the appropriate key symbols for the consonants. Copy the vowels as they are.

   sunk   photograph   know   alphabet   pheasant   cough

(See the Part II Answers section for the answers to Review 8, page 99.)

◇ *ch, sh, zh*

ch	**1.** We have no single letter in the alphabet to represent the first phoneme we hear in the key word *chair*. We will use the logical two-letter combination, the _____ , to identify this phoneme.

Study the digraphs in these sets of words:

1	2	3
chair	*character*	*chiffon*
chalk	*chord*	*machine*
churn	*chaos*	*chute*

no	Each word contains the grapheme *ch*. Does each grapheme represent the phoneme we associate with the key symbol *ch*? _____
no	Try pronouncing each one using the first phoneme in *chair* for each digraph. Is the digraph *ch* reliable? _____

ch	**2.** The digraph in each of the words in set 1 represents the phoneme we associate with the key symbol _____. The digraphs in set 2
k	represent the phoneme we associate with the key symbol _____.
If you guessed *sh*, you are right!	Can you guess what key symbol represents the digraphs in set 3? _____

no	**3.** Is the digraph *ch* reliable as to the phoneme it represents? _____ If we do not know the word, we cannot tell which
ch	key symbol to identify with it. It might be _____ , or
k, sh	_____ , or _____. (However, if you are an expert on language derivation, you will have clues.)

	4. The sound heard at the beginning of *ship* is very common, but there is no letter in the alphabet to represent it.
	We shall use the key symbol *sh* to represent the phoneme as heard in
ship	the key word _____.
	(ship, clip)

one no	**5.** When *s* and *h* appear together in this order in a syllable, we expect them to represent _____ phoneme(s). Can you hear the (How many?) separate phonemes represented by *s* and *h* in *shut?* _____ If you could, you would hear the word *hut* in *shut.*
/sh/ shure, shoe, moshon, shugar, mashine, speshal	**6.** *Sh* is very reliable in that when we see *sh,* we can be sure we will hear / /. However, the phoneme we represent by *sh* has a variety of graphemes; that is, it is spelled in a variety of ways. Examine the words below. Look at the underlined parts. Rewrite the words using *sh* to represent the underlined graphemes. *sure* _____ *shoe* _____ *motion* _____ *sugar* _____ *machine* _____ *special* _____
s, sh, ti s, ch, ci	**7.** The graphemes that we associate with the key symbol *sh* are: _____ in *sure* _____ in *shoe* _____ in *motion* _____ in *sugar* _____ in *machine* _____ in *special*
no	**8.** Now listen for the middle consonant sound as you say *treasure.* Is there a letter in the alphabet to represent this sound? _____
zh	**9.** We shall use the digraph *zh* as the key symbol to represent the phoneme heard in the key word *treasure,* although it is never represented in a word with the grapheme _____.
pleazhure vizhon sabotazhe azhure pich	**10.** Rewrite the words at the right to indicate, by using the key symbols, the sounds of the underlined letters. *plea̲sure* _____ *vi̲sion* _____ *sabota̲ge* _____ *a̲zure* _____ *pit̲ch* _____
seizure dozen	**11.** The *z* occasionally stands for the /zh/ as in _____. (*seizure, dozen*) Pronounce *seizure* and *dozen* aloud. Which has the phoneme you hear in *zipper?* _____

leisure, collage	**12.** The *s* and *g* are two other graphemes that occasionally represent the /zh/ as in _____ and _____. The *s* (*leisure, base*) (*collage, age*)
treasure	in the key word _____ represents the /zh/ phoneme. We (*treasure, sun*)
do not	_____ have a grapheme to represent the /zh/ phoneme. (do, do not)

decision *seizure* *beige* *garage* *measure*	**13.** Check the words at the right in which the underlined grapheme represents the /zh/. If you identify all of the words in which the /zh/ phoneme occurs, you are really thinking! *deci<u>s</u>ion* *sei<u>z</u>ure* *bei<u>g</u>e* *gara<u>g</u>e* *per<u>s</u>on* *mea<u>s</u>ure*

s, g	**14.** What letter represents the sound we associate with *zh* in *measure*? _____ In *rouge?* _____

never	**15.** *Zh* _____ appears in a word, so it is not appropriate to (never, seldom) make a statement regarding reliability.

✳◇✳ Review 9

1. Use the key symbol to indicate the sound of each consonant in the following words. Underline the digraphs that represent distinctive phonemes.

    a. *shiver*   **b.** *eggs*   **c.** *sure*   **d.** *share*
    e. *treasure*   **f.** *character*   **g.** *brazier*   **h.** *Christmas*
    i. *schools*   **j.** *ghosts*   **k.** *charge*   **l.** *chute*
    m. *quack*   **n.** *lotion*   **o.** *division*   **p.** *Chicago*
    q. *string*

2. How does the *zh* differ from the other digraphs?

    (See the Part II Answers section for the answer to Review 9, page 99.)

◇ *th, ₮h, wh*

no, no	**1.** Listen to the first phoneme while you pronounce *that* aloud. Compare it with the first phoneme in *thumb.* Do you hear the /t/ in either phoneme? _____ the /h/? _____
voiced	**2.** The /th/ heard in *thumb* is a whispered sound, a "voiceless" sound. However, we use our vocal cords when we say the first phoneme in *that.* We call it a _____ phoneme. (voiced, voiceless)

3. You have learned that the *th* digraph represents two phonemes. One phoneme is voiced (*that*), the other phoneme is voiceless (*thumb*). A voiced phoneme is produced when the vocal cords vibrate. A voiceless phoneme is produced when the vocal cords do not vibrate. Pronounce the words at the right. Write the words in which the *th* is voiced in Column 1 below. Write the words in which the *th* is voiceless in Column 2.

think

there

thick

these

those

thing

this

thank

Column 1 Voiced	Column 2 Voiceless
_____	_____
_____	_____
_____	_____
_____	_____

there   think

these   thick

those   thing

this   thank

4. You <u>must</u> say these words aloud or you will not hear the voiced quality. Note that the voiceless phoneme has a whispered sound even when you say it aloud.

The *th* in _____ has a whispered or voiceless sound. Our
                    (this, thorn)
vocal cords do not vibrate.

thorn

think	**5.** Many people do not realize that *th* is a grapheme that represents two sounds just as different as the sounds represented by *p* and *b* or *s* and *z*.	*think*
		the
thought		*though*
	They automatically use the correct sound for the words they have heard before. Check the words at the right in which the *th* represents the voiceless phoneme. You will not be able to tell the difference if you do not say them out loud!	*thought*
		them
		they
thank		*thank*
through		*through*
length		*length*
both		*both*

6. Repeat all the words in the previous frame in which the *th* represents the voiceless phoneme. Then say all the words in which the *th* represents the voiced phoneme.

We shall use *th̸* as the key symbol to represent the voiced sound. We shall use *th* as the key symbol to represent the voiceless sound.

Rewrite the following words; underline the digraphs that represent the voiceless phonemes and put a slash through the digraphs that represent the voiced phoneme.

toge̸th̸er, <u>th</u>ink, <u>th</u>row	together _____ think _____ throw _____

7. When we see an unknown word in our reading that contains the

digraph *th,* we have no way of knowing which _____ it represents. We can use the dictionary. Many dictionaries use the slash

to indicate that the *th* represents the _____ phoneme as

in _____.
     (their, worth)

phoneme

voiced

their

the, bath /t/	**8.** The *th* is not a reliable digraph. It may represent the voiced sound heard in _____ , the voiceless sound heard in _____ , (*the, third*) (*bath, bathe*) or, in rare instances, the / / as in *Thomas.*
wh *what*	**9.** Another phoneme composed of two letters is _____ as heard in *whale.* It is also heard in _____ . (*who, what*)
w You are correct, whatever your response.	**10.** This phoneme may give you some trouble because it is rapidly disappearing from our language. If you pronounce *weather* and *whether* exactly the same, you are following the trend in America. Many people make the phoneme represented by the key symbol *wh* sound like that represented by the single letter _____ . What do you do? Pronounce *whistle, white.* Do they sound like *wistle,* *wite?* _____
wh *while*	**11.** Most dictionaries note this trend but continue to indicate the pronunciation of words beginning with *wh* as *hw.* We will use the key symbol _____ to represent the sound of the digraph, although it actually is better represented by *hw.* *Wh* represents the phoneme heard in _____ . (Pronounce (*whom, while*) *whom* and *while* carefully so that you will hear the distinction.)
beginning	**12.** The *wh,* like the consonant *w,* appears at the _____ of the word or syllable and is followed by a vowel.

BOX 2.5

When Is a Bumkin a Pumpkin?
An Easy Way to Recognize Voiced and Voiceless Phonemes
and Some Insight into Invented Spelling

You have learned that your vocal cords vibrate when pronouncing voiced phonemes, and do not vibrate when pronouncing voiceless phonemes. However, sometimes it is difficult to determine from listening alone whether a particular phoneme is voiced or voiceless. To identify a voiced phoneme, you must find your voice. Here is a quick and easy way to do this:

1. Lightly place your hand over the lower part of your throat.

2. Pronounce each pair of words below:

   <u>z</u>ap <u>s</u>ap   <u>b</u>an <u>p</u>an   <u>d</u>en <u>t</u>en   <u>g</u>in <u>k</u>in   <u>v</u>an <u>f</u>an

3. Now pronounce each pair again, only this time draw out the phoneme that is represented by the underlined grapheme. When exaggerating the pronunciation of the phoneme, pay special attention to the vibration of your vocal cords. When you feel your vocal cords vibrate, you have found your voice, and you have also identified a voiced phoneme! Which phoneme in each word pair is voiced? Which is voiceless? (See answers below.)

4. To put this into a useful context for the teaching of reading, pronounce each pair once again, this time paying special attention to the way in which you form (articulate) each voiced and voiceless phoneme. Concentrate on your tongue, teeth, and lips. What do you notice about the way in which you articulate each voiced and voiceless phoneme pair?
   If you noticed that the phonemes in each pair represent the same articulation, and differ only in the presence or the absence of breath, you are very observant!

Understanding the voiced and voiceless phoneme pairs will help you to interpret children's misspellings. Sometimes, as children spell, they confuse phonemes that have the same articulation but differ in voicing. Suppose a child writes *bumkin* for *pumpkin*. This misspelling might be due to insufficient phonics knowledge, or to misperceiving the letters *b* and *p*. There is, however, another explanation: Perhaps the child, when thinking about the sounds of the English language, confused the /b/ and /p/ phonemes. After all, these phonemes are articulated in the same manner, and only differ in their voiced and voiceless qualities. Understanding the voiced and voiceless phonemes helps you, the teacher, recognize the many ways in which children combine their knowledge of the phonemes of the English language with their knowledge of phonics in order to spell words when writing.
   Answer to step 3: If you said that the voiced phonemes are /z/, /b/, /d/, /g/, and /v/, you are right!

✖◇✖ Review 10

1. We have identified each of the seven graphemes that serve as additions to our alphabet. Six of them are contained in the words below. Write the key symbol following the word in which each is found.

   swing _____   white _____   measure _____

   mother _____   flash _____   porch _____

2. One grapheme is missing from the group of digraphs above.
   It is found in _____.
   (breath, breathe)

3. We have identified all 18 single-letter phonemes. They are heard in the initial position in each of the following words: *boat, dog, fish, goat, hat, jeep, kite, lion, moon, nut, pig, ring, sun, table, van, wagon, yo-yo, zipper.* Select key words from those above to illustrate phonemes represented by the underlined graphemes in the following words. Those that have no key word may be left blank.

   Examples: <u>w</u>ork   <u>wagon</u>   <u>p</u>sychology _____

   (1) cou<u>l</u>d   _____   (9) o<u>f</u>   _____

   (2) <u>y</u>onder   _____   (10) <u>g</u>et   _____

   (3) <u>c</u>ircle   _____   (11) <u>h</u>onor _____

   (4) jumpe<u>d</u>   _____   (12) ta<u>ll</u>   _____

   (5) <u>g</u>ist   _____   (13) m<u>y</u>   _____

   (6) bom<u>b</u>   _____   (14) <u>wr</u>ong _____

   (7) pa<u>l</u>m   _____   (15) <u>l</u>ittle _____

   (8) <u>gh</u>etto   _____   (16) <u>r</u>ag   _____

4. The word *gem* _____ a key word because the *g* _____
   (is, is not)   (does, does not)
   represent the phoneme we associate with the key symbol *g*.

5. The word *try* is not a key word for the *y* phoneme because the *y* is not at the beginning of the syllable; it is, therefore, not a _____ letter.
   (consonant, vowel)

6. From the following words, select those that contain the /t͡h/ phoneme:

   path   thorn   write   wheel

   white   theme   this   author

   father   whip   mouth   cloth

   wrong   feather   them   whistle

7. Which of the words in question 6 contain the /wh/ phoneme?

8. What do the consonants *w* and *wh* have in common?

(See the Part II Answers section for the answers to Review 10, page 99.)

◇ *ng*

beginning		**1.** The phoneme /*ng*/ is different from the others represented by digraphs in that it is never heard at the _____ of a syllable, (beginning, ending)
follows		or, to put it another way, it always _____ the vowel. (precedes, follows)

	bang	**2.** Say the words at the right aloud. Does	*bang*	_____
yes	*ranjer*	each contain the letters *ng*? _____ Does	*ranger*	_____
no	*stung*	each contain the digraph *ng*? _____ Rewrite the words to show pronunciation of the consonants. (Copy the vowels,	*stung*	_____
	hinj	omit silent *e*).	*hinge*	_____
	hungry		*hungry*	_____

/ng/	*si<u>ng</u>*	**3.** Recall that *n* generally represents / / when followed by *g* or *k*. Rewrite these words, indicating pronunciation of the consonants. Use *ng* (but underline it) to represent the digraph. Work carefully. This takes a keen ear.	*sing*	_____
	pi<u>ng</u>k		*pink*	_____
	bla<u>ng</u>k		*blank*	_____
	fi<u>ng</u>ger		*finger*	_____
	jinjer		*ginger*	_____
	si<u>ng</u>k		*sink*	_____
	tria<u>ng</u>gle		*triangle*	_____

finger, triangle	**4.** In which words from the preceding frame do you hear hard *g*, /g/, as well as /ng/?

digraph
 	
gingham
 	
orange
	5. The letters *n* and *g* together in a word are most commonly a
	
	_____ , that is, a two-letter combination representing a
	
	single phoneme as in _____. However, they may represent
	                (*gingham, ungrateful*)
	
	two separate phonemes as in _____.
	              (*orange, among*)

digraphs
 	
chair
 	
sh
 	
zh
 	
th
 	
that
 	
whale
 	
ng
	6. We have identified the seven _____ that represent distinct phonemes not represented by the single letters in the alphabet. They are
	
	     (1) *ch* as in _____
	                  (*chair, choir*)
	
	     (2) _____ as in *ship*
	
	     (3) _____ sounded like the *s* in *treasure*
	
	     (4) _____ as in *thumb*
	
	     (5) ~~th~~ as in _____.
	                 (*that, thrill*)
	
	     (6) *wh* as in _____
	              (*whole, whale*)
	
	     (7) _____ as in *king*

STUDY GUIDE
Consonant Digraphs
ch, sh, th, wh, ng

Digraph	Key Symbol	Key Word
ch	*ch*	*chair*
sh	*sh*	*ship*
th	*th*	*thumb*
th	*t̶h̶*	*that*
wh	*wh*	*whale*
	zh	*treasure*
ng	*ng*	*king*

The consonant digraphs are two-letter combinations that represent unique phonemes. The phonemes that the digraphs represent are different from the sounds associated with either of the two consonant letters when they occur alone in words.

ch   The digraph *ch* is not reliable. *Ch* may represent the /ch/ (*chair*), the /k/ (*character*), or the /sh/ (*machine*).

sh   The /sh/ is a common sound in the English language. The *sh* (*ship*) is very reliable.

Voiceless th   The digraph *th* represents two distinct phonemes, one voiceless and one voiced. The /th/ in the key word *thumb* is a whispered sound, which we call the voiceless *th* (*thorn, thick*).

Voiced t̶h̶   We use our vocal cords to pronounce the /th/ phoneme in the key word *that,* which we refer to as the voiced *t̶h̶* (*there, father*). Dictionaries may use a slash, a line, or italics to indicate the voiced digraph *t̶h̶* (*t̶h̶, th, th*). We will use the slash (*t̶h̶*) as the key symbol.

wh   The digraph *wh* represents /hw/ (*why, white*). *Wh* occurs in the beginning of syllables, and is followed by a vowel.

zh   While /zh/ occurs in English words (*measure, vision*), the /zh/ is never represented in a word with the grapheme *zh*. The /zh/ may be represented by the *s* (*pleasure, vision*), the *g* (*collage*), or the *z* (*seizure*).

ng   The digraph *ng* is never heard at the beginning of a syllable, and always follows a vowel. The letters *ng* may represent /ng/ (*sing, among*). The letter *n* may also represent /ng/ when it is followed by the letter *g* (*finger—fing-ger*) or the letter *k* (*pink—pingk*). Your dictionary may use the symbol ŋ to represent /ng/.

✖◇✖ Review 11

1. Which of the seven representative digraphs never appears at the beginning of a word?

2. Rewrite these words showing consonant pronunciation. (This calls for acute hearing.)

   Underline the digraphs. Pronounce vowels as you would in the actual word.

   a. *mango, manger, mangy*
   b. *pin, ping, pink, ping-pong*
   c. *ban, bang, bank, banking*
   d. *ran, rang, rank, ranking*
   e. *rancher, range, fancy*

3. There are 25 consonant sounds in the American-English language.

   a. We identify 18 of them with single-letter symbols. Write the 18 consonant letters. _____

   b. We use _____ to identify the seven additional phonemes.

      Write the seven digraphs. _____

4. *C* was not included in question 3.a. because _____.

5. What other consonant letters were not included?

6. The digraph *ph* was not included in question 3.b. because _____.

7. Rewrite the following words using appropriate key symbols for the consonants. Omit silent consonants. Copy vowels as they are.

whole	_____	*high*	_____
quick	_____	*gopher*	_____
wholly	_____	*phone*	_____
thatch	_____	*that*	_____
taught	_____	*comb*	_____
glistening	_____	*daughter*	_____
rustle	_____	*doubt*	_____
knot	_____	*budget*	_____
wrap	_____	*thinking*	_____

   (See the Part II Answers section for the answers to Review 11, page 100.)

◇ Consonant Clusters and Blends

letters, digraphs bl	**1.** We have identified each of the 25 consonant phonemes of the American-English language: 18 of these are represented by single _____; 7 are represented by _____. Now let us turn our attention to consonants that form a cluster in a word. What **cluster** of consonant letters do you see in the word _blue?_ _____
2 b, l	**2.** Pronounce the word _blue._ How many consonant phonemes does _blue_ contain? _____ What are they? _____ _____
one **clusters**	**3.** A digraph is a two-letter grapheme that represents _____ speech sound. The word _blue_ does <u>not</u> contain a consonant digraph. Neither the _b_ nor the _l_ loses its identity. Both are sounded, but they are blended together. We call such combinations of consonant letters _____, and the sounds they represent we call **blends.** We need to study the consonant blends because in many ways they act as one phoneme.
bl, cl, fl, dr ft sk, fr, spr, spl Sh is a digraph. k	**4.** **A consonant cluster is composed of two or more consonants that blend together when sounded to form a consonant blend.** The letters do not form a digraph. The phonemes in the blend retain their individual identity. Pronounce the words below. Fill in the blanks with the letters that form the consonant clusters. black _____ clown _____ flying _____ draft _____ desk _____ fry _____ spray _____ splash _____ Why did you omit the _sh_ in _splash?_ _____ The _ck_ in _black_ represents the single consonant _____, not a blend.
s p l blends	**5.** Some reading series do not use the term _cluster._ In that case, _blend_ refers to both letters and sounds. In the word _splash,_ for example, the letters _____ _____ _____ as well as /_spl_/ are called _____.

6. Pronounce the words in each set below. Each set has one of the common "blenders." Write the letter common to each consonant cluster in the set.

	1	2	3
	brown	flame	skate
	street	claim	snow
	great	split	street
	_____	_____	_____

1. *r* 2. *l* 3. *s*

7. The common blenders are represented by the letters

r, l, s

_____ , _____ , and _____. However, there are clusters that do not contain these letters.

cluster

digraph

8. We distinguish a _____ from a digraph by the fact that it represents two or more phonemes blended together. The

_____ represents a single sound. Check those combinations in the following list which do <u>not</u> represent consonant blends.

sh

ch

th

bl	cr	qu	sc	scr
cl	dr	tw	sh	spr
gl	sk	ch	sm	spl
sl	pr	th	mp	str

9. It may seem strange to classify *qu* as a consonant cluster when *u* is a vowel. The *u* in this case, however, takes the sound of the consonant

w

equal, quart, queen, quick

_____. So this combination is actually a /*kw*/ <u>blend.</u> Select the words with the /*kw*/ blend from the following:

equal   quart   unique   queen   opaque   quick

10. Underline the consonant clusters in these words:

tr, tw, gr, spl, qu
pl, str, sl, pr, gr-sp
(<u>NOT</u> ch or sh!)

tree	twin	great	splash	chair	quilt
please	she	street	slow	pretty	grasp

11. The *sh* in *splash* and the *sh* in *she* cannot be blends because the

s, h

sounds represented by the _____ and the _____ are not heard.

field		*field*
		dish
lamp		*lamp*
bent		*bent*
task		*task*
fast		*fast*
hand		*hand*
		church
belt		*belt*
draft		*draft*

12. Many consonant clusters occur in the final position in English words or syllables. Read the words at the right. Underline the consonant clusters that occur at the end of the words.

(Left column underlined: fie**ld**, la**mp**, be**nt**, ta**sk**, fa**st**, ha**nd**, be**lt**, dra**ft**)

---

train
task

13. As you have seen, clusters may appear at the beginning of a word or syllable, as in *train,* or at the end of a word or syllable, as in *task.*

Underline the appropriate blend in both of these examples.

(tr**ain**, ta**sk**)

Clusters	Digraphs
speech	*speech*
rest	*church*
digraph	*digraph*
trash	*trash*
shield	*shield*

14. Arrange the words below in two columns: Clusters   Digraphs
those with clusters representing blends and
those with digraphs. Some words may be
used in both columns. Underline to indicate
the part in each word that qualifies it to be
in the particular column.

speech, church, rest, digraph, trash, shield

(Clusters: **sp**eech, re**st**, di**gr**aph, **tr**ash, shie**ld**; Digraphs: spee**ch**, chur**ch**, digra**ph**, tra**sh**, **sh**ield)

---

t

h, r,

th

15. There are many words in which a consonant digraph is a part of a cluster. Examine the word *throw.* The first three letters: _____ ,

_____ , and _____ compose a cluster. Within the

cluster is the digraph _____. All blend together: /thr/.

---

thr shr chr phr

ch   ph

16. Draw a single line under the digraph, and another line under the entire cluster in these words:

through   shrimp   chrome   phrase

Which of the digraphs in the above words are not one of the seven key symbols needed to complete the phonemes of our language?
_____ _____

str, str ngth, scr
bl nd, sm, thr ft
	17. All consonant clusters (written) represent blends (spoken). Underline the consonants that represent blends in these words:
	
	   string *strength* *scrap*
	
	   blond *small* *thrift*

strength */ng/* and */th/*	**18.** Which word in frame 17 has a cluster composed of two digraphs? _____ The two digraphs which blend together are / / and / /.

Blends Digraphs
 	
toas<u>t</u> *di<u>ph</u>thong*
<u>gr</u>apheme *gra<u>ph</u>eme*
<u>thr</u>ee *<u>th</u>ree*
<u>cl</u>anging *cla<u>ng</u>ing*
<u>str</u>ike *alto<u>g</u>ether*
    fa<u>th</u>er
	19. Arrange the words below in two columns: <u>Blends</u> <u>Digraphs</u>
	those containing clusters that represent blends and those containing digraphs. Some of these words, too, may be used in both columns, so underline to indicate the part of each word that places it in a column.
	
	  toast, diphthong, grapheme, three,
	
	  clanging, strike, altogether, father

phoneme	**20.** We have studied the single consonant phonemes, the consonant digraphs, and the consonant blends. We include the blends because in many ways, one blend acts as though it were one _____.

STUDY GUIDE
Consonant Clusters and Blends

Consonant Clusters
A consonant cluster is composed of two or more consonants that blend together when sounded to form a consonant blend (*clown*, *spray*). Some teachers' manuals do not use the term *cluster*. In that case, *blend* refers to both letters and sounds. We will use the more frequently used term, *blend,* in this study guide.

Beginning Consonant Blends
The most common blends that occur at the beginning of a word or syllable include the letters *r, l,* and *s.*

r Blends		l Blends		s Blends			
br	bright	bl	black	sc	scout	scr	scrap
cr	crayon	cl	class	sk	sky	spl	splash
dr	dress	fl	flower	sl	slip	spr	spring
fr	free	gl	glad	sm	small	squ	square
gr	green	pl	plan	sn	snow	str	string
pr	pretty			sp	spot		
tr	train			st	stop		
				sw	swim		

tw and dw   The *tw* (*twin*) and *dw* (*dwell*) blends are less common in English than the blends that include the letters *r, l,* or *s.*

qu   *Qu* is a consonant blend when it represents /kw/ as in *quick* and *quilt.*

Consonant blends are taught as units rather than as single graphemes (e.g., *st* as representing two blended phonemes rather than an isolated /s/ and an isolated /t/).

Consonant Digraphs and Consonant Blends
Blends that occur at the beginning of a syllable may include a consonant digraph and a consonant cluster, such as in *shr* (*shrimp*), and *thr* (*throw*).

Final Position Blends
Many consonant blends occur in the final position in English syllables. Some of the more common final blends include:[*]

ld	old	nd	end	st	most	mp	lamp	lt	salt
lk	milk	nt	went	sk	desk	ft	lift		

---

[*]In teaching, vowels may be combined with consonant blends to create letter patterns that we call rimes. You will learn about rimes in Part V of this book. Examples of vowel and consonant blend rimes include *old* (*told*); *ild* (*wild*); *ilk* (*milk*); *alt* (*salt*); *end* (*mend*); *ent* (*went*); *ost* (*most*); *esk* (*desk*); *amp* (*lamp*); *ift* (*lift*).

✖◆✖ Review 12

1. A cluster differs from a digraph in that _____

2. Why were no key symbols given to represent the blends?

3. Seven specific digraphs together with 18 single letters supply us with the consonant sounds of our language. Which of the seven digraphs appear in the following paragraph? List them in the order in which they make their first appearance.

    It started as a pleasure trip. The driver, nearing the exit leading through the city, changed lanes. He jerked the wheel too quickly and landed on the slick shoulder.

4. There are three unnecessary single letters in our alphabet. Illustrations are in the above paragraph. Rewrite these words to show how other letters could substitute.

5. What consonant blends are heard at the beginning of words in the above paragraph?

(See the Part II Answers section for the answers to Review 12, page 100)

For a helpful summary and review of the phonemes, turn to page 157. Work through the consonant section, using a separate sheet of paper. Then you will be able to have a complete review after you have studied the vowels.

◇ Recap I

25 phonemes word	**1.** In our study of consonants, we identified _____ consonant _____ (the smallest unit of sound that distinguishes one _____ from another).
symbol *b d f g h j k l m n p* *r s t v w y z* digraphs *ch sh th ͭh wh zh ng*	**2.** To know exactly to which sound we are referring, we assigned each phoneme a key _____ and a key word. As you go through the alphabet, write the 18 consonant letters that symbolize specific phonemes: _____ _____ _____ _____ _____ _____ _____ _____ _____ _____ _____ _____ _____ _____ _____ _____ _____. But we need 25 symbols. We use _____ to complete our representation of the consonant phonemes: _____ _____ _____ _____ _____ _____ _____.

phoneme	**3.** Although consonants are fairly reliable (there is a high relationship between grapheme and _____), there are irregularities:
	1. A letter (or grapheme) may represent more than one
phoneme	_____. For example:
/k/ /s/	the *c* in *camp* represents / /, and in *ace* / /
/d/ /t/	the *d* in *date* / /, and in *jumped* / /
/j/ /g/	the *g* in *age* / /, and in *go* / /
/n/ /ng/	the *n* in *ran* / /, and in *rank* / /
/s/ /sh/ /z/ /zh/	the *s* in *soap* / /, in *surely* / /, in *runs* / / and in *measure* / /
/s/ /z/ /zh/	the *z* in *waltz* / /, in *quiz* / /, and in *azure* / /

	4. A phoneme may be represented by more than one grapheme. Write the phoneme that is represented in each set of words. Then rewrite the words, using the key symbols. (frames 4 and 5)
/f/ *fase, lauf, fone*	/ / as in *face* _____ , *laugh* _____ , *phone* _____

/j/ *paje, joke,* *fuje, grajual*	**5.** / / *page* _____ , *joke* _____ *fudge* _____ , *gradual* _____
/k/ *ankor, antikue* *kue*	/ / *anchor* _____ , *antique* _____ , *cue* _____
/z/ *uzed, frozen,* *zylofone*	/ / *used* _____ , *frozen* _____ , *xylophone* _____

	6. A letter may represent no phoneme: it may be
silent	_____.
	Some common silent letter patterns are:
t	The second of two like-consonants, as the _____ in *letters,*
s	the _____ in *dress*
b	_____ following *m,* as in *bomb;* followed by *t* as in *doubt*
k	_____ followed by *n,* as in *know*
h	_____ following *g,* as in *ghost*

Use your dictionary to verify.	**7.** Did you feel there were any words that did not belong in the last 4 frames, words you would pronounce in a different way? List them here:
girl *give*	**8.** Repeat the generalization regarding the hard-soft sounds of *c* and *g*. Check the following words that do not follow the generalization. *music* *gem* *ghost* *girl* *comic* *success* *cycle* *give*
before F	**9.** The consonants *w* and *y* are found _____ the vowel in a (before, after) word. The consonant *y* is often a silent letter. T F
k	**10.** The key symbol for *q* is _____.
I hope so. That would be a real achievement.	**11.** Did you get all the exercises in this recap correct? What a sense of satisfaction you must have. Congratulations! We have been studying the consonants, the most regular of all the phonemes. But the consonants cannot get along without the vowels. We will now proceed with a study of the vowels and their relationships with the consonants.

Part I and II Answers to the Reviews

These reviews give you an indication of your mastery (or lack of mastery) of the material. WORK TO ACHIEVE 100% ON EACH REVIEW! Your success depends largely on your self-motivation. It takes very little more effort to achieve mastery than to fail, even while writing each answer. The difference depends on your mind-set. Reread the section INTRODUCTION. Good luck!

Review 1

1. decode **2.** phoneme **3.** 44 **4.** segment (or separate), blend
5. segmenting **6.** blending **7.** grapheme **8.** graphophonic
9. syntactic **10.** semantic

Scores:

Review 2

1. no **2.** phonemes (The key symbols represent sounds, never letters.)
3. *m* **4.** *m* **5.** 2, digraphs **6.** letters **7.** digraph, one

Scores:

Review 3

1. 5, 5 **2.** 3, 3 **3.** digraphs **4.** *c, q, x* They are represented by other letters; they have no distinctive phonemes of their own. **5.** symbols, words
6. *m, k, r, v* **7.** *u*, silent, *w* **8.** *m v r, k w v r* **9.** When we see a *v* in a word, we know it represents the same sound as that heard at the beginning of *van*.

Scores:

Review 4

1. **a.** no **b.** *saf* **c.** *mel* **d.** *plara* **e.** *gaeve* **f.** *lam*
g. *kak* **h.** *tovom* **i.** *rok* **j.** *rim* **k.** *kwimel* **l.** *klopem* **m.** *voter*
2. digraphs, one   3. We are apt to add a vowel sound.   4. The key symbols represent the sounds of our language. Each sound is represented once. *Q* would be a duplication.

Scores:

If you have missed any items in previous reviews, take that review now. Write the second score following the first. Does it show improvement?

Review 5

1. **a.** *b* **b.** *t f* **c.** *h j* **d.** *v* **e.** *f n* **f.** *t t* **g.** *g s t l*
h. *s l j r* **i.** *j n d r* **j.** *h f t* **k.** *p l n t d*
l. *k w l t* **m.** *z r* **n.** *s l* **o.** *k l m*   2. **a.** don't, ride, moved
b. *fine, graph, photo, off*   **c.** *wedge, soldier, Roger*   **d.** *knot, stranger*
e. *his, puzzle, does*

Scores:

If you missed any, turn to the appropriate pages and restudy. Select a previous review. Write the answers. Did you better your score or maintain a perfect score? Be sure you write your scores for each review and "review of reviews."

Review 6

1. A *g* followed by *e, i,* or *y* generally has the sound of /j/; a *g* followed by *a, o, u,* any consonant, or at the end of a word is /g/ as in goat.   2. **a.** *j n t*
b. *b ng k* **c.** *g r l* **d.** *b g* **e.** *s r k s* **f.** *k k* **g.** *h*
h. *m ch* **i.** *y l* **j.** *w* **k.** *k w k* **l.** *r t* **m.** *y t* **n.** *n k*
3. *girl*   4. C followed by *e, i,* or *y* generally has the sound of /s/; *c* followed by *a, o, u,* any consonant, or at the end of a word is /k/.   5. *ed, d, t*   6. The consonants *w* (as in *wagon,* /w/) and *y* (as in *yo-yo,* /y/) appear before the vowel in a syllable.   7. **a.** *g* **b.** *ch* **c.** *j* **d.** *k* **e.** *j* **f.** *k* **g.** *k*
h. *k* **i.** *k* **j.** *f*   8. digraphs   9. *ranje, ringkle, ransom; manjer, trianggle, lingks*   10. *e, i, y*   11. digraph, *go, j,* silent

Scores:

There were some tricky words in this review. Sincere congratulations if you had them all correct. If you did not, make sure you understand the principle involved. Restudy the appropriate section. Plan to "review this review" soon.

Review 7

1. a. *e, i, y   k   a, o, u*   **b.** *k*   **c.** *ks, gz, z*   **2. a.** hard *a, o, u*   **b.** soft *j   e, i, y*   **3. a.** some   **b.** *z*   **4.** *d   t*   **5.** *v*   **6.** *ch   sh*   **7. a.** *s, sh, z, zh; z; s, zh*   **b.** *c, z; z, s, x* (any two)   **c.** *k, g, h*   silent; *t*   silent
8. a. graphemes, phoneme   **b.** phonemes, grapheme   **c.** phoneme

Scores:

Review 8

1. digraph   **2.** *k   k,   h,   zh,   wh,   wh   ch,   th,   t͟h,   sh, sh   g,   w   sh,   v   zh, ng*   **3.** *weather, which, bring, wish, both, through* (If you omitted the *wh* of *which*, you are correct also.)   **4.** letter, 7, digraphs, *sh, ch, wh, zh, th, t͟h, ng*
5. *gh* in *tough, ch* in *chloroform, ph* in *phoneme*   **6.** *f, k, f*   **7.** *sungk, fotograf, now* (no), *alfabet, feazant, kouf*

Scores:

Continue those reviews of reviews so as to improve scores or maintain perfect scores!

Review 9

1. a. *s͟h   v   r*   **b.** *gz*   **c.** *s͟h   r*   **d.** *s͟h   r*   **e.** *t   r   z͟h   r*
f. *k   r   k   t   r*   **g.** *b   r   z͟h   r*   **h.** *k   r   s   m   s*   **i.** *s   k   l   z*
j. *g   s   t   s*   **k.** *c͟h   r   j*   **l.** *s͟h   t*   **m.** *k   w   k*   **n.** *l   s͟h   n*
o. *d   v   z͟h   n*   **p.** *s͟h   k   g*   **q.** *s   t   r   n͟g*   **2.** The digraph does not appear in a word.

Scores:

Review 10

1. *ng* (swing), *wh* (white), *zh* (measure); *t͟h* (mother), *sh* (flash), *ch* (porch)
2. *breath*   **3.** (1)—(*l* is silent), (2) *yo-yo*, (3) *sun*, (4) *table*, (5) *jeep*, (6)—(7)—
(8)—(9) *van*, (10) *goat*, (11)—(12)—(13)—(not a consonant); (14) *ring*, (15) *lion*,
(16) *ring*   **4.** is not, does not   **5.** consonant   **6.** *this father feather them*
7. *wheel white whip whistle*   **8.** Each appears at the beginning of a word or syllable and has a vowel following.

Scores:

Review 11

1. *ng*   **2. a.** ma*ng* go, man jer, man jy (The following are spaced only to make them more distinct, not to indicate syllables.) If you get these, you're good!
b. pin, pi *ng,* pi *ng* k, pi *ng*-po *ng*   **c.** ban, ba *ng,* ba *ng* k, ba *ng* k i *ng*
d. ran, ra *ng,* ra *ng* k, ra *ng* k i *ng*   **e.** ran *ch* er, ran je, fan sy   **3. a.** b, d, f, g, h, j, k, l, m, n, p, r, s, t, v, w, y, z   **b.** digraphs sh, ch, wh, zh, th, *th̶,* ng
4. C has no distinctive sound of its own. It is represented by the s and k.
5. q, x   **6.** Ph is represented by f.   **7.** hole, hi, kwik, gofer, holy, fone, thach, *th̶*at, taut, kom, glisening, dauter, rusle, dout, not, bujet, rap, thingking

Scores:

Review 12

1. You hear the sounds represented by the letters in the cluster; a digraph represents a new sound.   **2.** The blends are represented by phonemes we already know.   **3.** zh (*pleasure*) *th̶*(*the*) ng (*nearing*) th (*through*) ch (*changed*) wh (*wheel*) sh (*shoulder*)   **4.** egzit or eksit, kuickly (kwikly), sity   **5.** /st/, /pl/, /tr/, /dr/, /thr/, /kw/, /sl/.

Scores:

This is a good time to take stock of the reviews. Is there material you need to study? Do it now.

Part III

Vowels

A reminder: Do not pull the mask down until you have written your response to the entire frame.

vowels	**1.** The 26 letters of the alphabet are divided into two major categories: consonants and _____.
phonemes phonemes 19, phonemes	**2.** Although there are many variations due to dialect, individual speech patterns, and so forth, for all practical purposes in the task of teaching reading we can consider the American-English language to contain 44 separate and distinctive _____. We have noted that 25 of these are consonant _____. Therefore, there are _____ vowel _____.
vowels	**3.** **The letters *a, e, i, o, u,* and sometimes *w* and *y* are classified as _____.**
yo-yo	**4.** How can you tell when *y* is a consonant and when it is a vowel? You have learned that the key symbol *y* (consonant) represents the phoneme heard in _____. *Y* functions as a consonant <u>only</u> (yo-yo, say) when it represents the phoneme heard in *yo-yo.*

101

initial	**5.** The consonant *y* is always the _____ letter in a word (initial, final) or syllable. It is always found before the vowel.
consonant *yellow* vowel *yet* *beyond*	**6.** Study the words at the right. Underline each *y* that is a consonant. The _____ *y* is never a silent letter. (consonant, vowel) The _____ *y* is often a silent letter. (consonant, vowel) *they* *yellow* *yet* *may* *very* *beyond*
vowel	**7.** *Y* does not serve as a key symbol for a vowel phoneme. **Y represents no vowel sound of its own. When *y* is a** **_____ , its pronunciation is shown by the key symbols** **we associate with the *i* or the *e*.**
$\overset{c}{year}$ $\overset{v}{gym}$ $\overset{v}{my}$ $\overset{v}{ready}$ *canyon* $\overset{c}{canyon}$	**8.** Study the function of the *y* in the words at the right. Place a <u>c</u> or a <u>v</u> above each *y* to identify *y* as a consonant or as a vowel. Check each *y* consonant to see that it represents the same sound as the initial phoneme in *yo-yo*. In which word is the *y* the first letter in the second syllable? _____ *year* *gym* *my* *ready* *canyon*
wagon	**9.** Now let us examine the *w*. You have learned that *w* as a consonant represents the phoneme heard in _____ . (wagon, snow)
symbol	**10.** **As a vowel, the *w* represents no** **distinct phoneme of its own.** Therefore, it cannot be represented by a key _____. **W is always used in combination with another vowel** as in *few, cow, grow*.

thaw, threw	**11.** Underline the *w*s that function as vowels in the following words: *water, which, thaw, threw, dwarf* (Be sure that they do not represent the phoneme you hear at the beginning of *wagon.*)
follows	The vowel *w* always _____ another vowel. (precedes, follows)
w, y	**12.** Two of the seven vowels are not identified by distinctive key symbols because they do not represent sounds of their own. These are the vowels _____ and _____.
a, e, i, o, u	**13.** Now let us turn our attention to the vowels that do represent phonemes and can be assigned key symbols to distinguish them from each other. The vowel phonemes are represented by five letters. They are _____ , _____ , _____ , _____ , _____ .
cannot be	**14.** These five vowels, alone and in combination with another vowel, represent the 19 vowel phonemes of our language. Therefore, there _____ a one-to-one correspondence between phoneme (is, cannot be) and letter.
a 5	**15.** Study the words at the right. Pronounce the sound represented by the underlined vowel. We can see that one vowel, the _____ , represents at least _____ different phonemes. *s<u>a</u>me* *d<u>a</u>re* *c<u>a</u>n* *<u>a</u>rm* *<u>a</u>bout*
phoneme vowels	**16.** Each vowel letter represents more than one _____ . If we meet an unfamiliar word, how will we know which sounds its vowels represent? There are some patterns (with exceptions, of course) that will give us some help in determining the sounds represented by the _____ in unknown words.

phonemes vowel	**17.** Our task, then, is twofold: (1) To identify the vowel _____ of the American-English language and assign each a key symbol. (2) To become acquainted with the generalizations that will aid us in associating the correct phonemes with the _____ letters in unknown words.
letters	**18.** For our study, we shall divide the vowel phonemes into two major groups: (1) those represented by single vowel letters (2) those represented by combinations of vowel letters Each of the single letters (as in group 1) and each of the combinations of _____ represent <u>one</u> phoneme.
letter	**19.** We shall begin our study of the vowel phonemes with group 1: those represented by a single vowel _____ . (letter, phoneme)

✕◇✕ Review 13

1. The vowel letters are _____ , _____ , _____ , _____ , _____ , and sometimes _____ and _____ .

2. We need not select key symbols to represent the sounds of _____ and _____ , because they duplicate the sounds of other vowels.

3. Indicate whether the *w* and the *y* in these words are consonants or vowels by writing <u>C</u> or <u>V</u> following each word:

   yet _____   *type* _____   *play* _____

   wide _____   *draw* _____   *when* _____

4. The *w* in *white* is part of a _____ _____ .
                    (consonant, vowel) (blend, digraph)

5. There are _____ vowel phonemes than there are vowel letters.
                    (fewer, more)

6. How many vowel phonemes will we need to identify?

   (See the Part III Answers section for the answers to Review 13, page 155.)

◇ Short Vowel Sounds

a	ă	ăpple
e	ĕ	ĕdge
i	ĭ	ĭgloo
o	ŏ	ŏx
u	ŭ	ŭmbrella

ă *(apple)*   ĕ *(edge)*   ĭ *(igloo)*   ŏ *(ox)*   ŭ *(umbrella)*

1. One set of phonemes represented by single vowel letters includes those that stand for "short" vowel sounds. The **breve** is a diacritical mark used to indicate the specific pronunciation of each vowel in this group. Its linguistic relationship to "short" can be noted in such words as *abbreviate* and *brevity.* It is the custom, in phonics, to call the vowel sound whose key symbol contains a breve a **short** vowel sound.

1	2	3
a	ă	apple
e	ĕ	edge
i	ĭ	igloo
o	ŏ	ox
u	ŭ	umbrella

short

The vowels in column 3 at the right represent the _____ sounds. Each key symbol (2) consists of the vowel marked with a

breve

_____.

Mark the initial vowel in each key word.

2. Because, in actuality, these sounds are not held for a shorter period of time than certain other vowel phonemes, some prefer to call them **unglided phonemes.**

If you write "unglided" and this text gives the answer as

short

"_____" (or vice versa), you may count your answer correct.

ĭ, ŏ, ŭ

3. The key symbols that identify the vowels when they represent their short sounds are: ă, ĕ, _____, _____, _____. Reading would be easier if

phonemes

five additional characters representing these _____ were
(letters, phonemes)

added to our alphabet.

m

4. Pronounce the word *map.* Listen for three phonemes, the consonant phoneme represented by _____, the vowel

a, consonant

phoneme represented by _____, and the _____

p

phoneme represented by _____. Pronounce the vowel

apple

sound alone. The same vowel sound is heard in _____ .
(apple, far)

măp	**5.** Pronounce the vowel phoneme in *map*. Rewrite *map* using key symbols: _____. It is important to note that various dictionaries indicate pronunciation in different ways. We must study the pronunciation key of the particular dictionary we use. For example, many dictionaries indicate the pronunciation of all short vowel sounds with the letter and no diacritical mark. In these
map	dictionaries, the pronunciation of *map* is written _____. Pronounce the following words. Circle those whose vowel phoneme is the same as that in *map*.
ran, grab, back	ran all car above grab back paw
3 *hĕn*	**6.** There are _____ phonemes in *hen*. Listen for the vowel phoneme as you say *hen* aloud. Rewrite *hen* using key symbols to indicate its pronunciation. _____
mĕt, hĕm, ĕnd	**7.** Mark with a breve each of the vowels in the words below that represent the same vowel phoneme heard in the key word *edge*. feed met rib hem end reward If you find this difficult, pronounce the first vowel phoneme heard in *edge,* then pronounce each word, substituting that sound for each vowel phoneme.
3 *rĕd*	**8.** Read this sentence aloud: *I read a book yesterday.* How many phonemes do you hear when you say "read" in the sentence above? _____ Rewrite *read* using a key symbol to indicate each phoneme. _____ You have written in code. Anyone who knows the code can pronounce *read* correctly without a sentence to clarify it.
pĭn, drĭp, lĭft, thĭk	**9.** Pronounce *igloo*. Now say the first vowel phoneme. Rewrite the following words using key symbols to code *each* phoneme: pin _____ drip _____ lift _____ thick _____

3
 	
ox
	10. Pronounce *hot.* It contains _____ phonemes. The
	                           (How many?)
	vowel phoneme sounds the same as that in _____ .
	                                         (boy, ox)

	11. Indicate the pronunciation of each short (unglided) vowel sound by using the correct diacritical mark in these words:
lĭp, tŏp, pŏp,	lip top note pop lap graph pod home
lăp, grăph, pŏd	The vowel letters with the marks you placed above them are the
key, symbols	_____ _____ for the phonemes they represent.
breve or *ŭ*	**12.** Pronounce *umbrella.* We use the _____ to indicate that the *u* represents a short (unglided) sound. Now, pronounce the vowel sound alone. Place the correct diacritical marks above all the vowels in the following words that represent the same sound as the first vowel phoneme in the key word *umbrella.*
jŭmp, ŭs, dŭk, cŭp, tŭb	jump use us duck cup house tub

	13. Pronounce the vowel phoneme represented by the vowel letter in each of the words in column 1 at the right.	1	2
		an	*car*
short *fĕnce*	Each vowel represents its _____ phoneme. Now pronounce the vowel phoneme in each of the words in column 2. Place a breve above each vowel in column 2 that represents its unglided sound. Check carefully.	*fed*	*fence*
		pin	*pine*
		hot	*cow*
dŭg		*cup*	*dug*

hĕd	**14.** Pronounce the words at the right. Listen carefully for the vowel phonemes. Rewrite each word, using the key symbols that indicate the sounds we associate with the vowel and consonant phonemes.	head	_____
sĕd		said	_____
sĕnts		cents	_____
ĕnd		end	_____

	15. To obtain a better understanding of the short vowels, we will consider them as they usually occur within the English syllable. A syllable is the smallest unit of speech that has one vowel phoneme.
1	When you say the word *mat,* you hear _____ vowel
	(How many?)
1	phoneme(s). The word *mat* consists of _____ syllable(s).
	(How many?)
2	When you pronounce *mattress,* you hear _____ vowel
	(How many?)
2	phoneme(s). *Mattress* has _____ syllable(s). A syllable in
	(How many?)
phoneme	the English language has only one vowel _____.

	16. **The most common vowel-consonant pattern is that of CVC (consonant-vowel-consonant) in which the V (vowel) represents its short sound.**
	There are many one-syllable words and many accented syllables in multisyllable words that follow this pattern.
	These words and syllables are made of an initial consonant, a middle
vowel, consonant	_____ , and a final _____ .
	17. The C (consonant) in the pattern may represent a digraph or a blend. Circle the syllables (or one-syllable words) that have the CVC pattern.
ring, this, rab bit, big	*ring this rab bit be side rain big*
short (unglided)	**18.** VC, in which the vowel represents the _____ sound as in *an*, is also a common pattern. It functions the same as the
C	CV_____ pattern.
short (unglided)	**19.** **The CVC and the VC patterns give clues to the pronunciation of unknown words. In both cases we would expect the vowel to represent the _____ sound.**
	To indicate the pronunciation of the vowel, we place a
breve	_____ above it.
	20. Do the vowels in all CVC patterns represent the short sound? Study the following words and syllables.
yes (Blends and digraphs are considered as Cs.) no *sĕt, lŏt*	*far ther long set lot her*
	Do all of them have the CVC pattern? _____ Do all the
	vowels represent the short sound? _____ Mark the vowels that represent the short sounds with breves. Work carefully.
	21. The key words given at the beginning of this section will help us remember the phoneme for each vowel. A sentence that contains each of the short vowel phonemes may be easier to remember. Would the sentence below furnish a key word for each of the short
yes	vowel phonemes? _____ . (Check each word with the set at the beginning of this section.) Mark the vowels with breves.
Dăn kĕpt hĭs pŏp gŭn.	*Dan kept his pop gun.*

4
 	
Năn's pĕt ĭs nŏt fŭn.
Săm's nĕt ĭs nŏt cŭt.
Săd Tĕd ĭn hŏt hŭt.
All mĕn ĭn hŏt bŭs.
	22. Look at the groups of words below. Mark the vowels that represent the short sound. Number _____ is not a good key phrase.
	
	       (1) *Nan's pet is not fun.*
	       (2) *Sam's net is not cut.*
	       (3) *Sad Ted in hot hut.*
	       (4) *All men in hot bus.*

chim   men
 	
sun
 	
can   win
 	
wish   gin
	23. We often find the vowel phoneme in a closed syllable to be short. *chim ney men*
	                                    tree sun
	   A closed syllable ends with a
	   consonant <u>phoneme</u>. *can win dow*
	
	Study the words at the right. Underline the *wish be gin*
	closed syllables, including closed one-syllable words.

short *don't, bird*	**24.** One vowel in a closed syllable (or in a closed one-syllable word) usually represents its _____ sound. With your key sentence in mind (frame 21), check the vowel phonemes in the following words. Which words do not have the short vowel phoneme? *clap don't skin sick trust fed bend bird*
yes *but ton* *pen cil* yes	**25.** Study the words at the right carefully. Is each syllable a *but ton* closed syllable? _____ Write the closed *pen cil* syllables here: Is there a single vowel in each syllable? _____
        unaccented	**26.** We might expect that we can properly indicate *but' ton* the pronunciation of each of the vowels with a breve. If you pronounce the words too carefully—that is, *pen' cil* artificially—you might indicate their pronunciation that way. Say a sentence aloud containing the word *button,* then one with *pencil.* You will notice that the vowel in the _____ syllable (accented, unaccented) represents more of an "uh" sound and not the phonemes you hear in the words *ox* and *igloo.*

closed	**27.** Syllables with the CVC pattern are _____ syllables; those (closed, open)
closed	with the VC pattern (such as *ant*) are _____ syllables. (closed, open)
	28. The generalization for the short vowel phoneme is most useful when it is stated: **A single vowel in an accented closed syllable usually represents the short sound of the vowel.** Indicate the pronunciation of the syllables that follow this generalization:
lĕm băn hŏp	re pay lem on ban jo hop per
	29. We have noted the sounds represented by *a, e, i, o, u.* *gym* How about the *y?* *sys tem* Study the words at the right. Each contains *sym bol*
vowel	a _____ *y* within the syllable. The *y* represents (consonant, vowel)
short, *i*	the _____ sound of the letter _____. (long, short)
	30. Let us review the short sounds of the vowels. *date* *put* Check the words at the right against the key
(Any errors? *fĭt* Recheck the *păn* sound!) *stŏp* *pĕg*	words you have learned. Place a breve above *want* *fit* each of the vowels that represent the short *pan* *stop* sound of that vowel. *peg* *cute*
	31. We can expect that single vowels in closed accented syllables will
short	usually represent _____ sounds. Remember that all one-syllable words are considered accented syllables.

shelve	**32.** There are many words in which the vowel is followed by two consonants and a final *e* (VCCe). Note that in words ending with a vowel that is followed by two consonants and a final *e,* the first vowel phoneme is usually	*shelve*
pulse		*pulse*
fence		*fence*
short	_____.	*ride*
	(short, long)	*rinse*
rinse	Which words have the VCCe pattern?	*smile*

	33. Study the words at the right. We can make a generalization concerning these words.	*dance*
		plunge
	When a word (or syllable) has two vowels, one of	*dodge*
e	which is a final _____ , and the two vowels are	*fence*
consonants	separated by two _____ , the first	*bronze*
short (unglided)	vowel usually represents the _____ sound	*lapse*
silent	and the final *e* is _____.	*bridge*
		smudge

	34. The generalization is applied to words that have the ending pattern of VCCe (with exceptions, of course!). The word *lapse* is an example of the VCCe pattern: vowel-consonant-consonant-final *e.*
	When a word (or a syllable) has two vowels, one of which is a final *e,* and the two vowels are separated by two consonants, the final *e* is silent and the first vowel usually represents its short sound.
VCCe	*Since* and *judge* end with the _____ pattern.

	35. Check the words below that end with the VCCe pattern.
chance, ridge, since	chance _____ ridge _____ telephone _____ since _____ could _____
sentence, prince	shape _____ tree _____ sentence _____ toy _____ prince _____

	36. Study the words at the right. Note that in words ending with -*dge* the first vowel phoneme is	*bridge*
		dodge
short	usually _____.	*smudge*
	(short, long)	*wedge*

✕◇✕◇✕   *STUDY GUIDE*   ✕◇✕◇✕
                        Short Vowels

Short Vowel	Key Symbol	Key Word
a	ă	apple
e	ĕ	edge
i	ĭ	igloo
o	ŏ	ox
u	ŭ	umbrella

Breve (˘)   The breve (˘) is the diacritical mark used to indicate the specific pronunciation of the short vowels. *Unglided* is another term that refers to the short vowel phonemes.

CVC Pattern   The most common vowel-consonant pattern is that of the CVC (consonant-vowel-consonant) in which the V (vowel) represents its short (unglided) sound (*pat, pet, pig, pot, puff*).

VC Pattern   The V (vowel) in the VC pattern represents the short sound (*ant, etch, itch, odd, up*). The VC pattern functions the same as the CVC pattern.

VCCe Pattern   When a word or a syllable has two vowels, one of which is a final *e*, and the two vowels are separated by two consonants, the first vowel usually represents the short sound and the final *e* is silent (*dance, fence, since, dodge, fudge*).

Closed Syllable   A closed syllable ends with a consonant phoneme (*at*). A single vowel in an accented, closed syllable usually represents the short (unglided) sound of the vowel.

Ww as a Vowel   As a vowel, the *w* represents no distinct phoneme of its own. The vowel *w* always follows another vowel in English words, and is used in combination with the other vowel (*new, cow, saw*).

Yy as a Vowel   As a vowel, *y* represents no distinct phoneme of its own. When *y* is a vowel, its pronunciation is shown by the key symbols we associate with the *i* and the *e*. The vowel *y* is often silent (*play*).

---

	37. Now consider the following words.
	fence range paste hinge prance fudge
no	Is the VCCe pattern completely reliable? _____
	(yes, no)

38. Now take time to study your own dictionary. Look up *bed.* Does the breve appear above the *e* in the pronunciation guide? Since the unglided vowel sound is so common, many dictionaries indicate the pronunciation of all short sounds with the letter alone (no diacritical mark). How would the pronunciation of *bed* be shown in these

bed, pin

dictionaries? _____ Of *pin?* _____

ă ĕ ĭ ŏ ŭ

ăpple, ĕdge, ĭgloo

ŏx, ŭmbrella

39. Write the key symbols we are using in this text to represent the short

vowel phonemes. _____ _____ _____ _____ _____

Write the key words for each short vowel. Mark the initial vowel in each key word.

Pronounce the short vowel phonemes. Can you say them rapidly? Practice them. Since they are so common, you should be familiar with them.

✖◇✖ Review 14

1. Can you state the major generalization concerning short vowel sounds?

   pet

   in

   a. Write the generalization that applies to the first two words at the right.

   since

   b. State the generalization that applies to the vowel-consonant ending pattern in the last two words at the right.

   dance

2. We are studying the vowel phonemes that are represented by a single letter. We have learned to associate 5 of the 19 vowel phonemes with their key pronunciation symbols. Mark the vowels to indicate their pronunciations.

   bed   next   lot   cat   trip   skin   mop   us   send   bug

3. Write the vowel-consonant pattern for the following words.

   up   hat   lapse   tub   ad   rinse

4. We expect the single letter *g* to represent its hard sound, except when it is followed by _____ , _____ , or _____ .

   (See the Part III Answers section for the answers to Review 14, page 155.)

◇ Long Vowel Sounds

	ā (apron) ē (eraser) ī (ice) ō (overalls) ū (unicorn) **1.** This section introduces the long vowel sounds as shown above. Thus far we have identified five other vowel sounds. We call them "short" or unglided sounds. We distinguish the short vowels (as in the dictionary) from other
breves	vowel sounds by placing _____ over them.

	ā (apron) ē (eraser) ī (ice) ō (overalls) ū (unicorn)

a	ā	apron
e	ē	eraser
i	ī	ice
o	ō	overalls
u	ū	unicorn

2. One set of phonemes represented by single vowel letters is those that "say their own names." The key symbol for these vowel phonemes is a macron (-). Pronounce the first word at the right. Make the sound represented by the underlined vowel; then say the name of the underlined vowel.

1	2	3
a	ā	<u>a</u>pron
_____	_____	<u>e</u>raser
_____	_____	<u>i</u>ce
_____	_____	<u>o</u>veralls
_____	_____	<u>u</u>nicorn

The sound represented by the vowel is the same as the

_____ of the vowel. Pronounce the rest of the key words (3), vowel phonemes (key symbols) (2), and letter names (1) the same way. Complete the table.

(Many dictionaries are now using an equivalent symbol, the ȳōō, to indicate the ū. Check your dictionary.)

name

3. We indicate the pronunciation of the vowel letter that "says its own name" by placing a **macron** (-) over it. Therefore the key symbol, as found in the dictionary, for the a in apron is ā. What would the key symbol be for each of the other underlined vowels in frame 2?

ē, ī, ō, ū

_____ _____ _____ _____

4. "Macron" contains the word element *macro*, which means "long" or "great." It has been the custom, in phonics, to call the vowel sound whose key symbol is a macron over the vowel letter a "long vowel sound."

pine

Therefore, we would say the *i* in _____ represents a long
(*pin, pine*)
vowel sound.

long	**5.** It would seem that, in the normal pronunciation of words, we would hold long vowel sounds for a greater length of time than short vowel sounds. This is not necessarily true. Some texts now use the term "**glided sound**" rather than _____ to indicate the (long, short) sound of a vowel that "says its own name." We will use these terms interchangeably.
tāke, gō, fīne, bē, sāme (If you had any incorrect, study them carefully. Does the _a_ in _many_ "say its own name"?)	**6.** Place a macron above the vowels that represent long (glided) sounds in these words. Be sure the vowel "says its own name." _take go many fine once all be same_
no yo͞o is not o͞o	**7.** Though we will use the macron ($\bar{u}$), we will briefly consider the use of the yo͞o and the o͞o to indicate the long $\bar{u}$. Some teachers' manuals use the yo͞o to indicate the pronunciation of the long $\bar{u}$ in _cube_, and the o͞o to indicate the pronunciation of the long $\bar{u}$ in _tune_. Say _cube_ and _tune_. Listen carefully. Do you hear different pronunciations of the long _u_ in _cube_ and _tune_? _____ (yes, no) A /y/ precedes the /oo/ in _cube_. This long vowel sound is therefore represented by _____. The sound that the _u_ represents in _tune_ (yo͞o, o͞o) _____ preceded by /y/. (is, is not) We would expect this sound to be represented by a(n) _____. (yo͞o, o͞o) (Consult your teacher's manual for the symbols that are used to represent the long $\bar{u}$.)
cake, be, time _home, huge_	**8.** These five vowel phonemes are represented by the key symbols $\bar{a}, \bar{e}, \bar{i}, \bar{o}, \bar{u}$. Select a word from the list at the right that illustrates each. $\bar{a}$ _____ $\bar{e}$ _____ $\bar{i}$ _____ $\bar{o}$ _____ $\bar{u}$ _____ be up cake home huge time run

nāmé, thēsé, cūté, bōné, *tōé, pīné*	**9.** Study the words below. Indicate those vowels that represent their long (glided) sounds by placing macrons above them. Put a diagonal line (/) through each vowel that is silent. name these cute bone toe pine
     e, e long (glided)	**10.** There are many one-syllable words with two vowels in which *e* is the second vowel as well as the final letter of the word. We can make a generalization concerning these words. Study the words *name* and *pine;* then complete this generalization: When a one-syllable word has two vowels, one of which is a final _____ , the _____ is silent and the first vowel usually represents its _____ sound.

 VCe
 	
 yes
	11. This generalization most often applies to words that have the ending pattern of VCe. The word *use* is an example of VCe: vowel-consonant-final vowel *e.*
	
	 Time and *plate* have the ending pattern of _____ . Does this
	
	 generalization apply to them? _____
	
	      When a one-syllable word has two vowels,
	      one of which is the final *e*, the *e* is silent and the
	      first vowel usually represents its long sound.

     VCe	**12.** The C in the vowel-consonant-final vowel *e* (VCe) pattern may signify a single consonant letter or a consonant digraph, but only one consonant phoneme. Since *ph* represents a single consonant phoneme, the nonsense word *sophe* has an ending pattern _____ .
dīné, hōpé, fācé, rīdé, *cūbé, phōné* VCe	**13.** Mark each vowel in the following words with the proper diacritical mark. Put a slash (/) through the silent letters. dine hope face ride cube phone All of the above have the vowel-consonant ending pattern _____ .

When a one-syllable word has two vowels, one of which is the final *e*, the *e* is silent and the first vowel usually represents its long sound.	**14.** Write the generalization concerning vowel sounds illustrated by the words: ate game ice
come, some there	**15.** It is well to remember that the generalization is very helpful but not infallible. Check the words in the following set that <u>do</u> <u>not</u> follow the generalization. (Is the final *e* silent? Does the first vowel "say its own name"?) come _____ place _____ these _____ some _____ there _____ late _____ clothe _____ same _____
dance pāste fence VCCe VCCe VCCe wāste pulse VCCe VCCe	**16.** This generalization is of little value in helping to determine the vowel sound in words ending with the vowel-consonant pattern of VCCe, even when such words are of one syllable. Study the words below. Indicate the vowels that represent the long sound by using the macron. dance paste fence waste pulse _____ _____ _____ _____ _____ Write the ending pattern (begin with the vowel) under each of the words.
dăns, rīd, sāf, brĭj kāk, fĕns long (glided) short (unglided) silent	**17.** Write the words below to show pronunciation, using the key symbols we associate with each vowel and consonant letter. Omit each silent letter. dance ride safe bridge cake fence We can see that in one-syllable words that end with the pattern of VCe the first vowel is usually _____ ; in one-syllable words that end with the pattern of VCCe the first vowel is usually _____ . The final *e* in both patterns (VCe and VCCe) is usually _____ .

	lāte	**18.** Mark the vowels in the last syllable in each of the words at the right to show pronunciation. The last syllable in each of these words has the vowel-consonant ending pattern of _____ . With these words (VCe, VCCe) in mind, our generalization might be extended to read: When a word or an accented syllable has two vowels, one of which is a final _____ , the _____ is silent and the first vowel usually represents its _____ sound.	*re late*
	pēde		*stam pede*
VCe	*rāde*		*pa rade*
	cāse		*book case*
	tāke		*mis take*
e, e			
long			

	19. All of the two-or-more syllable words at the right have a final *e* which is silent. The consonant letter before the silent *e* in these words is either _____ or _____. Does the last syllable in each of these words follow the generalization we have been studying? _____ Underline the word(s) that does follow the generalization. Be sure you don't use an artificial pronunciation.	*active*
v, l		*objective*
		motive
no		*forgive*
		legislative
		outlive
arrive		*arrive*
		sterile
		automobile

	20. When a word or an accented syllable has two vowels, one of which is a final *e*, the *e* is silent and the first vowel usually represents the long (glided) sound. If we omit those words ending with *ve* and *le,* this generalization is of value in determining the vowel sounds in two-or-more syllable words that have the ending pattern of VCe. **The *ve* and *le* endings are too irregular to be considered a reliable pattern.** Which of the following endings is most apt to follow the generalization at the beginning of this frame?
ine	ale ive ave eve ine ole

21. In frame 20, you identified *ive* and *ave* as too irregular to be of value in determining the vowel sounds of words that have the ending pattern of **VCe.** Rewrite the words below, omitting the final *e:*

love	prove	have	give	glove

lov, prov, hav, giv, glov

_____ _____ _____ _____ _____

Puzzle: Why do these words end in a final *e* if the **VCe** pattern does not help us determine the pronunciation of the vowel sound?

Hint: Look at the words that you have rewritten. Do they look like

No

English words? _____

The final *e* follows the letter *v* in words such as *love, have,* and *give* because English words do not end in the letter *v.*

Follow	Do Not Follow
stove	come
cone	one
throne	none
globe	some

22. Let us consider another exception. Say the words at the right. Listen carefully to the sound that the vowel *o* represents. Arrange the words in two columns: (1) those in which the ending pattern **VCe** is of value in determining the pronunciation of the vowel, and (2) those in which the ending pattern **VCe** does not help us determine the pronunciation of the vowel.

stove
cone
come
one
throne
none
globe
some

Words do not follow the generalization when the vowel letter *o* is pronounced like the sound of "uh" in the word *done.*

---

long (or glided)

(All words below must have a silent, final *e.*)

rōle, remāke, extrēme

prīce, cūbe

23. We have identified five vowel phonemes that represent the

_____ sounds of the letters.

We have also learned one generalization that gives a clue to that sound. Select one word for each of the five vowels to illustrate this generalization. Place a macron above the vowels selected.

shady	one	role	piece	remake
extreme	come	price	cube	dance

---

consonant

long (glided)

VCe

24. We have noted that when we see a word or an accented syllable with the pattern of a single vowel followed by a single

_____ and final *e,* the single vowel is likely to represent its

_____ sound. The vowel-consonant ending pattern we

expect to see is _____.

BOX 3.1

Final *E* Solves Four Spelling Problems

Before spelling was finalized in the 17th century, early writers used the final *e* to solve several tricky spelling problems. We will consider four ways in which the final *e* came to the rescue.

1. English words ending with a /v/ or a /z/ phoneme presented a sticky spelling problem for early writers. Although English words can end with a /v/ or /z/ phoneme (*groove, breeze*), spelling conventions did not provide for a single *v* or *z* to be the final letter (*groov, breez*). The inventive writers added a final *e* to avoid ending words with a final *v* or *z* grapheme (e.g., *starve, swerve, bronze, snooze*).

2. Early writers needed a way to indicate when the *th* is voiced (*teethe*) and when it is unvoiced (*teeth*). In solving their problem, the inventive writers once again used the final *e*, adding it to words such as *teethe* and *clothe* so as to avoid confusion with words such as *teeth* and *cloth*.

3. The final *e* also came in handy when spelling words that end in /s/. Sometimes the /s/ is part of the root word (*dense*); sometimes it is part of a suffix (*dens*). In using the final *e*, the writers of yesteryear generously provided the reader with a helpful visual cue for sorting out when the letter *s* is part of a root word (*tens + e = tense, brows + e = browse*) and when the final *s* is part of a suffix (*horse + s = horses; lapse + s = lapses*).

4. Thanks to the final *e*, it is clear when to use the soft *c* (key word: *sun*) and *g* (key word: *jeep*) in words such as *choice* and *damage*. Without the final *e*, the reader might be tempted to pronounce *choic* (choice) as /choik/ and *damag* (damage) as /damag/.

English is a dynamic and evolving language in which spelling changes occur over relatively long periods of time. Will the final *e* eventually drop away from words in which the *e* neither contributes to pronunciation nor gives the reader an important visual clue? No one knows—but we might speculate. Generally speaking, American spelling changes make words simpler, such as dropping the *u* from the British *colour* or the trendy *nite* for *night*. So perhaps the writers in some future century will spell *groove* and *breeze* as *groov* and *breez*.

	pīne *cūte*	**25.** All the vowels at the right represent the	*pin* *cut*
short	*rāte* *strīpe*	_____ sound. Check each one to make sure.	*rat* *strip*
	kīte *pāle*	Now add a silent *e* to the end of each word to	*kit* *pal*
	hāte *āte*	see what happens. To show the new pronunciation, mark the first vowel in each of the new words you've made with the appropriate diacritical mark.	*hat* *at*
long		The vowels now represent their _____ sounds.	

e	**26.** We can see that the silent _____ at the end of a word *cut*
	has a purpose. *cute*
pronunciation (or	It changes the meaning of the word as well as *strip*
sound)	the _____ of the word. *stripe*

so	**27.** Another situation in which we often find the *so* *sup pose*
so lo *fe ver*	vowel to be long is that of the open syllable. *so lo* *fe ver*
ti ger	**An open syllable ends with a** *pine* *ti ger*
	vowel <u>phoneme</u>. *me* *pa per*
me *pa per*	Study the words at the right. Underline the open
	syllables, including open one-syllable words.

	28. This generalization most often applies to words and syllables that have the vowel-consonant pattern of CV. Study the words and the underlined syllables below.
	me *<u>be</u> long* *<u>ma</u> ple* *so*
	The words and the underlined syllables have the vowel-consonant
CV	pattern of _____. Each of the above words and underlined
open	syllables is a(n) _____ syllable.
	(open, closed)

consonant	**29.** The first syllable of *sup pose* ends with a _____ phoneme.
	The second syllable of *sup pose* is not an open syllable because it does
phoneme	not end with a vowel _____. The last letter is a vowel, but it
	(letter, phoneme)
silent	is _____.

yes	**30.** Is the first syllable of *fe ver* an open syllable? _____
	What key symbol represents the final phoneme of the first
ē	syllable? _____ The first syllable in *fe ver* has the
CV	vowel-consonant pattern of _____. Is the second
no	syllable an open syllable? _____ What key symbol
r	represents the final phoneme? _____

long		**31.** Study these words: hel l<u>o</u> b<u>e</u> m<u>e</u> ter t<u>i</u> ger The underlined vowels represent their _____ sounds. (long, short)

open glided (or long) CV	fā hē sī tō hū	**32.** Place a macron above the five vowels (*a, e, i, o, u*) that represent their glided sounds in the words at the right. We might generalize: A single vowel in an _____ syllable often represents its _____ sound. The vowel-consonant pattern for an open syllable is _____.	fa vor he si lent to tal hu man

s<u>ō</u> l<u>ō</u> b<u>ē</u> long d<u>ī</u> graph h<u>ā</u> l<u>ō</u> hel l<u>ō</u> d<u>o</u>	**33.** Study the words at the right. Draw a line under the single vowels in the open syllables. Place a macron above those vowels you underlined that represent the long sound. Work carefully. You may find exceptions.	so lo be long di graph ha lo hel lo do

e open	**34.** Although the *a* in *about* and the _____ in *debate* *a bout* are single vowel letters in _____ syllables, they do *de bate* (closed, open) not represent long sounds. **We tend to shorten the vowel sounds in unaccented syllables.**

long (glided)	**35.** The generalization has more application when we limit it to accented syllables: A single vowel in an open accented syllable usually represents its _____ sound. We will study this more fully later.

	36. We should note, however, that sometimes single vowel letters in open <u>unaccented</u> syllables do represent the long sounds. *so' lo* *ha' lo*
lō, lō	Two syllables from the words at the right that illustrate this are _____ from *solo* and _____ from *halo*. Mark the vowels in these unaccented syllables.
<u>pa</u> pa <u>to</u>	**37.** We should also note that not all vowels in open accented syllables represent long sounds. (Exceptions, exceptions!) Underline the syllables that are exceptions to the generalization: *no* *pa' pa* *to* **Single vowel letters in open accented syllables usually represent their long sounds.** *she*

short
 	
no
 	
long
silent
	38. We will now consider long vowel exceptions to the closed syllable generalization. We expect that single vowels in closed syllables—the CVC and VC *sight*
	
	high
	
	right
	patterns—will usually represent _____ sounds. *sight*
	               (long, short) *sigh*
	
	Do the words at the right follow the closed syllable
	generalization? _____
	
	An exception to the closed syllable generalization is found in words in which the *i* is followed by *gh*.
	
	The *i* represents the _____ sound and the *gh* is
	
	_____ in such words.
	  (long, short)

ld	**39.** The words below represent another exception to the closed syllable generalization. *child* *wild* *mild* *sold* *told* *hold* We can summarize: **When *i* or *o* is followed by _____, the vowel usually represents the long sound.**

closed
 	
closed
 	
open
 	
phoneme
	40. Let us review. Syllables with the CVC pattern are _____
	                                                                    (closed, open)
	syllables; those with the VC pattern (such as *ant*) are _____
	                                                                    (closed, open)
	syllables. Syllables that have the CV pattern are _____
	                                                                    (closed, open)
	syllables. An open syllable ends with a vowel _____.
	                                                                    (phoneme, letter)

a, e, i, o, u	**41.** The previous frames in this section contain examples of the five vowels, _____, _____, _____, _____, and _____, in which they represent their long sounds.
vowel	**42.** We have learned that the vowel *w* always appears with another _____ letter. Therefore, there would be no instances in which we could apply the <u>single</u>-vowel open syllable generalization to the *w*.
bī *mī* *whī* *flī* *ī* *krī* CV	**43.** Let us examine the generalization with *by* _____ respect to the vowel *y*. Look at the words at the right. *my* _____ In each instance the *y* represents the *why* _____ phoneme we associate with the key *fly* _____ symbol _____. *cry* _____ The vowel-consonant pattern for these words is _____. Rewrite these words. Use the key symbol we associate with each vowel and consonant phoneme.

long *e*	**44.** Study the words at the right. Complete *happy*
	the generalization:
	                                                                  lucky
	When *y* is the final letter of a two-syllable word, it
	                                                                  baby
	represents the _____ sound of _____.
	                                                                  windy

bī pas	**45.** *Y* is not always the final letter in a word. Study the words at the right. Rewrite them to show the pronunciation of the consonants and of the vowels representing the long sounds.	*by pass* _____
sī pres		*cy press* _____
pī thon		*py thon* _____

46. If *y* represents the long sound of the *e* when it is the final and only vowel in the last syllable of a multisyllabic word, then the open syllable generalization we have been studying applies to *a, e, i, o, u,* and *y.*

cry   The *y* would represent the sound of the long *i* in _____ and
                                                                  (*cry, happy*)

lucky   the long *e* in _____ .
                              (*my, lucky*)

A single vowel in an open accented syllable often represents its long sound.	**47.** State the generalization that concerns a single vowel in an open accented syllable.

BOX 3.2   ✖◇✖◇✖

The Extra *E*

Exception words such as *gone* and *done,* which we expect to be pronounced with a long *o,* are a consequence of the quirky way in which the English spelling system developed. Before the 14th century, the final *e* represented an "uh" that was pronounced at the end of words. To get a sense of how contemporary words would sound with a final "uh," say *gone* and *done,* and then add an extra "uh" to the end—"gonuh" and "donuh." Sometime around the 14th century the "uh" was dropped from pronunciation, and the final *e* became the silent letter in words spelled with the VCe pattern.

Then something curious happened. For some unknown reason, the early writers began to attach a final *e* to short vowel words that ended in a consonant letter. The writers usually doubled the final consonant, suggesting that they knew that the final *e* in the VCe pattern signaled that the preceding vowel is long. Put into a contemporary context, the word *pit* might be spelled *pitte,* and *pin* as *pinne.* For some time, English spelling was cluttered with extra consonants and final *es.* Spelling was eventually untangled in the 17th century when the practice of adding an extra *e* to the end of short vowel words was discontinued. However, some of the words from this earlier period still continue to be spelled with the unnecessary final *e,* which is the reason why we have words such as *gone* and *done* in our English language dictionary today.

✕◇✕◇✕   *STUDY GUIDE*   ✕◇✕◇✕
Long Vowels

Long Vowel	Key Symbol	Key Word
a	ā	apron
e	ē	eraser
i	ī	ice
o	ō	overalls
u	ū	unicorn

Macron (-)   The macron (-) is the diacritical mark used to indicate the specific pronunciation of the long vowels. *Glided* is another term that refers to the long vowel phonemes.

Long ū   Some dictionaries are now using the (y)$\overline{oo}$ to indicate the ū. Some teachers' manuals use two symbols to indicate the ū—the y$\overline{oo}$ for the ū in *unicorn* and *cube,* and $\overline{oo}$ for the ū in *tune* and *true.*

VCe Pattern   When a word or an accented syllable has two vowels, one of which is a final *e,* the *e* is silent and the first vowel usually represents the long (glided) sound (*ape, hope*).

le and ve Exceptions to the VCe Pattern   The *le* or *ve* endings are too irregular to be considered reliable representations of the VCe pattern (*have, love*).

o Pronounced as "uh" Exception to the VCe Pattern   Words do not follow the VCe generalization when the vowel letter *o* is pronounced like the "uh" in the words *done* and *come.*

Open Syllable   An open syllable ends with a vowel phoneme (*be, try*). Single vowel letters in open, accented syllables usually represent their long (glided) sounds (*she*).

Unaccented Syllables   We tend to shorten vowel sounds in unaccented syllables (*a bout'*).

CV Pattern   The CV pattern is an open syllable in which the vowel usually represents its long sound (*be, tree*).

Yy as a Vowel   When *y* is the final letter in a one-syllable word (*my*), it usually represents the sound we associate with long *i* (key word: *ice*). When *y* is the final letter in a two-syllable word (*happy*), it usually represents the long sound of *e* (key word: *eraser*).

igh Exception to the Closed Syllable Generalization   When the *i* is followed by *gh* in a word or a syllable, the *i* usually represents the long sound and the *gh* is silent (*light*).

i or o Followed by ld to the Closed Syllable Generalization   When *i* or *o* is followed by *ld,* the vowel usually represents the long sound (*wild, fold*).

✻◇✻ Review 15

1. We have been studying five phonemes that represent the long sounds of the vowels: ā, _____ , _____ , _____ , _____ . We can show their pronunciation by placing a _____ (name of diacritical mark) over each of them.

2. *Y* can represent a long sound also, but it does not have a key symbol: It is a duplication of either the long _____ (as in *cry*) or the long _____ (as in *lucky*).

3. We have learned to recognize two patterns that may give clues as to the vowel sound in an unknown word. One is the vowel-consonant-silent _____ pattern (VCe). State the generalization:

4. The other is a single-vowel, open syllable pattern: The single vowel in an open, _____ syllable is often _____ .

5. Another way we can state the same generalization is: When the only vowel in a word or accented syllable comes at the _____ of the syllable, that vowel usually represents its _____ sound.

6. The long sounds of the vowels are easiest to recognize in known words because the name of the vowel is the same as the _____ it represents.

7. Pronounce the words at the right.

   a. Place a C behind each word that ends with a consonant phoneme.

   b. Place a V behind each word that ends with a vowel phoneme.

   c. Indicate the pronunciation of the final phoneme by writing the key symbol. If the word ends with a consonant blend, use only the symbol that represents the final phoneme in the blend.

   d. Underline the words in which the final syllable is an open syllable.

dine	*table*
tack	*go*
way	*tight*
watch	*enough*

8. We are studying the vowel phonemes that are represented by a single letter. We have learned to associate 10 of the 19 vowel phonemes with their key pronunciation symbols. Mark the following vowel graphemes to indicate their pronunciation.

   bite   bit   can   cane   pet   Pete   us   fuse   cot   code

(See the Part III Answers section for the answers to Review 15, page 155)

◇ Schwa (ə)

			(comma, chicken, family, button, circus)	1	2	3
a	ə	comma	**1.** Say the words at the right aloud. Listen to the phoneme represented by the underlined letter. When you say the words slowly and distinctly (and artificially), they may sound quite different from one another; but when these words are used in ordinary speech, the underlined part represents a very soft "uh."	_____	ə	comma
e	ə	chicken		_____	ə	chicken
i	ə	family		_____	ə	family
o	ə	button		_____	ə	button
u	ə	circus		_____	ə	circus
a, e, i, o, u			The letters that represent the "uh" sound in the words at the right are _____, _____, _____, _____, _____. Place them properly in column 1.			

	2. Dictionaries usually indicate the soft vowel sound found in unaccented syllables with a **schwa (ə)**.
ə	The pronunciation is shown by the sign _____ (an inverted e).

	3. How is the *schwa* pronounced? The *sch* grapheme in *schwa* represents the phoneme we associate with the key symbol *sh*.
blend	The *sh* and the consonant *w* form a _____ . The *a* represents
	(digraph, blend)
	an "ah" sound.

commə	**4.** Rewrite the words at the right to show the pronunciation of the vowel in the *unaccented* syllable.	com' ma	_____
chickən		chick' en	_____
faməly	Without the schwa, each of these vowels would need a separate diacritical mark.	fam' i ly	_____
buttən		but' ton	_____
circəs		cir' cus	_____

	5. **The schwa is used to indicate the pronunciation of the vowel phoneme in many unaccented syllables.**
	Study the word below. Rewrite it, indicating the sound of each letter.
bā' kən	ba' con _____

pĕn səl	**6.** Say the words at the right in a natural manner. *pencil* _____
lī ən	Rewrite them, using key symbols to indicate each of the phonemes. *lion* _____
sĕk ənd	Check the vowels that can represent the schwa *second* _____
prŏb ləm	phoneme: *problem* _____
a, e, i, o, u	*a* _____ *e* _____ *i* _____ *o* _____ *u* _____

	7. The use of the schwa for each vowel that represents the short "uh" sound, along with the frequent use of the short *i* (ĭ), has simplified pronunciation keys greatly.
unaccented	Almost all vowels in _____ syllables represent one of these (accented, unaccented) two short, soft sounds.

ə	**8.** Let us examine the words *distant* and *village.* The dictionary may indicate the pronunciation as dĭs′ tənt and vĭl′ ĭj. The _____
i	and the _____ indicate the two soft phonemes regardless of spelling.

	9. The following words are written to show their pronunciation. What are the words?
facet, sicken	*făs′ ĭt* _____ *sĭk′ ən* _____
banquet, melon	*băng′* kwĭt _____ *mĕl′ ən* _____

	10. Examine the words below. They are written the way they might appear in your dictionary. What are the words?
vegetable, possible	*vĕj′ tə bəl* _____ *pŏs′ ə bəl* _____
	Note that we pronounce the syllable *ble* as though a very short vowel precedes the *l: bəl.*

	11. Although the word part *er* has only a touch of a vowel sound, the schwa is used with the *r* to indicate the pronunciation of the word
er, tī gər	part _____. Thus the key symbols for *tiger* are _____. (Check your dictionary to see how it treats this word part.)

stā′ bəl, mī′ nəs _bŏt′ əm, dĭf′ ər_	**12.** Rewrite the words below to show pronunciation. Omit the silent letters. sta′ ble _____ mi′ nus _____ bot′ tom _____ dif′ fer _____
sō′ fə, plĕzh′ ər _kwiv′ ər, drān′ ĭj_ _kō′ kō, bī′ sĭ kəl_	**13.** Are you ready to code some more difficult words? Rewrite the words below to show pronunciation. They should be written as they might appear in parentheses following the boldface entry word in the dictionary. To avoid artificial pronunciation, check each one by saying it in a sentence. so′ fa _____ pleas′ ure _____ quiv′ er _____ drain′ age _____ co′ coa _____ bi′ cy cle _____
sĭm′ fə nē (or nĭ) _ĭ mŭl′ shən_ _dĭf′ ə kŭlt, ăn tēk′_	**14.** Rewrite the words below to show pronunciation. They should be written as they might appear in parentheses following the boldface entry word in the dictionary. To avoid artificial pronunciation, check each one by saying it in a sentence. sym′ pho ny _____ e mul′ sion _____ dif′ fi cult _____ an tique′ _____
short _i_	**15.** The first vowel in _decay_ represents the _____ phoneme. This use represents the trend toward simplification. It is not _e_. Try it in a sentence to check this. Now try it using _i_ as a guide in pronouncing the first syllable.
hăp′ ən (or hap′ ən)	**16.** It is necessary to note that various dictionaries indicate pronunciation in different ways. We must study the pronunciation key of the particular dictionary we use. For example, many dictionaries indicate the pronunciation of all short sounds with the letter and no diacritical mark. The pronunciation of _happen_ is written _____ .
village _pilot_	**17.** Let us review. We have learned that a vowel grapheme in an unaccented syllable could reasonably be expected to represent the sound we associate with the unglided _i_ (short _i_) or with the sound represented by the schwa (ə). The _i_ would identify the vowel phonemes in the last syllable of _____ . The ə would (candy, program, village, hotel) identify the last syllable of _____. (pilot, locate, liquid, railroad)

✖◇✖◇✖   STUDY GUIDE   ✖◇✖◇✖
                          Schwa

Vowel in an Unaccented Syllable	Key Symbol	Key Word
a	ə	comm<u>a</u> (soft "uh")
e	ə	chick<u>e</u>n (soft "uh")
i	ə	fam<u>i</u>ly (soft "uh")
o	ə	butt<u>o</u>n (soft "uh")
u	ə	circ<u>u</u>s (soft "uh")

Vowels in Unaccented Syllables   The vowels in unaccented syllables can reasonably be expected to represent a soft "uh," or the sound we associate with an unglided (short) ĭ.

Schwa   The dictionary uses a schwa (ə) to indicate the soft "uh" sound found in many unaccented syllables. Without the schwa (ə), the vowels that represent the soft "uh" in unaccented syllables would each need a separate diacritical mark to indicate pronunciation.

Short ĭ   The vowels in unaccented syllables may also represent the unglided (short) ĭ, such as in *manage* (măn' ĭj). The vowels in unaccented syllables represent the soft "uh," the schwa, more often than the short ĭ.

✖◇✖ Review 16

1. The key symbol used to represent many of the vowel phonemes in

unaccented syllables is called a _____ (ə).

2. This symbol is very useful because _____.

3. The ə*r* is used to indicate the pronunciation of a word part in

_____.

   (*river, erase*)

4. The words below are written to show their pronunciation. How are they correctly spelled?

rē' gəl   hănd māď sěl' ə brāt   ěp' ə sōd

(See the Part III Answers section for the answers to Review 16, page 156.)

◇ Other Single Vowels

5, schwa
 	
phoneme
	1. Thus far we have identified 11 vowel phonemes using only
	
	_____ vowel letters and a _____.
	  (How many?)
	We can readily tell which _____ is represented when
	                          (letter, phoneme)
	diacritical marks are used, as in a dictionary, glossary, or other pronunciation guide.

short (unglided)	**2.** We also have examined patterns common to the English language so that we can make a reasonable guess as to the sound of certain vowels. For example, we expect the vowel letter in the pattern CVC to represent its _____ sound.
apple	**3.** If the vowel in the CVC pattern is *a,* then we would expect *a* to represent the same sound as the vowel phoneme heard in _____ . (*said, car, ball, apple, date, saw*)
glided (long) silent	**4.** We expect the first vowel grapheme in the ending pattern VCe to represent its _____ sound and the final *e* to be _____.
sew	**5.** If the first vowel grapheme in the VCe ending pattern is an *o,* then we would expect *o* to represent the same vowel phoneme as that heard in _____. (*done, gone, boy, sew*)
schwa sofa	**6.** A vowel in an unaccented syllable could reasonably be expected to represent the sound we associate with the unglided (short) *i* or with the _____. The ə would identify the vowel phoneme in the last syllable of _____ . (*sofa, remit, require, insect*)

a	*â*	*care*	
u	*û*	*fur*	
a	*ä*	*father*	
a	*ô*	*ball*	

graphemes

7. There are still other single vowel phonemes as shown at the right. Some are influenced by the consonant following the vowel. We will identify these vowel phonemes and suggest a key word by which each can be remembered. However, we commonly use the pronunciation key given at the bottom of the page in the dictionary for these more difficult phonemes. Each of these phonemes is represented by a

	1	2	3
a	_____	*câre (kâr)*	
u	_____	*fûr*	
a	_____	*fäther (fäthər)*	
a	_____	*ball (bôl)*	

variety of spellings, in other words, by a variety of _____.
(sounds, graphemes)
Complete the table by filling in the key symbols (2). We have noted that various dictionaries use different ways to indicate pronunciation. Check the pronunciation key in your dictionary for the key symbols for these four vowel phonemes.

---

r

8. Let's examine the vowel phoneme in the key word *care*. The key symbol we will use to represent this phoneme is *â*.

We can hardly separate it from the following consonant phoneme, so we call it _____ -controlled.
(r, l, w)

---

yes

6

9. Study the words at the right. Pronounce each word aloud. Is the vowel phoneme the same in each word?

_____.

In these examples, one vowel phoneme is represented by

_____ graphemes.
(How many?)

chair

share

their

there

bear

prayer

---

ai, a, ei, e, ea, ay

10. Underline the graphemes that represent the same vowel phoneme heard in *care*. They represent vowel phonemes, so do not underline the controlling consonant.

chair   share   their   there   bear   prayer

You can see that our table, frame 7, is greatly oversimplified. Column 1 should show the six graphemes that, when followed by *r*, represent the vowel phoneme we hear in *care*.

11. Rewrite the words below, using the key symbols to indicate the pronunciation of consonants and vowels. Omit silent letters.

kâr, whâr, fârē

care _____   where _____   fairy _____

shâr, hâr, băt

share _____   hair _____   bat _____

bat

The word out of place in this list is _____.

12. The following words are written as they would appear in a dictionary to show pronunciation. Spell them correctly.

air, anchor, square

âr _____   ăng′ kər _____   skwâr _____

pile, scarce, chair

pīl _____   skârs _____   châr _____

race, civic, their

rās _____   sĭv′ ĭk _____   t͟hâr _____

or there

You can interpret the dictionary code!

13. Another vowel phoneme which is *r*-controlled is the one heard in *fur*. In fact, it is impossible to separate it

i

e

r

ea

from the _____.

o

Say the words at the right. What graphemes represent the vowel phoneme heard in *fur* as shown by the words at the right? Underline them.

u

y

thirst

germ

learn

worm

purple

myrtle

14. Rewrite the words above using the *û* to show the pronunciation of that part of the word.

thûrst, jûrm, lûrn

_____   _____   _____

wûrm, pûrpəl, mûrtəl

_____   _____   _____

15. Note that this phoneme is not the same as that heard as a separate syllable, generally a suffix, as in *farmer, lower.* We will identify this separate syllable by ər.

Rewrite the following words to show pronunciation:

wûrkər, wûrkt, snâr

worker _____   worked _____   snare _____

sûrv	**16.** Rewrite the words at the right to show their pronunciation. *serve* _____
pāpər	*paper* _____
skûrt	*skirt* _____
hâr	*hair* _____
several different	**17.** The phoneme that we associate with the key symbol *û* may be represented by _____ graphemes. The key word chosen (only one, several different)
fur	to help us remember this phoneme is _____.
several different	**18.** The phoneme that we associate with the key symbol *â* may be represented by _____ graphemes. Its key word is (only one, several different)
care	_____.
graphemes (or spellings)	**19.** The phoneme that we will identify with the key symbol *ä* and the key word *father* may be confusing because of regional differences in pronunciation. It is represented by many different letters and combinations of letters. Dictionaries reveal anywhere from 3 to 11 different _____ that represent this phoneme.
ä	**20.** Pronounce the words at the right. If you do not hear the vowel phoneme you hear in *father,* your pronunciation is simply reflecting a regional difference. You are not wrong. *arm* *calm* *hearth* *sergeant* *bazaar* Now pronounce them so that you can hear the phoneme we represent by the key symbol _____ in each one.
a, al, ea, e, aa	**21.** In the words below, underline the graphemes that represent the phoneme we identify by *ä.* Include the silent letters that could be considered a part of the grapheme. *arm* *calm* *hearth* *sergeant* *bazaar*

fär, täcō, pläzə *cäm, gärd, dâr*	**22.** If you cannot agree with the pronunciation, use your dictionary. Your pronunciation may reflect that of your region. Use the key symbols to show the pronunciation of these words: far _____ taco _____ plaza _____ calm _____ guard _____ dare _____
kärnāshən, bärnyärd, bâr *pârənt, kāk, hûrt*	**23.** Rewrite these words to show pronunciation: carnation _____ barnyard _____ bear _____ parent _____ cake _____ hurt _____
raw, caught, walk, broad *fought, tall, order*	**24.** Pronounce *ball.* Listen to the vowel phoneme. We will represent this phoneme with the key symbol ô. Say the words below. Check those in which you hear the phoneme heard in *ball.* raw _____ caught _____ walk _____ broad _____ bead _____ fought _____ tall _____ order _____ Some of the answers here may also be affected by regional variations in pronunciation. Check your dictionary. Do you have trouble with the word *order?* Would you believe that many dictionaries use *order, for,* and *horn* as the key words?
aw, au, al, oa, ou, a, o	**25.** What graphemes in frame 24 represent the vowel phoneme heard in *ball?* _____ _____ _____ _____ _____ _____ _____
rô, kôt, wôk, brôd *bēd, fôt, tôl, ôrder*	**26.** Rewrite the words in frame 24 using key symbols to indicate pronunciation. _____ _____ _____ _____ _____ _____ _____ _____
ball *sô*	**27.** Pronounce *saw.* The *a* represents the vowel phoneme in _____ . (*ball, sat*) When *a* is followed by an *l* or *w* in the same syllable, the *a* may represent the sound we associate with the key symbol ô. Rewrite *saw* to show pronunciation. _____

28. These words are written to show their pronunciation. What are the words?

shawl, small

shôl _____   smôl _____

false, drawn

fôls _____   drôn _____

29. Let us review: Four single-vowel phonemes are represented by the underlined letters at the right.

1. â   c<u>a</u>re
2. ä   f<u>a</u>ther
3. ô   b<u>a</u>ll
4. û   f<u>u</u>r

Indicate the pronunciation of the underlined vowels in the words below by using the number of the word in which the vowel has the same pronunciation.

3, 1, 3, 2, 4

f<u>au</u>lt _____   rep<u>ai</u>r _____   Ut<u>a</u>h _____   s<u>e</u>rgeant _____   t<u>e</u>rm _____

1, 3, 4, 4

th<u>e</u>re _____   br<u>oa</u>d _____   c<u>ou</u>rage _____   w<u>o</u>rk _____

30. There are a few broad generalizations that may be of some help in determining the pronunciation of these vowels in unknown words.

car

farmer

curl

If the only vowel letter in a word or syllable is followed by *r*, the vowel will be affected by that *r*.

first

Say the words at the right. The vowel sounds are neither

corn

short

long nor _____. They are almost lost in the

r

consonant letter _____.

31. If the only vowel in a word or syllable is an *a* followed by *l* or *w*, the *a* is affected by that *l* or *w*.

draw

saw

Study the words at the right. Which word does not belong

late

late

in the list? _____ Do any of the others represent

fall

no

the long or short sound of *a*? _____ Does the *a* followed by *l* represent the same sound as the *a* followed by

small

yes

w? _____

Again, regional variations in the pronunciation of these words may cause you some difficulty.

STUDY GUIDE
Other Single Vowels

Vowel Letter	Key Symbol	Key Word
a	*â*	*care*
u	*û*	*fur*
a	*ä*	*father*
a	*ô*	*ball*

R-Controlled Vowels   When the only vowel letter in a word or syllable is followed by *r*, the vowel will be affected by that *r*. When pronouncing a vowel followed by the *r*, the vowel phoneme is almost lost in the consonant.

R-Controlled â(r)   It is impossible to separate, in normal pronunciation, the /â/ from the /r/. Six graphemes represent the *â* when followed by *r*: c*are*, h*ai*r, h*ei*r, w*ea*r, wh*e*re, and pr*ay*er.

R-Controlled û(r)   It is impossible to separate, in normal pronunciation, the /û/ from the /r/. Several graphemes represent the *û(r)*, as we see in the words f*i*rst, g*e*rm, l*ea*rn, w*o*rm, p*u*rple, and m*y*rtle.

R-Controlled ä(r)   The *a*, when preceding the letter *r*, represents an *r*-controlled vowel. Examples of the *r*-controlled *a*, pronounced as /är/, may be heard in the words *a*rm, y*a*rd, *a*rch, and l*a*rge. This phoneme may also be spelled with the *ea* grapheme, as in h*ea*rth, and the *er*, as in s*er*geant.

R-Controlled ô(r)   The *o*, when preceding the letter *r*, represents an *r*-controlled vowel. Examples of the *r*-controlled *o*, pronounced as /ôr/, may be heard in the words m*o*re, c*ou*rt, and *o*rder.

ä   The *ä*, key word *father*, does not always precede the letter *r* in English words. Several graphemes represent the *ä*, as shown in the words c*a*lm, c*o*t, sh*a*h, and baz*aa*r.

ô   The *ô*, key word *ball*, is heard in c*au*ght and br*oa*d. Several graphemes represent the *ô*, as shown in the words s*a*w, c*au*ght, w*a*lk, br*oa*d, f*ou*ght, and *o*rder.

a Before l or w (ô)   When the letter *a* is the only vowel in a word or syllable, and precedes the letter *l* or the letter *w*, the *a* is affected by the *l* or *w*, and is pronounced /ô/. Notice the difference in the phonemes that the letter *a* represents in *bald* (*bôld*) and *bad* (*băd*), and in *jaw* (*jô*) and *jam* (*jăm*). Examples include *call, almost, talk, draw, awful,* and *shawl.*

❊❖❊ Review 17

1. We have been studying the vowel phonemes that can be represented by single-vowel key symbols. The first group of five (example, *apple*) we labeled

the _____ vowel phonemes. Write their key symbols:

2. The second group of five (example, *ice*) we labeled _____ vowel phonemes. Write their key symbols:

3. The third (example, *comma*) was given a key symbol not in the alphabet, called the _____. This key symbol, _____, represents each of the vowels when they have the sound heard in _____ .
   (happy, agree)

   It is very useful because _____.

4. That left us with four additional single vowel phonemes, which cannot be grouped except for the influence on them of the phoneme _____
   (following, preceding)

   the vowel. We found that they were affected by phonemes represented by the _____, _____, and _____.

5. The key words for these vowel phonemes can be placed in the following sentences. Fill in the blanks and mark the vowels.

   a. She hit the _____ over the fence.

   b. The kitten has soft, fluffy _____.

   c. Tom's _____ will take Tom on a fishing trip next Saturday.

   d. The mother dog takes good _____ of her puppies.

   (See the Part III Answers section for the answers to Review 17, page 156.)

◇ Diphthongs

	oi (oil) *ou (house)*
	1. We have been studying the vowel phonemes that are represented by single vowel letters. We will now turn our attention to those that are represented by combinations of letters. Say *oil.* The word *oil* is
consonant	composed of two phonemes: one vowel and one _____.
l	They are represented by the graphemes *oi* and _____.
	2. The *oi* functions as one phoneme called a **diphthong.**
	A diphthong is a single vowel phoneme, represented by two letters, resembling a glide from one sound to another.
	A study of **phonetics** (the science of speech sounds) would show that many single-letter vowels are actually diphthongs. They represent more than a single sound. Note the gliding sound of the *u* in *use.* You may be using "glided" rather than "long" for this vowel phoneme.
diphthongs (Check the spelling.)	We will call only the <u>two</u>-letter gliding combinations _____.

diphthong	**3.** In this study we have made the arbitrary statement that there are 44 phonemes. It really is not that simple! Say *few.* Is the vowel phoneme equivalent to the phoneme heard at the beginning of *use,* or should we consider *ew* a separate diphthong, not a duplication of any single vowel phoneme? Our decision is to consider that *few = fū.* So we will <u>not</u> call *ew* a _____.
oi, ou	**4.** It seems most helpful to classify only two of the vowel phonemes as diphthongs. These are the vowel sounds heard in *oil* and *house.* The _____ and the _____ then represent 2 of the 44 speech sounds in our language.

		b<u>oi</u>l	**5.** Examine the words at the right. Underline the grapheme in each word that represents the diphthong *oi.* There are two spellings that represent this diphthong: _____ and _____. boil boy coin enjoy toy
oi oy		b<u>oy</u>	
		c<u>oi</u>n	
		enj<u>oy</u>	
		t<u>oy</u>	

boil, boi, koin, ĕnjoi, toi *oi*	**6.** Rewrite the five words above using the marks of pronunciation (the diacritical marks). _____ _____ _____ _____ _____ The key word for this diphthong is *oil,* the key symbol _____.

h<u>ou</u>se		**7.** The second diphthong is that heard in the key word *house.* The key symbol is *ou.* Read the words at the right. Underline the diphthongs. This diphthong is also represented by two spellings: the _____ and the _____. house brown cow mouse blouse owl
br<u>ow</u>n		
c<u>ow</u>	*ou*	
m<u>ou</u>se	*ow*	
bl<u>ou</u>se		
<u>ow</u>l		

8. Complete the table at the right with the two spellings of each diphthong (1), key symbols (2), and key words (3).

1	2	3
oi, oy	oi	oil
ou, ow	ou	house

1	2	3
oi, _____	oi	_____
_____ , _____	_____	house

ou *kloun*	**9.** The key symbol for the vowel phoneme heard in *clown* is _____. Rewrite *clown* to show its pronunciation. _____

two   two
 	
two
 	
no   *ou*
 	
oi
	10. We are recognizing _____ diphthongs. Each has _____ spellings.
	                              (How many?) (How many?)
	The key symbol for each diphthong is composed of _____ letters
	                                                                              (How many?)
	with _____ diacritical marks. These letters will be either _____
	        (one, two, no) (*ou, ow*)
	or _____ because they are the <u>key</u> symbols. We find them
	        (*oi, oy*)
	used in most dictionaries for pronunciation purposes.

koi *noiz* *broil* *snow* *snō* *kou*	**11.** Study the words at the right. Rewrite *coy* _____ them using key symbols to indicate the pronunciation of all the phonemes. Underline *noise* _____ the diphthongs. *broil* _____ There is no diphthong in _____. *snow* _____ *cow* _____
powder, proud, how, soil	**12.** Underline the diphthongs in the following words. Work with care. The *ou* and *ow* often represent other phonemes. Be sure you underline only those which have the vowel phonemes found in *oil* and *house.* *powder proud course how soil courage gracious*
short	**13.** The *ous* ending, as in *gracious,* is more likely to represent the phonemes we associate with the key symbols _____ *u* and (long, short) *s* (or the schwa and *s*) than with the diphthong *ou* and the *s*. If we do not have the word in our speaking vocabulary, however, it is difficult to determine whether the *ou* (*ow*) is a diphthong.

✖◇✖ Review 18

1. Two of the 44 phonemes are classified as diphthongs. What are the key symbols of these two diphthongs? _____ , _____

2. The diphthongs are _____ phonemes.
     (vowel, consonant)

3. Copy the words that contain diphthongs (Write the key symbol of the diphthong following each.):

   cough   owl   grow   cow   through   moist   oyster

4. Use key symbols to show the pronunciation of the following words; omit silent letters, underline diphthongs:

   house   boy   ounce   enjoy   noise   brow

   (See the Part III Answers section for the answers to Review 18, page 156.)

◇ Vowel Digraphs

	ōō *(food)* o͝o *(hook)*
two one	1. The second category of phonemes represented by two-letter vowels is that of the **vowel digraph**. A digraph is a _____-letter grapheme that represents _____ phoneme(s).
two digraph	2. Listen to the vowel sound as you pronounce *food* aloud. Separate the phonemes as you pronounce *food* again: f oo d. Say the vowel phoneme aloud. The key symbol we use to identify the vowel sound heard in *food* is ōō. This is a _____-letter vowel grapheme representing a single phoneme. We call it a vowel _____.
ōō o͝o ō ō o͝o ŭ o͝o ō ōə or ōĭ ō	3. Write the key symbol to indicate the pronunciation of the vowels in each of the following words. Omit silent letters. Work carefully. *school* _____ *broom* _____ *rowboat* _____ *soon* _____ *flood* _____ *through* _____ *so* _____ *poet* _____ *though* _____
no no, *flood*	4. Does ōō represent the same phoneme as ō? _____ When we see *oo* in a word, can we be sure that it has the sound heard in *food*? _____ The word _____ above contains two *os*, but has the sound of a short *u*.

no *through*	**5.** Is the sound indicated by the key symbol $\overline{oo}$ always spelled with two *os*? _____ Which word in frame 3 contains /$\overline{oo}$/ but is not spelled with two *os*? _____
ou $\overline{oo}$ $\overline{oo}$ $\bar{o}$ $\overline{oo}$ $\overline{oo}$ $\overline{oo}$ $\overline{oo}$ oi $\bar{a}$ $\overline{oo}$ $\overline{oo}$	**6.** Examine the following words carefully. On the line following each, write the key symbol that represents its vowel-pair. *mouse* _____ *cool* _____ *kangaroo*_____ *dough* _____ *drew* _____ *due* _____ *glue* _____ *moon*_____ *coil* _____ *main* _____ *soup* _____ *cartoon* _____
yes no breve	**7.** A second digraph that cannot be represented by a single letter is found in the word *hook*. Pronounce *food,* then *hook.* Pronounce the vowel phoneme in each word. Are they spelled the same? _____ Do they sound alike? _____ Since the key symbol for the sound heard in *food* is two *os* covered by an elongated macron ($\overline{oo}$), it is logical to represent the short phoneme heard in *hook* with an elongated _____ over the two *os* ($\overline{oo}$).
1 2 3 oo $\overline{oo}$ food oo $\overline{oo}$ hook	**8.** **A vowel digraph is a two-letter grapheme that represents one vowel phoneme.** Complete the table at the right with the most common spelling of each digraph (1), key symbol (2), and key word (3) for each digraph. | 1	2	3
---	---	---
_____	$\overline{oo}$	_____
_____	$\breve{oo}$	_____	
foot, goose, took, look, soon, pool, wood, tooth, loose	**9.** Using *food* and *hook* as key words to aid you, mark the words below to show pronunciation. *foot* *goose* *took* *look* *soon* *pool* *wood* *tooth* *loose*
digraph no $\overline{oo}$, $\breve{oo}$	**10.** When we see the vowel _____ oo in a word, can we be sure of the phoneme it represents? _____ The double-*o* is most likely to represent the _____ in *food* or the _____ in *hook*. $\qquad\qquad\qquad\qquad$ ($\overline{oo}$, $\breve{oo}$) $\qquad\qquad\qquad\qquad$ ($\overline{oo}$, $\breve{oo}$)

goose	**11.** When you see a double-*o* in an unknown word, the only clue to pronunciation is that it most often represents the $\overline{oo}$ as in _____. *(goose, book)* You may wish to choose other key words to help you remember the phonemes. *Hook* serves as a good key word for the phoneme we represent by $\overline{oo}$ if we see a resemblance between an elongated breve and a hook! A mental image of the flat surface of a stool may help you remember
$\overline{oo}$	that the key symbol _____ represents the sound heard in *stōol* (or a *plāte* of *fŏod*!).
blŭd *stŏod* *zōo* *flŭd* *drōop*	**12.** Not all *oo*'s represent the sounds heard in *food* and *hook*. Rewrite the words at the right to show the correct pronunciation of each. *blood* _____ *stood* _____ *zoo* _____ *flood* _____ *droop* _____
phonemes consonant, vowel	**13.** The /$\overline{oo}$/ and /$\overline{oo}$/ represent 2 of the 44 _____ of the American-English language. We now have identified all of the phonemes: 25 _____ phonemes and 19 _____ phonemes! However, we must study still another category of vowel combinations.

✖◇✖ Review 19

1. What is a digraph?
2. What are the key symbols that identify each of the vowel digraphs?
3. When you see a double *o* in an unknown word, how will you know what sound it represents?
4. Using key symbols, indicate the pronunciation of each of these words: *tooth, spoon, book, loose, stood, moo, shook.*
5. Show, through the use of key symbols, how you would expect this nonsense word to be pronounced: *clood*
6. Write the symbols, consonants, and vowels to indicate the pronunciation of these words. Omit silent letters.

    boot, fudge, down, toy, shook, cocoa, night, fruit, throw, through, though, thought, quit, book, smooth, fool, breath, breathe, knight

(See the Part III Answers section for the answers to Review 19, page 156)

◈ Other Vowel Pairs

grapheme	**1.** A digraph is a _____ composed of two letters that
phoneme	represent one _____.
/o͞o/	<div align="center">*oo* in *food* represents / / </div>
/o͞o/	<div align="center">*oo* in *hook* represents / / </div>
	2. We have a special name for the digraphs represented by a "gliding
diphthongs	phoneme" as found in *mouse* and *toil.* They are called _____.
	3. Now examine the following words. Each has two vowels that
one	represent _____ phoneme(s). What phoneme does each vowel pair represent? Be sure to use the diacritical mark to identify the phoneme.
ā ē ā	_____ *rain* _____ *heat* _____ *fail*
ē ō ī	_____ *green* _____ *coat* _____ *pie*
	4. All the words in frame 3 contain a vowel digraph: Each has a
grapheme, phoneme	two-letter _____ that represents one _____; but
long	each of these vowel pairs represents a sound already studied: the _____ sound we associate with a single vowel letter. None (long, short)
	of these pairs has a distinctive sound of its own. We will call them **vowel pairs** to distinguish them from the digraphs that represent distinctive sounds: o͞o and o͝o.
	5. We need to give further study to this large group of vowel pairs because they form one of the common patterns in the English language. First, examine the word *rain.*
	Underline the pair of vowels. Indicate the silent vowel by drawing a slash through it. Mark the long vowel.
rā*i̷*n	*Rain* has _____ phonemes represented by _____, (how many?)
3, *r,*	
a, n	long _____, and _____.

	_tā/l_	**6.** Study the words at the right. Underline the pair of vowels in each word.	_tail_
	_sā́y_		_say_
macron	_sēat̸_	As you say each word, place a _____ over the first vowel. (macron, breve)	_seat_
	_fḗed_		_feed_
silent	_cṓat̸_	Indicate that the second vowel is _____ by drawing a slash through it.	_coat_

	7. A syllable must have only one vowel phoneme.	_rain_
	Many syllables (and one-syllable words) have two vowel letters.	_feed_
		hue
	Note the words at the right. In these cases, the first vowel	_toe_
long	represents its _____ sound and the second vowel	
silent	is _____.	

two	**8.** We can make a generalization about the vowel pairs in the words you have studied. When _____ vowels appear together in a
long	syllable (or one-syllable word), the first usually represents its _____
silent	sound and the second is _____.

	9. Mark each vowel in these words to show the pronunciation.
beạ́ch, plāý, mā́/l, ēạ́ch	beach play mail each

	_i_	_e_	**10.** Study the words at the right. The first _pine_ _____ _____
	_o_	_e_	two follow the pattern VCe, the last two _rose_ _____ _____
CVVC	_o_	_a_	follow the pattern _____. Place the vowel _boat_ _____ _____
	_e_	_e_	that represents the long sound in the first column following the word and the silent _jeep_ _____ _____
			letter in the second.

	11. If the vowel pairs were as regular as those represented by the VCe ending pattern, we could form a generalization to include both types:
	When there are two vowel letters in a word or syllable,
long	**the first usually represents its _____ sound**
silent	**and the second is _____.**

diphthong	**12.** The generalization does not apply to *boil* because *oi* is a _____. It has a distinctive sound of its own.
digraph br$\overline{oo}$k	**13.** The generalization does not apply to *brook* because *oo* is a _____ with a distinctive sound. Use the diacritical mark to show pronunciation. _____
sounded	**14.** If the only exceptions to the "first-vowel-long" generalization were the diphthongs and the double-*o* digraphs, we might consider them "phonemes represented by single letters" because in each case only one of the letters is _____. (silent, sounded)

no   *pail*
    toe
    snow
	15. Study the words at the right. Can we depend upon the "first-vowel-long" generalization for all but vowel diphthongs and double-*o* digraphs? _____
	Underline the words that follow the generalization:
	When two vowels appear together in a word
	or syllable, the first usually represents the
	long sound and the second is silent.
	
	pail *said* *auto* *toe* *piece* *snow* *few*

silent f/$\bar{e}$
long   f/$\bar{e}$
       f/$\bar{e}$
       ¢/$\bar{a}$
	16. Place diacritical marks on the vowel pairs in the words at the right. In this set, the first vowel is _____ and the second represents the _____ sound.
	
	field *believe* *niece* *great*

ai, oa, ee, ea, ay	**17.** Although it is true that more words fall under the "first-vowel-long" generalization than any other, there are many exceptions. It can only be used as a clue to the possible pronunciation of a word. However, there are some pairs that follow the generalization more consistently than others. Those that are most consistent appear in these words: *rain, boat, keep, each, play.* The pairs that follow the generalization a greater percentage of the time are _____, _____, _____, _____, _____.

18. However, even these are not without exception. One of the most common sets (*ai*) appears in *said*.

Rewrite *said* using needed diacritical marks to show its pronunciation.

sĕd

said _____

19. Indicate the pronunciation of all the vowels and consonants by using the key symbols. A part of a dictionary key is given below to provide a bit of assistance.

nā bər, bâr	neighbor _____	bear _____
ôt, brĕd	ought _____	bread _____
sô, pēs	saw _____	peace _____
grōn, grōō	grown _____	grew _____
lăf, oul	laugh _____	owl _____
fŏŏt, fēl	foot _____	feel _____

Dictionary Key

â care   ä father   ô ball, order   û fur

ōō food   ŏŏ hook

---

thrōō

thō

bou   no

rŭf

kôf

20. Examine the spelling of the words at the right. They look as though they should rhyme. Do they? _____ To show the inconsistencies in our language, indicate the pronunciation of all the graphemes in these words.

through _____

though _____

bough _____

rough _____

cough _____

21. The words below seem to consist of rhyming couplets. Say the words in set 1 aloud; in set 2; set 3. Do they rhyme? _____ Indicate the pronunciation of all the graphemes in these words. Work set by set.

no

1	2	3
brāk brĕd shōō	break _____	bread _____	shoe _____
frēk bēd tō	freak _____	bead _____	toe _____

STUDY GUIDE

Diphthongs, Vowel Digraphs, and Other Vowel Pairs

Vowel Diphthongs

Diphthong	Key Symbol	Key Word
oi, oy	*oi*	*oil*
ou, ow	*ou*	*house*

A diphthong is a single vowel phoneme, represented by two letters, resembling a glide from one sound to another. Examples of vowel diphthongs include *coin, boy, mouse,* and *how.*

Vowel Digraphs

Vowel Digraph	Key Symbol	Key Word
oo	$\overline{oo}$	*food*
oo	$\overset{\smile}{oo}$	*hook*

A vowel digraph is a two-letter grapheme that represents one vowel phoneme. The key symbol $\overline{oo}$ represents the sound heard in *food* and *school,* while the key symbol $\overset{\smile}{oo}$ represents the sound heard in *hook* and *book.*

Other Vowel Pairs

Vowel Pair	Key Symbol	Key Word
ai (rain)	ā	*apron*
ay (play)	ā	*apron*
ea (each)	ē	*eraser*
ee (keep)	ē	*eraser*
oa (boat)	ō	*overalls*

When two vowels appear together in a word or syllable, the first usually represents the long (glided) sound and the second is silent. Some vowel pairs follow the generalization more consistently than others. Pairs that are the most consistent appear in the words *rain, play, boat, each, keep,* and *pie.*

no
 	
kou   kōm   pād
lō   tōōm   sĕd
    bŏm
	22. Do these sets consist of rhyming words? _____ Show their pronunciation.
	
	1 2 3
	cow _____ comb _____ paid _____
	low _____ tomb _____ said _____
	                               bomb _____

though *freak, bead, toe* *low, paid*	**23.** List the words in the last <u>three</u> frames (20–22) that follow the "first-vowel-long" generalization.
diphthong digraph dictionary hearing	**24.** We have been working with words you know to help you to get a background. But in your reading, if you come across an unknown word with a two-vowel combination, you might first check for *ou, oi, oo,* and so forth, to see if it might be a _____ or a double-o _____. Next, try the "first-vowel-long" generalization, since it is the most common. If that doesn't give you a clue, use your reference book, the _____. For phonics to be of help, the word must be in your _____ vocabulary. (writing, hearing)

✕◇✕ Review 20

1. There are many vowel pairs that follow a pattern: a _____ has a gliding sound as _____ (key symbol) in *oil* and _____ in _____; a _____ in which the _____ represents the vowel sound in *food,* and _____ in _____.

2. Then there are pairs that do not have distinguishing key symbols because they represent single vowels that already have key symbols. For example: *boat, lean, chain.* These words contain vowel pairs that often follow the generalization:

3. The vowels may be separated as in the pattern VCe. What is the generalization?

4. A syllable may have more than one vowel _____, but only one vowel _____.

(See the Part III Answers section for the answers to Review 20, page 156)

◇ Recap II

		Vowel phonemes represented by
phonemes digraphs phonemes	**1.** We have been studying 44 _____ (sound units) of the American-English language. The consonants fell into two groups: the 18 represented by single letters and the 7 _____. The 19 vowel _____ also fall into groups, 15 represented by single vowel letters and 4 by two-letter combinations.	

short
 	
long
	2. We put our greatest emphasis on the five _____ sounds (as in *hop*), and the five _____ sounds (as in *hope*). (As you work through these frames, complete the outline at the right. Write the diacritical marks for the short vowels in I.A., and the diacritical marks for the long vowels in I.B.)	I. Single letter symbols
		  A. Short
		    1. ă
		    2.
		    3.

ə
 	
unaccented
 	
schwa
	3. We use a nonletter symbol (_____) to designate the soft sound heard in the _____ syllable of many two- or three-syllable words. We call it the _____. (Fill in C.1.)	4.
		    5.
		  B. Long
		    1.
		    2. ē
		    3.

r
 	
câre, ärm, ôt, hûrt
	4. There are four other single-letter phonemes that are often controlled by the letter following them, generally *l*, *w*, or _____. These phonemes represent a large variety of graphemes (e.g., â may represent *ai, a, ei, e, ea, ay*) in various words. Mark the four key symbols in this sentence: *Take care of your arm, you ought not hurt it.* (C.2, 3, 4, 5.)	4.
		    5.
		  C. Other
		    1. ə
		    2.
		    3.
		    4.
		    5.
		II. Double letter symbols
		  A. Diphthongs
		    1.
		    2.

diphthongs
 	
oi, ou
 	
house
	5. We also studied four vowel phonemes represented by two vowel letters. Two of these are gliding sounds called _____. They are represented by _____ in *oil* and _____ in _____. (Part II. A.)	B. Digraphs
		    1.
		    2.

digraphs o͞o, o͝o	**6.** The other two-letter combinations with distinctive sounds needed to complete the 19 vowel phonemes are called _____. They are found in _____ as in *food* and _____ as in *hook.* (Part II.B.) You have now completed the outline of the key symbols that represent the vowel phonemes. Turn to page 168 to correct. You have mastered all the phonemes!
symbols o͞a, e͞e, e͞a, a͞i ō, ē, ē, ā long, silent	**7.** There are other vowel pairs that do not have distinguishing key _____ because they represent single vowels with their own phonemes. For example: *coat, fleet, dean, main.* What vowel phoneme is represented in each of these? _____, _____, _____, _____. Mark the vowels in each word. In general, the first vowel represents its _____ sound and the second of the pair is _____.

ō
 	
 ŏ, ə
 	
 ô, û
 	
 y
 	
 ĭ
 	
 ə silent
 	
 a, e
 	
 e
 	
 listening
	8. Vowel letters are not very reliable.
	     a. A letter may represent more than one phoneme:
	         For example, an *o* may represent _____ as in
	         hope, _____ as in *hop,* _____ as in
	         mammoth, _____ as in *ought,* _____ as in *worm.*
	     b. A phoneme may be represented by more than one vowel letter:
	         The *ĭ* may be represented by _____ in *myth,*
	         _____ in *fin.*
	     c. A letter may represent no phoneme, it may be _____
	         as the _____ in *roam,* the _____ in *race,* or
	         the _____ in *doe.*
	 Although vowels are not very reliable, the use of certain generalizations will help us to identify words already in our _____ vocabulary.
	                           (reading, writing, listening)
	 (Of course, there are exceptions to the generalizations, too!)

long, silent	**9.** Some of these generalizations have been referred to previously, others follow. When a one-syllable word or accented syllable contains two vowels, one of which is the final *e,* the first vowel usually represents its _____ sound and the final *e* is _____ (the VCe pattern).
phoneme *echo, say, though, be* consonant *open, thought, rate, once* hearing the final phoneme	**10.** An open syllable ends with a vowel _____ (the CV pattern). (phoneme, letter) Underline the words that end with an open syllable: *echo, open, say, though, thought, rate, be, once.* A closed syllable ends with a _____ phoneme (the CVC, VC pattern). Which of the words above have closed syllables? Whether a syllable is open or closed depends upon _____. (hearing the final phoneme, seeing the final letter)
long *he, why* CV	**11.** A single vowel in an open accented syllable often represents its _____ sound. Which words follow this generalization? *he, why, pen, road, do* The vowel-consonant pattern is _____.
short *pin, sent, cat* VC	**12.** A single vowel in a closed accented syllable usually represents its _____ sound. Which words follow this generalization? *pin, sent, cat, hope, thought* The vowel-consonant pattern is _____.
never (at least in English words) yes	**13.** Is *y* a vowel or a consonant? The vowel *y* _____ (always, never, you can't tell) comes at the beginning of a word. Is the above true of a vowel *w?* _____
phoneme, vowel	**14.** Although a syllable may have more than one letter, it has only one vowel _____. The _____ has the most influence on the syllable. (vowel, consonant)

accented ə (*schwa*)	**15.** Vowels behave differently in accented and unaccented syllables. The vowel is most clearly heard in the _____ syllable. The vowel in most unaccented syllables represents the _____ or the ĭ.
mē lēpé, phā tŏg, rĕl nō, phō, ŏt, drāɪf, skōōs	**16.** The generalizations we have studied in connection with these vowel phonemes should aid in the pronunciation of words we do not recognize. The words below are nonsense words. Take a chance that the vowel phonemes follow the rules even in unaccented syllables or have their most common sound. Mark every vowel in these "words" to show pronunciation: me lepe pha tog rel no pho ot draif skoos

Part III
Answers to the Reviews

Review 13

1. *a, e, i, o, u, w, y*   **2.** *w, y*   **3.** C, V, V, C, V, C   **4.** consonant digraph
5. more   **6.** 19

Scores:

Review 14

1. **a.** When there is a single vowel in a closed accented syllable, that vowel phoneme is usually short.   **b.** When a word or a syllable has two vowels, one of which is a final *e,* and the two vowels are separated by two consonants, the first vowel usually represents the short sound and the final *e* is silent.   **2.** *běd, něxt, lŏt, căt, trĭp, skĭn, mŏp, ŭs, sěnd, bŭg.*   **3.** VC, CVC, CVCCe (or VCCe), CVC, VC, CVCCe (or VCCe).   **4.** *e, i, y*

Scores:

Review 15

1. *ē, ī, ō, ū* macron   **2.** *i, e*   **3.** *e* When a vowel or accented syllable has two vowels, one of which is the final *e,* the *e* is silent and the first vowel usually represents its long (glided) sound.   **4.** accented, long   **5.** end, long
6. sound (or phoneme)   **7.** d*in*e C n, tack, C k, <u>way</u> V a, watch, C ch, table C l, <u>go</u> V o, tight C t, enough C f   **8.** bīte, bĭt, căn, cāne, pět, Pēte, ŭs, fūse, cŏt, cōde.

Scores:

155

Review 16

1. *schwa*   2. it saves assigning separate diacritical marks to each vowel to indicate a phoneme all share.   3. *river*   4. *regal, handmade* or *handmaid, celebrate, episode*

Scores:

Review 17

1. short or unglided, ă, ĕ, ĭ, ŏ, ŭ   2. long or glided, ā, ē, ī, ō, ū   3. *schwa,* ə, *agree* (ə grē), it saves assigning separate diacritical marks to each vowel to indicate a phoneme all share.   4. following *r, l,* and *w*   5. a. ball (bôl)
b. fur (fûr)   **c.** father (fäthər)   **a.** care (kâr)

Scores:

(How did you do? You can feel a *real* sense of accomplishment if you had all of these correct. They are not easy!)

Review 18

1. *oi, ou*   2. vowel   3. *owl-ou, cow-ou, moist-oi, oyster-oi*   4. *hous boi ouns ĕnjoi noiz brou*

Scores:

Review 19

1. A digraph is a two-letter grapheme that represents a single phoneme.
2. o͞o, o͝o   3. You cannot tell. The only clue is that it is most often o͞o as in *food.*   4. *to͞oth, spo͞on, bo͝ok, lo͞os, sto͝od, mo͞o, sho͝ok*   5. *klo͞od*   6. *bo͞ot, fŭdj, doun, toi, sho͝ok, kō kō, nīt, fro͞ot, thrō, thro͞o, tho, thôt, kwĭt, bo͝ok, smo͞oth, fo͞ol, brĕth, brēth, nīt*

Scores:

Review 20

1. diphthong, *oi, ou, house;* digraph, o͞o, o͝o, *hook.*   2. When two vowels appear together in a word or syllable, the first usually represents the long sound and the second is silent.   3. When a one-syllable word has an ending pattern VCe, the first vowel is generally long and the *e* is silent.   4. letter, phoneme

Scores:

Part IV

A Review of the Phonemes

phonemes (or sounds)	**1.** Our written language is not based on pictorial representations of objects or ideas. It is a phonetic language in that there is a relationship between the letters of the alphabet and the _____ of the spoken language.
consonants	**2.** In fact, many of the _____ are fairly reliable as to sound. (consonants, vowels)
phonemes letters	**3.** However, there are so many inconsistencies in the sound-letter relationship that the English language is not an easy one to learn to read. If it were a consistent, strictly phonetic language, then (1) there would be one and only one letter to represent each of the _____ of the spoken language; (2) there would be one and only one phoneme represented by each of the _____ of the alphabet.

	4. The truth of the matter is:
	(1) **A letter may represent more than one sound.**
	For example, each vowel represents several sounds. Our alphabet has
26	_____ letters (and some of them are useless) to represent
phonemes	the 44 _____.
	(2) **The same sound may be represented by more than one letter.**
phonemes	The 44 _____ are represented by 251 different graphemes. For example, we spell the first consonant phoneme we hear in *chute*
sh	(key symbol: _____) in 14 different ways!
	(3) **A letter may represent no sound.**
silent	Almost any letter may, at some time or another, be _____.
spoken	**5.** We have identified the 44 phonemes that, for all practical purposes in the teaching of reading, make up the sounds of our _____ (spoken, written) language.
	6. We have designated a key symbol for each of these phonemes to serve as our pronunciation guide.
	These key pronunciation symbols, then, provide us with a one-to-one
symbol	correspondence between sound and _____.
j	For example, we use the _____ to symbolize the sound heard in *jam,* even though it may be represented by *g* as in *gentle, d* as in *graduate,* or *dg* as in *judgment.*
	7. Let us review, through the following outline, the 44 phonemes we
key symbols	have identified and the _____ _____ we have designated for each. Study and make responses as indicated. When choices appear in parentheses, underline the correct answer. For example, there are 44 (<u>phonemes,</u> graphemes).

◇ Review Outline

	I. CONSONANT PHONEMES

<table>
<tr><td></td><td>I. CONSONANT PHONEMES</td><td>Key
Symbol</td></tr>
<tr><td></td><td>A. Represented by a single consonant letter</td><td>1. b</td></tr>
<tr><td>boat</td><td>b as in _____ (page 43).
(boat, comb)
Complete this generalization:</td><td></td></tr>
<tr><td>silent, m</td><td>b is usually _____ when it follows _____</td><td></td></tr>
<tr><td>t</td><td>(comb) or precedes _____ (doubt) in the same syllable.</td><td></td></tr>
<tr><td>syllable</td><td>The b in submit is not silent because it is not in the same _____.</td><td></td></tr>
<tr><td></td><td>Say rabbit aloud. How many phonemes do these two like-</td><td></td></tr>
<tr><td>one</td><td>consonants represent? _____</td><td></td></tr>
<tr><td></td><td>Complete this generalization:</td><td></td></tr>
<tr><td>consonants</td><td>Two like-_____ appearing together in a word or syllable</td><td></td></tr>
<tr><td>one</td><td>generally represent _____ phoneme (pages 38, 43).
(How many?)
Make a slash through the second like-consonant to depict the silent letter.</td><td></td></tr>
<tr><td>lesson, better, hammer</td><td>lesson _____   better _____   hammer _____</td><td></td></tr>
<tr><td>happen, puddle, puff</td><td>happen _____   puddle _____   puff _____</td><td></td></tr>
</table>

symbol, word	
	c has no key _____ or _____.
	c usually represents the sound we associate with the *k*
a, o	when it is followed by _____ (*cat*), _____ (*coat*),
u, end	or _____ (*cut*) or when it appears at the _____
letter	(*comic*) of a word and when followed by any other _____ (*clasp*) (page 71).
e	*c* usually represents /s/ when it is followed by _____ (*cent*),
i, y	_____ (*city*), or _____ (*cycle*) (page 71).

Hard *c* Soft *c*	Use the words below to complete the table at the right by selecting words in which *c* represents the hard sound or the soft sound.	Hard *c* Soft *c*
cabin cell		_____ _____
cot city		_____ _____
cube cycle	*cycle city cabin cube cell cot close mice*	_____ _____
close mice		_____ _____
silent	*c* can be a silent letter when it follows _____ as in *scene*.	
	We could replace the letter *c* with *k* and *s* were it not for the	
ch	_____ digraph.	

dog	*d* as in _____ is fairly dependable.	2. *d*
	(key word)	
ladder, /t/	*d* may be silent as in _____ or may represent _____
	(*ladder, laden*) (/f/, /t/)
	when part of the *-ed* suffix.	
dg	*d* also represents /j/ as part of the combination _____ (*bridge*),
ld	and _____ (*soldier*) (page 52).

	f as in *fish* is a fairly reliable letter, with the notable exception in the word *of,* in which the letter *f*	3. *f*
/v/	represents _____ (page 52).	
	This phoneme is sometimes spelled	
gh, ph	_____ as in *enough,* or _____ as in *graph* (page 52).	

goat, hard	*g* as in _____ represents the _____ sound. 4. *g*
	(*goat, giant*) (*hard, soft*)
	This sound is usually heard when *g* is followed by the vowels
a, o, u	_____ (*game*), _____ (*goat*), or _____
letter	(*gum*), and when followed by any other _____ (*glad*) or
end	appearing at the _____ of a word (*drag*) (page 71).
soft	*g* usually represents a _____ sound when it is followed by the
	(*hard, soft*)
e, i, y	vowels _____ (*gerbil*), _____ (*giant*), or _____
	(*gym*) (page 71).
gift	The word _____ does not follow this generalization.
	(*gym, gift*)

Study the words below. For each set, choose a word from the six at the right in which *g* represents the same phoneme as the other underlined letters in the set and has the same vowel following it.

gypsy
good
gentle
guard
ginger
gate

1	2	3	4	5	6
game	gent	giant	goal	gulp	gym
gave	germ	margin	gold	guess	gyrate
____	____	____	____	____	____

1. *gate*   2. *gentle*
3. *ginger* 4. *good*
5. *guard*   6. *gypsy*

hat	*h* as in _____. 5. *h*
	(*ghost, hat, honor*)
end	*h* is never heard at the _____ (*oh*) of a word or syllable.
beginning	Sometimes *h* is silent (*honor*) at the _____ of a word.
g	The *h* is silent when it follows the consonants _____
k, r	(*ghost*), _____ (*khaki*), and _____ (*rhyme*) (page 43).
vowel	*h* is also silent when it follows a _____ (*oh*) in a word or syllable.
	Put a slash through the silent *h*s.
honor, oh, hurrah, rhyme	honor _____ oh _____ hurrah _____ rhyme _____
habit, pooh, ghost, khaki	habit _____ pooh _____ ghost _____ khaki _____

	j as in jeep. 6. *j*
	The /j/ phoneme is often represented by a *g* followed by
e, i, y	the vowels _____ , _____ , or _____ (page 52).
ld	(The /j/ phoneme may also be represented by _____
dg	(*soldier*) and _____ (*fudge*).)
king	*k* as in _____. 7. *k*
	(key word)
silent	*k* is _____ (*knight*) at the beginning of a word or syllable when
n	followed by _____ (page 43). Put a slash through the silent *k*s.
k̸not, k̸now	knot _____ key _____ know _____ keep _____
lion	*l* as in _____. 8. *l*
	(*lion, calm*)
	The letter *l* is sometimes silent when followed, in the same syllable,
m, k, d	by _____ (*calm*), _____ (*chalk*), and _____ (*should*) (page 43).
moon, reliable	*m,* as in _____ , is a _____ letter. 9. *m*
	(key word) (reliable, unreliable)
nut	*n* as in _____. 10. *n*
	(*nut, condemn*)
m	*n* can be silent when preceded by _____ (*autumn*) (page 52).
/ng/	*n* generally represents _____ when it is followed by *g* (*sing*) or *k* (*thank*).

	p as in *pig*. 11. *p*
reliable	As a single letter, *p* is _____.
	(reliable, unreliable)
s, t	When *p* is followed by _____ (*pseudo*), _____
n, silent	(*pterodactyl*), or _____ (*pneumonia*), the *p* is usually _____
	(page 43).
symbol	*q* has no key _____.
k	The dictionary uses a _____ to indicate its pronunciation.
	The *que* at the end of a word (*antique*) represents the phoneme we
k	associate with _____. The letter *q* is almost always
	(k, s)
u, silent	followed by the letter _____. The *u* may be _____ or
w	represent the sound we associate with the key symbol _____
	(page 43).
plak, kwēn, kwit	Rewrite *plaque, queen,* and *quit* to show pronunciation.
	r as in *ring*. 12. *r*
reliable	*r* is very _____. When we see *r*, we can
	(reliable, unreliable)
	be sure that it represents the sound we associate with the key
r	symbol _____ (page 43).
sun	*s* as in _____. 13. *s*
	(his, sure, sun)
	Except when acting as a plural at the end of words, *s* represents the
/s/	phonemes we associate with _____ (*miss*) or
/z/	_____ (*his*) with about equal frequency.
/sh/	*s* also represents the phonemes _____ (*sugar*), and
/zh/	occasionally stands for _____ (*treasure*) (page 71).

table	*t* as in _____. 14. *t* (*table, than*)
s	*t* may be silent when it follows the letter _____ (*listen*), or
f, ch	_____ (*soften*), and when it precedes _____ (*catch*).
ch	In connection with a vowel, *t* may represent _____ (*future*)
sh, silent	or _____ (*station*) (page 71). *t* may be _____ in words adopted from the French language (*ballet*).
mother	*t* is often part of the consonant digraph *th* as in _____ , (*mother, fast*) in which case the /t/ is not heard.
van	*v* as in _____ is very reliable (page 43). 15. *v* (*van, off*)
wagon	*w* as in _____ (page 71). 16. *w* (*two, why, wagon, who*)
consonant	*w* serves as a _____ and as a vowel. As a consonant, it
vowel, follows	precedes the _____ (*was*). As a vowel, *w* _____
silent	the vowel (*snow*). Sometimes *w* is _____ (*wrote*).
blend	*w* may also be part of a consonant _____ (*dwell*) or
digraph	_____ (*which*). Occasionally, *w* appears to be part of a
silent	digraph (*wh*), but is _____ (*who*).
	x has no phoneme of its own (page 71).
/ks/, /gz/	It represents the _____ in *six*, the _____ in *exam*,
/z/	or the _____ in *xylophone*. We are more apt to use
/gz/	_____ when *x* appears between two vowel phonemes (*exam*).

yo-yo	y as in _____ (page 71). 17. *y*
	(*day, yo-yo*)
vowel	y serves as a consonant and as a _____.
	y at the beginning of a word or syllable represents the sound we
/y/	associate with _____. *y* within a syllable acts as a vowel and
silent	may be _____ (*day*) or may represent a vowel sound (*rhyme*).
zipper	z as in _____ (page 52). 18. *z*
	(*quartz, zipper*)
/s/, /zh/	Occasionally, z represents _____ (*waltz*) or _____ (*azure*).

B. Represented by consonant digraphs

chair	ch as in _____. 19. *ch*
	(*choir, chair, machine*)
is not, /ch/	ch _____ reliable. *ch* may represent the _____ (*change*),
	(*is, is not*)
/k/, /sh/	the _____ in *choir,* or the _____ in *chiffon* (page 87).
/j/	dg represents no phoneme of its own. It often represents the key
	symbol _____ (*fudge*) (page 52).
	gh represents no phoneme of its own.
silent	gh is usually _____ (*bright*) when it precedes *t* in a syllable.
/f/	gh is silent (*through*) or represents _____ (*enough*) when it
	follows the vowel in a word or syllable (page 52). When it appears at
h	the beginning of a word or syllable, the _____ (*ghost*) is silent.

king beginning /ng/ thangk	*ng* as in _____ (page 87). 20. *ng* (*king, congest*) *ng* is never heard at the _____ of a syllable, and always follows a vowel. The letter *n* may also represent _____ when it is followed by a *g* or *k* (*bring, blank*). Write *thank* to show pronunciation.
f	*ph* has no phoneme of its own (page 52). The key symbol _____ commonly represents the sound, as in *phone*.
ship	*sh* as in _____ (page 87). 21. *sh* (*ship, division*)

thumb
 	
voiceless
	th as in _____ (page 87). 22. *th*
	         (*that, thumb*)
	
	The /th/ in *thin* is _____.
	        (voiceless, voiced)

that	*th* as in _____ (page 87).	23. *th*
	(*that, thumb*)	
voiced	*th* represents a _____ (page 87).	
	(voiceless, voiced)	

Pronounce the words at the right. Write the words in which the *th* is voiced in Column 1 below. Write the words in which the *th* is voiceless in Column 2.

thaw
their
thief
theme
these
this
thing
those

Column 1 Voiced	Column 2 Voiceless
their thaw	_____	_____
these thief	_____	_____
this theme	_____	_____
those thing	_____	_____

whale	*wh* as in _____ (page 87).	24. *wh*
	(*who, whale*)	

wh appears at the beginning of a word or syllable and is followed by a

vowel _____ (*which*).

treasure	*zh* as in _____ (page 87). 25. *zh*
	(*treasure, edge*)
	The /zh/ is never represented in a word with the grapheme *zh*.
s	The /zh/ may be represented by the _____ (*pleasure*), the
g, z	_____ (*collage*), or the _____ (*seizure*).
	II. VOWEL PHONEMES
	A. Represented by single vowel letters
a, e, i, o, u,	The letters _____, _____, _____, _____, _____, and
w, y	sometimes _____ and _____ are classified as vowels (page 101).
	Two of the seven vowels are not represented by key symbols because
sounds	they do not represent _____ of their own.
y, w	These are the _____ and the _____ (page 112).
	y as a vowel represents no sound of its own.
	When *y* is a vowel, its pronunciation is shown by the key symbols we
i, e	associated with the _____ or the _____ (page 112).
silent	The vowel *y* is often _____ (*play*).
	As a vowel, *w* is always used in combination with a preceding
vowel	_____ (*threw*) (page 112).

	1. Short sounds	
apple	*a* as in _____ (page 112). *(date, apple, all)*	26. ă
edge	*e* as in _____ (page 112). *(edge, even)*	27. ĕ
igloo	*i* as in _____ (page 112). *(ice, igloo)*	28. ĭ
ox	*o* as in _____ (page 112). *(over, ox)*	29. ŏ
umbrella	*u* as in _____ (page 112). *(umbrella, use)*	30. ŭ

Breve

The breve (˘) is the diacritical mark used to indicate

short — the pronunciation of _____ vowels (page 112).

wĕt, kăt — Write *wet* and *cat* to show pronunciation.

Many dictionaries indicate the pronunciation of the short
vowel sounds with the letter alone. How would the

hit, hat — pronunciation of *hit* and *hat* be indicated in these dictionaries?

Closed syllable

consonant — The closed syllable ends in a _____ phoneme (page 109).
 (consonant, vowel)

The vowel in a closed syllable represents its

short, *hid* — _____ sound, as in _____.
 (long, short)   *(hid, hide)*

CVC	**CVC pattern**
	The most common vowel-consonant pattern is that of the
	_____ (consonant-vowel-consonant) in which the
	V (vowel) represents its short (unglided) sound (page 112).
consonant	The CVC (or VC) syllable ends with a _____ phoneme.
	(consonant, vowel)
single	Complete this generalization:
short	A _____ vowel in an accented, closed syllable usually
	represents the _____ sound of the vowel (page 110).
two	**VCCe pattern**
	Complete this generalization:
	When a word or syllable has _____ vowels, one of which is
	a final *e,* and the two vowels are separated by two consonants, the
silent, first	final *e* is _____ and the _____ vowel usually
short	represents its _____ sound (page 112).

	2. Long sounds
apron	*a* as in _____ (page 126). 31. ā
	(*apron, ant*)
eraser	*e* as in _____ (page 126). 32. ē
	(*every, eraser*)
ice	*i* as in _____ (page 126). 33. ī
	(*ice, itch*)
overalls	*o* as in _____ (page 126). 34. ō
	(*overalls, over*)
unicorn	*u* as in _____ (page 126). 35. ū
	(*up, unicorn*)
	y has no vowel phoneme of its own. Its key symbol can
ī, ĭ	be the _____ as in *my,* the _____ as in *myth,*
ē	and the _____ as in *happy* (page 126).

long	We use a macron (¯) to indicate the pronunciation of _____
	vowel sounds (page 126). Some dictionaries and teachers' manuals use
yo͞o	the _____ to indicate the pronunciation of the long *u* in
o͞o	*cube* and the _____ to represent the pronunciation of the
	long *u* in *tune.*

vowel long, *hide*	**Open syllable** An open syllable ends in a _____ phoneme (page 126). 　　　　　　　　　　(consonant, vowel) We hear a _____ vowel phoneme, as in _____. 　　　　　(short, long)　　　　　　　　　　　(hid, hide)
CV no	**CV pattern** The open syllable generalization most often applies to words and syllables that have the _____ vowel-consonant pattern, as in _____ (page 126). 　　(no, not)
two silent long *mice, bone, make, hide*	**VCe pattern** Complete this generalization: When a one-syllable word has _____ vowels, one of which is a final *e,* the *e* is _____ and the first vowel usually represents its _____ sound (page 126). Mark each vowel in the following words with the proper diacritical mark. Put a slash through the silent letters. 　　　　　mice　　bone　　make　　hide

	CVVC pattern
	Complete this generalization:
two	When _____ vowels appear together in a word
	(How many?
	or syllable, the first usually represents its
long	_____ sound and the second
silent	is _____ (page 149).
	The pairs that follow the generalization a greater percentage
ai, oa, ee	of the time are _____ (rain), _____ (boat), _____ (street),
ea, ay	_____ (beach), and _____ (play) (page 149).

	Other vowel sounds	
	Schwa	
	ə represents the soft, unaccented sound of the	36. ə
a, e	vowel _____ in comma, _____ in chicken,	
i, o	_____ in family, _____ in button,	
u	and _____ in circus (page 131).	

	â is the vowel phoneme we associate with the key word	37. â
care	_____ (page 138).	
c<u>a</u>re, ch<u>ai</u>r, th<u>e</u>re	Underline the portion(s) of the words care, chair, and there that, when combined with r, represent this phoneme.	

	û is the vowel phoneme we associate with the key word	38. û
fur	_____ (page 138).	
h<u>u</u>rt, t<u>e</u>rm, co<u>u</u>rage	Underline the portion(s) of hurt, term, and courage that, when combined with r, represent this phoneme.	

vowel l w	Complete these generalizations: If the only vowel in a word or syllable is followed by r, the _____ is affected by that r, as in car, hurt, and orbit (page 138). If the only vowel in a word or syllable is an a followed by l or w, the is a affected by that _____ or _____ , as in _saw_ and _fall_ (page 138).
father _h<u>ea</u>rt, t<u>a</u>co, pl<u>a</u>za_	ä is the vowel phoneme we associate with the key 39. ä word _____ (page 138). Underline the portion(s) of _heart, taco,_ and _plaza_ that represent this phoneme.
ball _c<u>au</u>tion, t<u>a</u>ll, c<u>o</u>st_	ô is the vowel phoneme we associate with the key 40. ô word _____ (page 138). Underline the portion(s) of _caution, tall,_ and _cost_ that represent this phoneme.

oil
 	
_oy_
 	
house
 	
_ow_
	B. Vowel sounds represented by vowel combinations
	
	   1. Diphthongs
	
	     _oi_ as in _____. This phoneme is also
	
	     represented by the letters _____ (page 149). 41. _oi_
	
	     _ou_ as in _____. This phoneme is also
	
	     represented by the vowels _____ (page 149). 42. _ou_

food
 	
hook
	2. Vowel digraphs
	
	     o͞o as in _____ (page 149). 43. o͞o
	           (_food, flood_)
	
	     o͝o as in _____ (page 149). 44. o͝o
	           (_food, flood, hook_)

	3. Other vowel pairs The key symbols for other vowel pairs—_ai, oa, ee, ea,_ and _ay_—have already been given.

Part V

Onset and Rime

	at ight old ig
26	**1.** Thus far we have been studying the _____ letters and
44	_____ phonemes of the American-English language. We have learned
vowels, consonants	that the arrangement of _____ and _____ within the syllable affects the pronunciation.
	2. We will now turn our attention to the consonant(s) at the beginning of the syllable, and the vowel and the consonant(s) that follow it at the end of the syllable.
consonant	The **onset** is the _____ letter(s) that precedes the vowel in a syllable. The dictionary defines an onset as a beginning or
begins	commencement. Therefore, a syllable _____ with an onset. (begins, ends)
	3. The onset is the single consonant, consonant blend, or consonant digraph that begins a syllable. Study these words: _bat, street, thorn_.
single consonant	The onset in _bat_ is a _____. (single consonant, consonant blend)
blend	The onset in _street_ is a consonant _____. (blend, digraph)
digraph	The onset in _thorn_ is a consonant _____. (blend, digraph)

pig, <u>smile</u>, <u>chip</u>, <u>wish</u>,
<u>splash</u>, <u>bold</u>, <u>strain</u>, <u>pill</u>
 	
three
	4. Underline the onset in the one-syllable words below. Count the letters in each of the onsets you underline.
	
	  pig smile chip wish splash bold strain pill
	
	You can see that there are from one to _____ consonant
	  (How many?)
	letters in an onset.

c, k, cat *kn, n, knight* *bl, bl, black* *gh, g, ghost* *ph, f, phone* *wh, wh, white* *sk, sk, skin* *p, p, pink* consonant	**5.** Complete the table by filling in the onset (1) and key symbol (2) for each one-syllable word (3). | 1	2	3
---	---	---
__	__	cat
__	__	knight
__	__	black
__	__	ghost
__	__	phone
__	__	white
__	__	skin
__	__	pink	 An onset may consist of one or more _____ letters. (vowel, consonant)
no consonant yes ch	**6.** There are many syllables and one-syllable words in the English language that do not begin with an onset. Examine the one-syllable word *at*. Does *at* begin with an onset? _____ *At* does not begin with an onset because there is no _____ letter preceding the vowel. Does the one-syllable word *chat* begin with an onset? _____. The onset in the word *chat* is the consonant digraph _____.
off, it, add, out, up, elf	**7.** We have noted that a word or syllable may not always begin with an onset. Mark the one-syllable words below that <u>do not</u> begin with an onset. off show it add out split up elf queen

th t, p k, g d, m	**8.** Study the two-syllable words below. Write the onset that begins each syllable.
	thir teen pump kin gar den mag ic
ic	___ ___ ___ ___ ___ ___ ___ ___
	Which syllable in the words above <u>does</u> <u>not</u> begin with an onset? _____
consonant	**9.** We have learned that an onset is the _____ letter(s) that
precedes	begins the syllable. We have also learned that an onset _____
	(precedes, follows)
	the vowel in a syllable. Do we expect every syllable to begin with an
no	onset? _____
rime	**10.** We call the vowel and the consonant(s) that follows it at the end of the syllable the _____. *Rime* is a variation in the spelling of the word *rhyme.* The dictionary defines *rhyme* as "the agreement among the ending vowel and consonant sounds in words." Therefore,
vowel, consonant(s)	the rime consists of the _____ and the final _____ in a syllable.
spend, beg, strut	**11.** Study the one-syllable words below. Underline the rime in each word.
drink, stop, flat	spend beg strut drink stop flat
	How many vowel phonemes do you hear in each one-syllable
one	word? _____
	12. Use the number of the rime at the right to indicate the rime in the words below. **1.** *ug*
	2. *ant*
	3. *op*
2, 1, 2, 1, 3, 2	plant ____ bug ____ slant ____ dug ____ top ____ grant ____
3, 3, 2, 1, 1, 3	drop ____ hop ____ chant ____ plug ____ rug ____ mop ____
	You can see that our written language has many words that have the
rime	same _____.

c<u>an</u>	**13.** Study the rime in the words at the right to see if the rime always consists of one consonant that follows the vowel phoneme. Underline the rime in each one-syllable word.

can

m<u>atch</u>

match

k<u>ept</u>

kept

t<u>ent</u>

tent

h<u>am</u>

ham

s<u>alt</u>

salt

tr<u>ust</u>

trust

---

consonant

14. We can see from the words in frame 13 that a rime may have more than one _____ letter following the vowel phoneme. Mark the rimes in the one-syllable words below.

l<u>amp</u>, sw<u>ift</u>, p<u>ush</u>, c<u>all</u>,
th<u>ought</u>, s<u>old</u>

        lamp   swift   push   call   thought   sold

---

amb

15. The rime in the one-syllable word *lamb* is _____. This rime consists of one vowel, *a*, and two consonant letters, *m* and *b*. Say *lamb* out loud. How many consonant phonemes do you hear in this

one, silent

rime? _____ The last consonant letter is _____.

---

	l<u>ook</u>	**16.** Study the rimes in the words at the right. Underline the rime in each one-syllable word.	*look*
	sl<u>eep</u>		*sleep*
	m<u>ouse</u>		*mouse*
	wr<u>ite</u>		*write*
	bl<u>ame</u>		*blame*
no	tr<u>ain</u>	Does the rime always consist of one vowel letter? _____	*train*
yes	r<u>ide</u>	Does each rime consist of one vowel phoneme? _____	*ride*

	17. There are many rimes in written English that have more than one vowel letter. Say the one-syllable words below aloud.
	b<u>oa</u>t m<u>ade</u> st<u>ore</u> s<u>eed</u>
two	The rimes in the words above consist of _____ vowel letters.
	(How many?)
one	How many vowel phonemes do you hear in each rime? _____

<u>sure</u>	**18.** Underline the rime in each word at the right. Now pronounce the words aloud. Notice that you hear only one vowel phoneme.	sure
d<u>ance</u>		dance
st<u>ore</u>		store
h<u>ome</u>		home
l<u>eave</u>		leave
m<u>ouse</u>		mouse

rime	**19.** We have noted that there is one _____ in each syllable.
consonant	The rime consists of the vowel and the _____ letter(s) at the end of the syllable. Write the rime in each one-syllable word below. Work carefully. (If you correctly identify all the rimes, you are really thinking!)
ore, our, ent, aste	more our cent taste rain star starve point
ain, ar, arve, oint	____ ____ ____ ____ ____ ____ ____ ____

yes yes	**20. Phonogram** is another term for the rime in a syllable. Study the words at the right. Do the words rhyme? ____ Are the words spelled with the same rime? _____ Therefore, in the teaching of reading, phonograms are words with a common rime and rhyming sound.

bat
hat
cat

	21. Indicate the phonogram (rime) in each group below.
	
	    had seed fun cold
	    bad need run bold
	    mad feed sun hold

ad, eed, un, old

    ____   ____   ____   ____

four	**22.** In the teaching of reading, we also use the term **word family** to describe words that share a common rime and a common rhyming sound. How many word families are in frame 21? _____

	23. Group the words at the right into word families.

bed   *fan*   *run*
man   *red*   *led*
sun   *fun*   *ran*

Family 1   **Family 2**   **Family 3**

1. *bed, red, led*   _____   _____   _____

2. *fan, man, ran*   _____   _____   _____

3. *run, sun, fun*   _____   _____   _____

consistently	**24.** Study the word families in frame 23. The rime in each word family _____ represents the same sounds. (consistently, inconsistently)

rime, yes	**25.** *Cat* and *mat* contain the same ____. Do *cat* and *mat* rhyme? ____
yes	Do *cat* and *mat* belong in the same word family? _____
yes	**26.** Now let us consider *bed* and *head*. Do *bed* and *head* rhyme? _____
no	Are *bed* and *head* spelled with the same rime? _____ Do *bed* and *head*
no	belong in the same word family? _____
rhyme	**27.** We have noted that when words have the same rime, the words may also _____, as in *bug* and *dug*. There are exceptions (of course!), as we see in *cough* and *bough*.
	28. Now pronounce the sets of words below to see if the words that rhyme also contain the same rime. Mark the sets of words that have the same rime.
fish, wish	*fish joke pail deed*
deed, feed	*wish oak stale feed*
yes	Does each set of words rhyme? _____ Does each set of
no	words have the same rime? _____
rhymes	**29.** Each set of words in frame 28 _____. That is, in each set there is agreement among the ending vowel and the consonant
phonemes	sounds. We have learned that the same _____ may be represented by different graphemes. Therefore, words that rhyme
rime	may not always consist of the same _____.

en el, ase all, am age, *ump in* one	**30.** Write the rime in each of the two-syllable words below. *ken nel* *base ball* *dam age* *pump kin* ___ ___ ___ ___ ___ ___ ___ ___ Each rime consists of _____ vowel phoneme(s). (How many?)
two one	**31.** There are many rimes in written English that have more than one vowel letter. Say the one-syllable words below aloud. <u>boat</u> m<u>ade</u> st<u>ore</u> s<u>eed</u> The rimes in the words above consist of _____ vowel letters. (How many?) How many vowel phonemes do you hear in each rime? _____
vowel phoneme rime	**32.** We have seen that the rime consists of one _____ phoneme and the consonant(s) that follows the vowel phoneme in the syllable. We have learned that each syllable contains one vowel _____. Therefore, each syllable must contain one and only one _____. (onset, rime)
two two	**33.** Say the two-syllable words below aloud. *ti ger* *pic nic* *in tense* *blan ket* How many vowel sounds do you hear in each word? _____ Each word has _____ rimes.
two syllables rimes	**34.** If you hear two vowel phonemes in a word, you can be sure that the word has _____ rimes. You can also be sure that a word (How many?) with two rimes has two _____. Therefore, the number of _____ in a word is equal to the number of syllables in a word.

		35. Pronounce the one-syllable words at the right. Complete the table by filling in the onset (1), and the rime (2) for each word (3).	1	2	3
r	ight		____	____	right
s	ave		____	____	save
s	at		____	____	sat
l	ook		____	____	look
d	ish		____	____	dish
f	ind		____	____	find
b	ig		____	____	big
gr	een		____	____	green

36. Let us review. We have learned that the onset is the

consonant(s)

_____ at the beginning of the syllable (*boat*), and the rime is

vowel, consonant(s)

the _____ and _____ that follows it at the end of the syllable (*boat*).

onset

A word or a syllable may not have an _____ (*oat*).

rime

However, the syllable must have a _____. The rime has one

vowel

_____ phoneme, and may have more than one

consonant

_____ letter that follows the vowel (*dish*).

37. Now use your knowledge to combine the onset (1) with the rime (2) and write the one-syllable word (3) on the line at the right.

	1	+	2	=	3
scratch	scr	+	atch	=	____
bird	b	+	ird	=	____
street	str	+	eet	=	____
am		+	am	=	____
twig	tw	+	ig	=	____
shrine	shr	+	ine	=	____
chick	ch	+	ick	=	____

STUDY GUIDE
Onset and Rime, and 50 Common Rimes

Onset
The onset is the consonant that precedes the vowel in a syllable. The onset may have one (*cat*), two (*chat*), or three (*string*) consonant letters.

Rime
The rime consists of a vowel and the final consonant(s) in the syllable. The rime may have more than one vowel letter, but only one vowel phoneme (*reach*).

Rhyme
Rhyme is the agreement among the ending vowel and consonant phonemes in words (*rain, train* or *head, bed*). Words that share a rime (*rain, train*) may rhyme. Words that rhyme may not always share the same rime (*head, bed*). Furthermore, words that share the same rime may not always share the same ending vowel and consonant sounds (*head, bead*).

50 Common Rimes

Rime	Examples	Rime	Examples
ab	cab, grab, lab, tab	ell	bell, fell, sell, tell
ace	face, place, race, space	en	den, hen, men, pen
ack	back, black, sack, track	ent	bent, sent, tent, went
ad	bad, had, mad, sad	est	best, rest, test, west
ade	grade, made, shade, trade	et	bet, set, pet, wet
ag	bag, flag, rag, tag	ice	dice, mice, nice, twice
ail	fail, mail, sail, tail	ick	brick, lick, quick, trick
ain	gain, main, pain, train	ide	bride, side, tide, wide
air	chair, fair, pair, stair	ig	big, dig, pig, wig
ake	bake, make, take, wake	ight	fight, night, right, sight
all	ball, call, fall, tall	ill	bill, fill, hill, pill
am	clam, ham, ram, slam	in	fin, pin, thin, win
ame	came, game, name, same	ing	king, ring, sing, sting
amp	camp, damp, lamp, stamp	ink	link, pink, sink, wink
an	can, fan, man, tan	ip	dip, hip, ship, slip
and	band, hand, land, sand	it	hit, pit, sit, slit
ang	bang, hang, rang, sang	ock	block, rock, sock, stock
ank	blank, drank, rank, sank	og	dog, frog, hog, log
ap	cap, lap, map, nap	old	cold, fold, hold, told
at	cat, fat, hat, sat	op	hop, mop, pop, stop
ate	date, gate, late, rate	ot	dot, hot, got, lot
eam	beam, cream, dream, team	ug	bug, dug, hug, tug
eat	beat, meat, neat, seat	ump	bump, dump, hump, pump
ed	bed, fed, led, red	un	bun, fun, run, sun
eed	deed, feed, need, seed	ut	but, cut, nut, shut

✳◇✳ Review 21

1. Write the onset for each of the one-syllable words below.

   wrong   could   shop   high   stay
   sun   bowl   school   stage   goat

2. Which of the one-syllable words below do <u>not</u> begin with an onset?

   ask   loss   fan   ouch   am
   blue   green   leave   old   if

3. The rime consists of one _____ phoneme and the _____ that follows in the syllable.

4. Write the rime for each of the one-syllable words below.

   train   sent   mice   swamp   flour
   child   bought   since   house   trip

5. Which of the one-syllable words above have rimes that include more than one vowel letter?

   (See the Part V and VI Answers section for the answers to Review 21, page 218.)

Part VI

Syllabication and Accent

pronunciation	**1. The syllable is the unit of pronunciation.** It is convenient to use one-syllable words to illustrate the vowel and consonant phonemes because a one-syllable word is, in itself, one unit of _____.
syllable	**2.** The generalizations that apply to a one-syllable word may apply to each syllable of a two-or-more syllable word and generally apply to the accented _____ of a word.
syllable	**3. There is one vowel phoneme in each unit of pronunciation,** that is, in each _____.
vowel two	**4.** Each syllable contains only one _____ phoneme. If you hear two vowel phonemes, you may be sure the word has _____ syllables.

phoneme p<u>i</u>ne ī b<u>oy</u> oi r<u>i</u>ght ī p<u>au</u>se ô (If you missed *pause* ô, reread the frame.)	**5.** Each syllable may have more than one vowel letter but only one vowel _____. The word *cause* (kôz) has one vowel phoneme: ô. Underline the vowel letters in the words at the right. Write the key symbol that represents the vowel phoneme in the space following each word; mark it to show pronunciation. pine _____ boy _____ right _____ pause _____

syllables

6. How many units of pronunciation (or _____) are there in each of these words? What is the vowel phoneme in each syllable? Mark the vowel(s), in the space at the right, to show pronunciation.

				No. of Syllables	Vowel Phoneme(s)
1	ĕ		red	_____	_____
1	ŭ	(jŭmpt)	jumped	_____	_____
2	ō	ĭ(or ə)	broken	_____	_____
2	ā	ĭ	raining	_____	_____
1	ou		house	_____	_____

syllable	**7. One syllable in a two-or-more syllable word receives more emphasis or greater stress than the other syllables.** We indicate this accented _____ by placing an accent mark (') at the end of the accented syllable.
accent (or stress)	**8. In multisyllabic words, more than one syllable may be stressed.** There will be one primary _____ (shown by ') and one or more secondary accents. The secondary accent is shown by '.
vowel	**9.** We have already noted that accent, or stress point, affects _____ sounds. (vowel, consonant)

	10. **The vowel phoneme is the most prominent part of the syllable. Vowels behave differently in accented and unaccented syllables.**
accented	The vowel is most clearly heard in the _____ syllable.
	11. Many syllables, when pronounced carefully in isolation, appear to follow the generalizations we have noted.
	In normal speech, however, we have a tendency to give most vowels
schwa	in the unaccented syllables the soft, short, indistinct _____ sound.
	12. We can clearly see this behavior of vowels in accented and unaccented syllables in words that are spelled alike but accented differently. Read these sentences:
ŏ	*Your <u>conduct</u> is exemplary.* (k _____ n' dukt)
ə	*I will <u>conduct</u> you through the factory.* (k _____ n dukt')
	Show the pronunciation of the vowel in each of the first syllables above.
	13. Write the first syllable of each of the underlined words to show its pronunciation. If the first syllable is the stressed syllable, include the accent mark.
kŏn'	*I signed the <u>contract</u>.* _____
kən	*"Can't" is a <u>contraction</u>.* _____
kəm	*The work is <u>complete</u>.* _____
kŏm'	*You are <u>competent</u>!* _____
phoneme	**14.** Each syllable has only one vowel _____. It may have
	(phoneme, letter)
letter	more than one vowel _____.
	(phoneme, letter)
yes	**15.** Is *boy* a one-syllable word? _____ Does it have more
yes	than one vowel letter? _____ Does it have one vowel
yes	phoneme? _____ What key symbol represents this
oi, diphthong	phoneme? _____ This vowel phoneme is called a _____.

accent	**16.** To decode a word not known at sight, we need to have some idea of where to place the accent. There are some clues to where the _____ may be found in unknown words.

◈ Clues to Placement of Accent

accent	**1.** Obviously, it is necessary to have some understanding of where to expect to find the accented syllable. **First, we consider one-syllable words to have a primary _____.**

yes (They are one-syllable words; therefore, they are the accented syllable.)	**2.** The vowel phoneme in the accented syllable tends to follow the generalizations we have studied concerning its sound. Would you expect the words at the right to conform to these generalizations? _____	*met* *rain* *rate* *cat* *hope* *boy*

accented	**3.** Dictionaries, in showing pronunciation, do not place accent marks on one-syllable words. It is taken for granted that they are _____.

ex chang' ing *play' ful* *slow' ly* *cold' est*	**4.** **In general, prefixes and suffixes (affixes) form separate syllables. The accent usually falls on or within the root word.** Place the accents in these words.	*ex chang ing* *play ful* *slow ly* *cold est*

suffix	**5.** The root word is more likely to be accented than the prefix or _____.

pre cook' *un know' able* *move' ment* *re wrote'*	**6.** Show the syllabic division and place the accent for the words at the right.	*precook* *unknowable* *movement* *rewrote*

accent	7. In compound words, the primary _____ usually falls on or within the first "word."	
snow' man	Rewrite these compound words to show the syllables; place the accents.	*snowman* _____
some' thing		*something* _____
cow' boy		*cowboy* _____

8. Accent within sentences will not be considered here. However, note that a change in accent in the following sentences changes the meaning. Place the accent on *black* or *bird* in each sentence:

black bird'	*I see a black bird; I think it is a crow.*
black' bird	*The blackbird built its nest in the marsh.*

9. We have noted that (1) one-syllable words are accented;

root	(2) accents usually fall on or within the _____ word rather
first	than on an affix; (3) the _____ "word" in a compound word is usually the accented one.

10. The place of the accent may differentiate between a noun and a verb in words that are spelled alike:

first	*What is this* <u>object</u>?	_____
second	*Do you* <u>object</u>?	_____
first	*This is a* <u>present</u> *for you.*	_____
second	*Please* <u>present</u> *this to your friend.*	_____

The accents usually fall on the first syllables of nouns.

Study the above sentences. Write <u>first</u> or <u>second</u> to show the syllable on which the accent falls in each of the underlined words.

bet' ter	**11. When there is a double consonant within a word, the accent usually falls on the syllable that closes with the first letter of the double consonant:** ta' ble, din' ner	bet ter
thun' der		thun der
trum' pet		trum pet
	Place the accent in these words.	

tim' ber	**12.** Place the accent in the words at the right.	tim ber
splen' did		splen did
shel' ter		shel ter
rab' bit		rab bit

ex ten' sion	**13. In most multisyllabic words ending in** *(t)ion* **or** *ic,* **the primary accent falls on the syllable preceding the** *(t)ion* **or** *ic* **ending.**	ex ten sion
mag net' ic		mag net ic
	Place the accent in these words.	

	14. Mark the primary accent in the words below.
na' tion	na tion car na tion no mad ic an gel ic
car na' tion	
no mad' ic	
an gel' ic	

	15. Pronounce the words in frame 14. Using your knowledge of phonemes, rewrite the words to show pronunciation.
nā' shən	
kär nā' shən	na tion car na tion no mad ic an gel ic
nō măd' ĭk	
ān jĕl' ĭk	———— ———— ———— ————

preceding	**16.** We expect the primary accent in multisyllabic words ending in *(t)ion* or *ic* to fall on the syllable _____ the *(t)ion* or *ic* ending.
	
	Pronounce the words below aloud.
	
	    poet nomad donate concept
	
	    poetic nomadic donation conception

first preceding	The accent is on the _____ syllable of the root word. When a word ends in *(t)ion* or *ic,* the accent is on the syllable _____ the *(t)ion* or *ic* suffix.
main tain' *be neath'* *ex plain'*	**17.** Let us make another generalization: **When the vowel phoneme in the last and closed syllable of a word is composed of two vowel letters, that syllable is most often accented.** Mark the accent in these words.

ex ceed', be neath'
 	
de cay', mer maid'
	18. Divide the words below into syllables and mark the accent.
	
	    exceed *beneath* *decay* *mermaid*
	
	    _____ _____ _____ _____

CV CVVC'
 	
VC CVVCC'
 	
CVC CVVC'
 	
V CCVVC'
	19. Mark the accent in the "words" at the right. CV CVVC
	
	                                                    VC CVVCC
	
	                                                    CVC CVVC
	
	                                                    V CCVVC

When the vowel phoneme in the last and closed syllable of a two-syllable word is composed of two vowel letters, that syllable is most often accented.	**20.** State the generalization that applies to the "words" in frame 19.

first consonant vowel (t)ion, ic	**21.** We have noted that (1) when a word is used as different parts of speech, the accent is usually on the _____ syllable of the noun; (2) the accent usually falls on the syllable that closes with the first letter of a double _____; (3) when the last (and closed) syllable of a word has two _____ letters, that syllable is accented; and (4) the accent falls on the syllable preceding the _____ ending.

fin' ish prac' tice scoun' drel cen' ter mon' key lis' ten	**22.** **When there is no other clue, note that the accent most often falls on the first syllable of a two-syllable word.** Study these words to see if they follow this generalization. Place the accents.	fin ish prac tice scoun drel cen ter mon key lis ten

accented	**23.** Let us review all the generalizations concerning the placement of the accent. Consider the word *day*. A one-syllable word is considered to be _____. (accented, unaccented)

sun' set compound first	**24.** Rewrite the word *sunset* and place the accent: _____. In _____ words, the accent usually falls on the _____ "word."

catch' ing root prefix	**25.** Rewrite the word *catching* and place the accent: _____. The accent usually falls on the _____ word rather than on the suffix or _____.
un faith' ful root	**26.** Consider this word: *unfaithful.* Place the accent. Sometimes a root word has more than one affix, or the word has so many syllables that two or more syllables are stressed. The primary accent, then, usually falls on or within the _____ word.
reb' el noun	**27.** Consider the word *rebel* in the sentence: *He is a rebel.* Place the accent: _____. Certain words that are spelled the same sometimes function as different parts of speech. The accent on the first syllable generally indicates that it is a _____.
noun verb *con tent'*	**28.** The word *con' tenl* is a _____. The word *con tent'* is a _____. How would you place the accent in this sentence? After many revisions, the novelist was finally *con tent* with the manuscript.
glit' ter consonant closes consonant	**29.** Consider this word: *glit ter.* Place the accent. When there is a double _____ within a word, the accent usually falls on the syllable that _____ with the first letter of the double (closes, opens) _____.
ob tain' last	**30.** Consider this word: *ob tain.* Place the accent. When two vowel letters appear within the last and closed syllable of a two-syllable word, the _____ syllable is most often accented. (first, last)

or gan' ic at ten' tion (t)ion ic	**31.** Divide the words *organic* and *attention* into syllables. Use what you have learned thus far to place the accent. Complete the generalization: In most multisyllabic words ending in _____ or _____ , the primary accent falls on the syllable that precedes the *tion* or *ic* ending.
for get' ting con' tract de mand' ed ap pear' ance o' pen ing can teen' show' boat	**32.** Using what information you have and remembering that it is not customary to place accent marks on one-syllable words, place accent marks in all the appropriate places in the following: *I was for get ting my con tract which de mand ed my ap pear ance at the o pen ing of the can teen on the show boat.*

✕◇✕ Review 22

1. The unit of pronunciation is the _____.

2. The basic speech sound, or the smallest sound-bearing unit, is the _____.

3. Can there be more than one vowel letter in a syllable?

4. Can there be more than one vowel sound in a syllable?

5. The vowel phoneme is most clearly heard in the _____ syllable.

6. We studied several generalizations concerning the placement of accent marks. State the generalization that applies to each of these words. Place the primary accent in each word.

   a. *in ter change a ble*   **e.** *na tion*
   b. *cow boy*   **f.** *dol lar*
   c. *fast*   **g.** *con ceal*
   d. *ex port, (noun)*   **h.** *pa per*

(See the Part VI Answers section for the answers to Review 22, page 218.)

STUDY GUIDE
Syllable Accent

Syllable Defined
The syllable is the unit of pronunciation. There is one vowel phoneme in each syllable (unit of pronunciation). Each syllable may have more than one vowel letter but only one vowel phoneme (*boy, pause*).

Accent or Stress
One syllable in a two-or-more syllable word receives more emphasis or greater stress than the other syllables. Accent, or stress point, affects the vowel sound.

Accent Marks
An accent mark indicates the primary stress (*ti' ger*). In multisyllabic words, more than one syllable may be stressed. The secondary accent is shown by (') (*cen' ti pede'*).

Vowels in Accented Syllables
Vowels behave differently in accented and unaccented syllables. The vowel is most clearly heard in the accented syllable (*pa' per, plan' et*).

Vowels in Unaccented Syllables
We have a tendency to give most vowels in the unaccented syllables the soft, short, indistinct *schwa* sound (*pen' cil, pĕn' səl*), or the short *i* (*bracelet, brās' lĭt*).

Clues to Placement of Accent
One-syllable Words   We consider one-syllable words to have a primary accent (*bed', boy'*).

Prefixes and Suffixes   In general, prefixes and suffixes (affixes) form separate syllables. The accent usually falls on or within the root word (*play' ful, slow' ly*).

Compound Words   In compound words, the primary accent usually falls on or within the first "word" (*cup' cake, snow' man*).

Nouns and Verbs   The place of the accent may differentiate between a noun and a verb in words that are spelled alike. The accent usually falls on the first syllable of nouns (*ob' ject*) and the second syllable of verbs (*ob ject'*). (*His con' duct was excellent. He will con duct' the tour.*)

Double Consonants   When there is a double consonant within a word, the accent usually falls on the syllable that closes the first letter of the double consonant (*let' ter, trum' pet*).

Words Ending with tion or ic   In most polysyllabic words ending in *(t)ion* or *ic,* the primary accent falls on the syllable preceding the *(t)ion* (*na' tion, di rec' tion*) or the *ic* spelling (*his tor' ic, ter rif' ic*).

Two Vowels in the Final Syllable   When the vowel phoneme in the last syllable of a word is composed of two vowel letters, that syllable is most often accented (*ex plain', be neath'*).

When There Is No Clue to Accent   When there is no other clue, the accent most often falls on the first syllable of a two-syllable word (*fin' ish, prac' tice*).

◇ Clues to Syllable Division

A single vowel in a closed syllable generally represents its short sound.	**1.** We have established some guidelines to help us decide upon which syllable an accent might fall. We still have this problem: Where do the syllabic divisions occur? There are generalizations to help but with many exceptions. First, we need to review two generalizations concerning vowel phonemes. State the generalization that applies to the vowel sound of *met*.
A single vowel in an open syllable generally represents its long sound.	**2.** State the generalization that applies to the vowel sound of *me* and *so*.
short (unglided)	**3.** Let us attempt to syllabicate the word *pupil*. If you divided it *pup il*, the first vowel would be expected to have its _____ sound.
long (glided), open	**4.** If you divided it *pu pil*, the first vowel would be expected to have its _____ sound: It is in a(n) _____ syllable. (open, closed)
last (unaccented) pū' pəl	**5.** Write the correct pronunciation of *pupil*, placing the accent and using the *schwa* in the _____ syllable. _____
When there is no other clue in a two-syllable word, the accent most often falls on the first syllable.	**6.** Which generalization concerning the placement of accent would seem to apply?

7. Now write *pupil* as it would appear in the dictionary. The entry word should show syllabication only. Follow this by rewriting the word to show pronunciation, using the key symbols and omitting silent letters (if any).

pu pil (pū′ pəl)   _____   _____

8. Let us make a generalization:

> **If the first vowel in a two-syllable word is followed**
> **by a single consonant, that consonant often**
> **begins the second syllable.**

In other words, the syllable division is between the single

vowel

_____ and the single consonant.

si lent (sī′ lənt)

ti ger (tī′ gər)

lo cal (lō′ kəl)

9. Follow the above generalization and write these words as they would appear in the dictionary entry word followed by pronunciation.

silent _____   _____

tiger _____   _____

local _____   _____

10. We have designated CV to represent an open syllable (page 121). But how might we represent the open syllable clue to syllabic division? We will use CV/CV to indicate the open syllable clue.

open

The first syllable in the word *pupil* (*pu pil*) is a(n) _____ syllable.

Using C to represent consonant and V to represent vowel, we might represent *pupil* as CV′ CVC.

Show the syllabic division, mark the accent, and indicate the consonants and vowels in *bagel.*

CV′ CVC

si′ lo, CV′ CV

ba′ con CV′ CVC

do′ nut, CV′ CVC

sea′ son, CVV′ CVC

11. Show the syllabic division and indicate the vowels and consonants in the words at the right.

Key: C is consonant.
     V is vowel.

silo

bacon

donut

season

vowel open closed	**12.** Study the words in frame 11. We can see that CV/CV indicates that the first syllable is an open syllable. The open syllable ends with a _____ phoneme. The second, unaccented syllable may be _____ (*co la*) or _____ (*ba con*).
co' la, CV' CV *ba' con*, CV' CVC	**13.** Place the accent and indicate the vowels and consonants in *cola* and *bacon*.
silent	**14.** Let us review another generalization: When two consonants appear together, the second is generally _____ (*rattle*).
short (unglided) long (glided) short (unglided)	**15.** Examine the word *puppet.* If we divide it *pup pet,* we would expect the first vowel to have its _____ sound. If we divide it *pu ppet,* we would expect the *u* to be _____. The *u* in the word *puppet* should be _____.
closed *pŭp pet*	**16.** For the *u* to have the correct sound in the word *puppet,* it should appear in a(n) _____ syllable. Write the word *puppet,* (closed, open) dividing it correctly. Mark the *u.* _____

pup pet (pŭp' ət or pŭp' ĭt)
 	
p
 	
short
	17. Now write *puppet* as it would appear in the dictionary—first the entry word, using syllabication but the correct spelling.
	
	        _____ _____ (_____ _____)
	Follow this with the correct pronunciation. Omit the second _____.
	Sometimes in an unaccented syllable the vowel is not a *schwa* but rather a related sound, the soft _____ *i.*
	                                    (short, long)

consonants
 	
consonants
	18. We can make a generalization:
	
	   When two vowel letters are separated by two _____,
	
	   the syllable division is generally between the _____.

closed
 	
short (unglided)
 	
VC/CV
	19. The first syllable in *after* (*af ter*) is _____. Therefore, we
	                                              (open, closed)
	
	expect the vowel sound in this syllable to be _____.
	
	We will use _____ to represent the closed syllable
	                          (CV/CV, VC/CV)
	generalization for syllabic division.

closed consonants VC/CV	**20.** The closed syllable generalization (expressed VC/CV) *normal* gives us a clue for syllabic division. Study the words at *better* the right. The first syllable is _____. We divide *bandit* (open, closed) *hammer* the syllable between the two adjacent _____. How do we represent the closed syllable generalization to syllabic division? _____
mat' ter *sig' nal* *shel' ter* *gos' sip*	**21.** Observing the open and closed syllable *matter* _____ generalizations, divide the words at the right *signal* _____ into syllables and place the accent. *shelter* _____ *gossip* _____
cri' sis, CCV' CVC *chi' na*, CCV' CV *pen' guin*, CVC' CVVC	**22.** Study the words at the right. 1 2 3 Divide the words into syllables and place *panda* pan' da CVC' CV the accent (2), and indicate the vowels *crisis* _____ _____ and consonants (3). *china* _____ _____ *penguin* _____ _____
CV/CV vowel VC/CV consonants	**23.** Let us review: We can use _____ to represent the open syllable generalization for syllabic division. The syllable division is between the single _____ and the single consonant. We can use _____ to represent the closed syllable generalization for syllabic division. The syllable division is between the two _____.

open long (glided) first	**24.** Note the relationship between the sounds of the vowels, the syllabication, and the accent. When we divide the word *diner;* the first syllable is a(n) _____ (open, closed) syllable with the division between the vowel and the consonant. The vowel has its _____ sound, and the accent is on the _____ syllable.
closed short (unglided) first	**25.** When we divide *dinner,* the first two letters are the same, but the pronunciation is different: The first syllable is _____ , the sound represented by the first vowel is _____ , and the accent is on the _____ syllable.
closed short (unglided)	**26.** The syllabic division between consonants is more dependable than the division between the single vowel and single consonant. There are many words in which the first single consonant ends the first syllable: *ex it, nov ice, hon or, fac et.* In these words, the first syllable is _____ and the vowel has (open, closed) its _____ sound.
second	**27.** When in doubt, however, try the generalization first: **If the first vowel in a two-syllable word is followed by a single consonant, that consonant often begins** **the _____ syllable,** as in *di ner.*
tī ger yes	**28.** Divide *tiger* into syllables: _____ _____. Mark the vowel in the first syllable to show pronunciation. If *tiger* were spelled with two *g*'s, would it be expected to rhyme with *bigger?* _____

lĕt′ ter	**29.** Study the words at the right. Is each a two-or-more syllable word? _____ Is there a single vowel in the first syllable? _____ Is the single vowel followed by two consonants? _____

yes   *nŭm′ ber*

   ĕf′ fort

yes   *shăl′ low*

yes

letter   _____ _____

number _____ _____

effort   _____ _____

shallow _____ _____

If so, divide the words between the consonants. Mark the first vowel in each to show its pronunciation. Mark the accent.

If the first vowel in a two-syllable word is followed by a single consonant, that consonant often begins the second syllable.

30. State the generalization for the syllabication of *meter.*

When two vowel letters are separated by two consonants, generally the word is divided between the consonants.

31. State the generalization for the syllabication of *member.*

---

hōp¢
hŏp

hŏp′ p̸ĭng

32. Show the pronunciation of these words by dividing them into syllables, marking the vowels, placing the accents, and drawing a slash through silent letters.

hope   _____

hop   _____

hopping   _____

If we did not double the *p* to form *hopping,* we might expect the last

long (unglided)

letter of the first syllable to represent a _____ *o.* This would
                                             (long, short)
not be our intention.

	33. Let us make a generalization:
	Divide a compound word between the two "words" that form the compound,
	as in *cowboy* (*cow boy*).
sun shine	Divide *sunshine* into syllables. _____
compound	**34.** The words at the right are _____ words. *sunshine*
two	Each compound word consists of _____ *seashore*
	(How many?) *backyard*
	one-syllable words. *seahorse*
two	Therefore, each of these compound words has _____
	(How many?)
	syllables.
	35. We expect each "word" in a compound word to represent one or more syllables. Now let us consider the compound word *battleship*.
two	How many syllables do you identify in *battle*? _____
bat tle	Divide *battle* into syllables. _____
one	How many syllables do you identify in *ship*? _____
three	Therefore, *battleship* consists of _____ syllables.
	(How many?)
	36. Use the compound word generalization and other generalizations to divide the words below into syllables. Place the accent.
match' book, rain' drop	*matchbook* *raindrop* *firecracker* *pancake*
fire' crack er, pan' cake	_____ _____ _____ _____

	37. Remember that a two-letter grapheme, a digraph, acts as a single letter.
	Do not syllabicate between letters of a digraph.
th	The word *together* is not *to get her* because the digraph _____ is not to be divided.
dol' phin, kitch' en *pan' ther, cash' ew*	**38.** Show the syllables and mark the accent in the words below.
	dolphin *kitchen* *panther* *cashew*
	_____ _____ _____ _____
	39. Consonant clusters represent phonemes that are blended together when pronounced.
	Consonant clusters are often in the same syllable.
cluster	The word *secret* is not *sec ret* because the consonant _____ generally is not divided.
con stant *lob ster* *sis ter* *com plete*	**40.** Divide the words at the right into syllables. *constant* _____
	lobster _____
	sister _____
	complete _____
sister	The word _____ is an exception. The syllables in *sister* are divided between the consonants in the cluster.
	41. Let us summarize.
	We generally do not syllabicate between the letters in a consonant digraph or consonant cluster,
	as in *dolphin* (*dol phin*) and *complete* (*com plete*).
	Consonant digraphs are more reliable clues to syllabic division than
clusters	consonant _____.
	42. Observing the consonant digraph, consonant cluster, and other generalizations, divide the words below into syllables. Mark the accented syllable.
go' pher, ar' cher, *mar' shal, bush' el*	*gopher* *archer* *marshal* *bushel*

phoneme phoneme	**43.** Remember that vowel pairs, also known as vowel digraphs or vowel teams, represent one _____ (*freedom, train, boat, day, green, seat*). We generally do not divide syllables between the vowel letters that represent one _____.
do not	**44.** Vowel diphthongs represent a glide from one sound to another (*announce*). Therefore, we _____ divide syllables between the (do, do not) letters in a diphthong.
	45. We can make another generalization: **We generally do not syllabicate between the letters in a diphthong or vowel pairs that represent one phoneme** as in *royal* (*roy al*) and *freedom* (*free dom*).
chee tah *voy age* We generally do not syllabicate between the letters in a diphthong or vowel pair that represents one phoneme.	**46.** How would we divide the word *cheetah* into syllables? _____ How would we divide *voyage* into syllables? _____ State the generalization for the syllabication of letters in a vowel digraph or diphthong.
	47. We are studying generalizations that pertain to syllabication. In this study we are using words we already know. Now pretend you do not know the words below. Divide them into syllables following the "open-syllable, long" and "closed-syllable, short" generalizations. Mark the vowel in the first syllable to show pronunciation. Place the accent.

slŭg' gish, măm' mal
mē' ter, lā' ter
mō' tive, lăt' ter
 	
yes
	sluggish _____ *mammal* _____
	    meter _____ *later* _____
	    motive _____ *latter* _____
	
	Are all of these words marked the way they really are pronounced? _____

pī' rət *păn' thər* *grā' vē* *hăp' pən*	**48.** Pretend you do not know the words below. Syllabicate them according to the generalizations we've been studying. Mark the vowels to show pronunciation. Place the accent. Follow the directions carefully. *pirate* _____ *panther* _____ *gravy* _____ *happen* _____
no	**49.** Reread the words in frame 48. Are they all marked the way they are really pronounced? _____. If any are not, correctly divide them into syllables and mark the vowel in the first syllable.
often	**50.** If the first vowel is followed by a single consonant, that consonant _____ begins the second syllable. (always, often) (Take time to check your results. Are you getting them all correct? Are you applying what you have learned? Do you complete a frame, writing all the answers before you move the mask down? You should be able to see the results of your study. May you have a great feeling of self-satisfaction!)
root syllables	**51.** We have observed that the accent is generally on the _____ word rather than on the prefix or suffix. It is natural, then, to expect prefixes and suffixes to form _____ separate from the root word.

de lay
 	
re lent less
 	
re o pen ing
	52. **Prefixes and suffixes usually form separate**
	              syllables from the root word.
	
	Divide the words at the right into syllables. *delay* _____
	
	      relentless _____
	
	      reopening _____

d, t *loaded, dieted gated*	**53.** Most prefixes and suffixes form separate syllables from the root word. We have learned that *ed* forms a separate syllable when it is added to root words that end in a _____ or a _____ phoneme (page 48). Indicate the words in which *ed* forms a separate syllable. *loaded* *laughed* *traveled* *dieted* *gated* _____ _____ _____ _____ _____

sī' dər sō' də stā' shən ŭn tīm' lē wĭn' dō	**54.** Observing the generalizations, divide the words at the right into syllables and mark them to show pronunciation. Place the accents. cider _____ soda _____ station _____ untimely _____ window _____
ble two cle ble	**55.** Examine the words *table, circle, marble*. Each of these words has _____ syllables. Write the last syllable in each word. We can show the pronunciation of these syllables as *bəl, kəl*. ta _____ cir _____ mar _____
consonant	**56.** A helpful generalization is: **If the last syllable of a word ends in *le* preceded by a _____, that consonant usually begins the last syllable.**
pur ple can dle mar ble cir cle ta ble	**57.** Divide the words at the right into syllables. purple _____ candle _____ marble _____ circle _____ table _____
consonant, unaccented schwa	**58.** Study the words in frame 57. The final syllable consists of a _____ and *le* (C + *le*). This syllable is _____. (accented, unaccented) The vowel sound in the C + *le* syllable is a _____.

ga ble (gā' bəl)	**59.** Write the complete pronunciation of *gable* as it would appear in the dictionary. _____ _____ (_____ _____)
pronunciation (*Meaning* is correct also.)	**60.** Now let us examine a word that is the same as *gable* except for an *m* that precedes the *ble*. Read this sentence: *Do not gamble with your health.* The letter *m* affects the _____ of the word.
b *gam ble*	**61.** The last syllable in *gamble* ends with *le* preceded by the consonant _____. Show how we would divide the word. (Note that other generalizations correctly apply to these words.) *gamble* _____
gam ble (găm' bəl)	**62.** Now write *gamble* as it would appear in the dictionary. _____ _____ (_____ _____)
consonants consonant root compound before diphthong blend	**63.** The syllable divisions are most commonly made **a.** between two _____ (as in *ladder*). **b.** between a single vowel and a single _____ (as in *paper*). **c.** between prefixes, suffixes, and _____ words (unhelpful). **d.** between words that form a _____ word (*snowman*). **e.** _____ the C + *le* (as in *stable*). (before, after) They are not made between letters representing a single phoneme, that is, between letters in a digraph or a _____ (as in *app<u>oi</u>nt*). They generally are not made between the letters in a consonant _____ (as in *secret*).

syllable are not	**64.** We have seen that syllables are units of pronunciation. The arrangement of vowels and consonants within the _____. affects the pronunciation. We have noted that generalizations about syllabication are helpful but _____ infallible. <div align="center">(are, are not)</div>
ā′ bəl *change a ble* *chānj′ ə bəl*	**65.** Sounds may change with the lengthening of the word: Divide *able* into syllables. Mark it to show pronunciation. _____ Divide *changeable* into syllables. _____ Rewrite it to show pronunciation. _____
long *schwa* unaccented	**66.** In *able* the *a* represents the _____ sound. In *changeable* the second *a* represents the _____ sound; it is now in the _____ syllable. (accented, unaccented)
	67. To check our understanding, let us use symbols. Study the key below at the left. Divide the "words" in the right column into syllables, marking the vowels as they would be found most commonly and as though all syllables were accented.

Cv̆C   Cv̆ ph   Key: C is <u>c</u>onsonant   C v C C v ph
v̆C   Cv̆C   V is <u>v</u>owel (other than *e*) *e̸* is silent *e*   v C C v C
blv̄   Cv̄   ph is digra<u>ph</u>   bl v C v
Cv̆ ph   Cv̄ph e̸   bl is cluster which is <u>bl</u>ended   C v ph C v ph e̸

Did you succeed?

STUDY GUIDE
Syllable Division

Four Clues to Pronunciation
The four important clues to the pronunciation of a given word are (1) the vowel phonemes, (2) the consonant phonemes, (3) the position of the vowel in the syllable, and (4) the accented syllable.

First Vowel Followed by a Single Consonant
If the first vowel in a two-syllable word is followed by a single consonant, that consonant often begins the second syllable (*ti' ger, si' lent*).

Two Vowels Separated by Two Consonants
When two vowels are separated by two consonants, the syllable division is generally between the consonants (*pup' pet, plan' et*). Syllable division between consonants is more dependable than the division between the single vowel and single consonant.

Prefixes and Suffixes
In general, prefixes and suffixes form separate syllables from the root word (*play' ful, un smil' ing*).

Last Syllable *le*
If the last syllable of a word ends in *le* preceded by a consonant, that consonant usually begins the last syllable (*ta' ble, han' dle*).

Compound Words
Divide compound words between the "words" that form the compound (*check' list, moon' light*).

Consonant Digraphs and Consonant Clusters
In general, do not syllabicate between consonant digraphs (*cash' ew, pan' ther*) and consonant clusters (*se' cret, vi' brate*).

Vowel Digraphs (Pairs) and Vowel Dipthongs that Represent One Phoneme
In general, do not syllabicate between the letters in a vowel digraph (*ex' ceed, free' dom*) or diphthong (*trow' el, thou' sand*).

✖◆✖ Review 23

1. Examine the following consonant-vowel word patterns. Place a slash where the syllable division would be most likely to occur. Make sure that there is a vowel in each syllable. Give the reason you divided the word as you did. There are no digraphs in these words.

   a. CVCVCC
   b. CVCCVC
   c. CVCCV
   d. CCVCVCC

2. How would you expect the following words to be divided? Why? (Pretend that you do not know the words; then you cannot say, "I can hear the pronunciation unit.")

   a. *playful*
   b. *capable*
   a. *father*

(See the Part VI Answers section for the answers to Review 23, page 218.)

◇ Recap III

26 consonants phonemes	**1.** Phonics is the study of the relationship of letters and letter combinations to the sounds they represent. There are _____ letters in our alphabet, classified as vowels and _____. These letters and combinations represent the 44 sounds, or _____ , used in the American-English language. (This is oversimplified, but adequate in this step of the process of teaching children to read.)
phoneme phoneme 44 phonemes	**2.** How easy the development of independence in decoding would be if each letter represented one and only one _____ , and each phoneme was represented by only one letter! You know that is not the case; however, you have gained an understanding of the patterns within the inconsistencies. You have also developed a one-to-one correspondence between grapheme and _____ by selecting a key symbol to represent each of the _____ _____ of the language.

	3. Another relationship is that of the syllable to the word. A syllable is
pronunciation	a unit of _____. Each syllable must have one and only one
phoneme	vowel _____. Each word has one syllable that receives the
accented	greatest amount of stress. We call this the _____ syllable. If a
accented	word has only one syllable, that is the _____ syllable. There
vowel	is a strong relationship between the _____ and the accented
	<div align="center">(vowel, consonant)</div>
vowel	syllable. The _____ in the unaccented syllable often is
i (ĭ), ə (schwa)	represented by the soft, short sound of _____ or by the _____.

	4. You have become acquainted with the clues that help you
syllables	(1) to divide a word into _____ , and
accented	(2) to determine which syllable is _____.
	The following frames present specific words, selected to illustrate your knowledge of the syllable-accent generalizations as well as to review other learnings.

	5. On the blanks after each word (1) rewrite it as an entry word in the dictionary (useful for end-of-the-line hyphenation); (2) rewrite, adding the accent; and (3) in parenthesis, using all your knowledge of phonemes, rewrite the word showing pronunciation. To make this study more effective, as you work, say the generalizations of syllables, accents, and other understandings to yourself. Also fill in the other blanks as indicated.
see-saw, see′ saw (sē′ sô)	*seesaw* _____ _____ _____
	Using the word *seesaw* as an example, say to yourself, "*Seesaw* is a
compound	_____ word; the syllabic division comes between the words of which it is composed." (Fill in the first blank.) "The accent usually
first, compound	falls on or within the _____ word of a _____ word." (Fill in blank two.) On blank three, mark the word for pronunciation.

s	**6.** Continue your conversation about *seesaw:* "We represent the consonant phonemes in *seesaw* with _____. The first syllable has
two	_____ vowel letters. We know that each syllable can have
one	only _____ vowel phoneme. When there are two vowel
long	letters in a syllable, generally the first is _____ and the
silent	second is _____. So the phoneme in the first syllable is
$\bar{e}$	represented by _____. In the second 'word' the vowel phoneme is
ô	*w*-controlled. The key symbol is _____ ; the key word is
ball	_____." (But maybe you prefer to use *ought* (ôt) as the key
(sē' sô)	word. Do you?) The third blank, frame 5, reads _____.

Examine the footnote. Turn to page 234. Read items V 10 and 9. Did you use them in your conversation? How about S1 and A2 on page 235?

V 10, V 9, S 1, A 3[*]

---

	7. The second word in your study is *citrus.* (Caution: Although you can achieve correct results immediately, don't do it that way. This is your opportunity to review by yourself your understandings of the generalizations; syllables, accents, and so on, including "*c* usually
s, i	represents the _____ phoneme when followed by _____.")
	Selected references to Appendix A are given. Check your "conversation" after each frame. Did you include these generalizations? Also note irregularities in consonant and vowel phonemes.
cit-rus, cit' rus	*citrus* _____ _____ _____
(sĭt' rəs)	C 2, V 3, V 14, S 5, A 5[*]

---

un but ton ing	**8.** Continue with the words as given in each of the following frames.
un but' ton ing	*unbuttoning*
(ŭn bŭt' ən ĭng) or	
(ən bŭt' ən ĭŋ)	_____ _____ _____
	V 3, V 14, S 2, S 5, A 2[*]

---

[*]Key to generalizations (Appendix A): C: Consonant, p. 233; V: Vowel, p. 234; S: Syllable, p. 235; A: Accent, p. 235.

ad mi ra tion *ad mi ra' tion* *(ăd mə rā' shən)*	**9.** *admiration* _____ _____ _____ S 2, A 6[*]
wrin kle wring' kle *(ring' kəl)*	**10.** *wrinkle* _____ _____ _____ C 1a.n, S 3, A 8[*]
1. *an nex an nex'* *(ə nĕks')* 2. *an nex an' nex* *(ăn' ĕks)*	1. 2. **11.** We will *annex* the land on which the new *annex* was built. 1. _____ _____ _____ 2. _____ _____ _____ A 4[*]
ti ger ti' ger *(tī' gər)*	**12.** *tiger* _____ _____ _____ S 4[*]
weath er weath'er *(wĕth' ər)*	**13.** *weather* _____ _____ S 6[*]
con tain con tain' *(kən tān')*	**14.** *contain* _____ _____ _____ C 2, V 10, A 7[*]

[*]Key to generalizations (Appendix A): C: Consonant, p. 233; V: Vowel, p. 234; S: Syllable, p. 235; A: Accent, p. 235.

yel low yel' low	**15.** *yellow*
(yel' ō)	_____ _____ _____
consonant	Is this *y* a vowel or a consonant? _____
	C 6, S 5, A 5[*]
	16. Turn to Appendix A[*]. Restudy the generalizations to check your thinking. I hope you are saying, "I did very well." ("perfect"—?) The problem we face is that you know these words. If you were attacking
reading (Children should know the words at the hearing level.)	words not in your _____ vocabulary, you would have a
	(reading, listening)
	better test of your phonics ability.
	17. Another way to analyze the syllable is to divide it into the
onset, rime	_____ and the _____. You know that the onset is
consonant	the _____ letter(s) that begins the syllable, and the rime is
phoneme	the vowel _____ and the consonant letter(s) that
follows	_____ the vowel phoneme.
	18. Using your knowledge of the onset and the rime in the syllable, divide the word *pencil* into syllables. Then analyze the two syllables into onsets and rimes.
pen	The word *pencil* consists of the two syllables _____ and
cil	_____.
p	The first syllable, *pen,* consists of the onset _____ and the
en	rime _____.
c	The second syllable, *cil,* consists of the onset _____ and the
il	rime _____.

[*]Key to generalizations (Appendix A): C: Consonant, p. 233; V: Vowel, p. 234; S: Syllable, p. 235; A: Accent, p. 235.

	19. Now continue to identify the onset and the rime in each of the syllables in the following words.
sur	The word *surprise* consists of the two syllables _____ and
prise	_____.
s, ur	The first syllable, *sur,* consists of the onset _____ and the rime _____.
pr	The second syllable, *prise,* consists of the onset _____ and the rime
ise	_____.
lav	The word *lavender* consists of the three syllables _____ ,
en, der	_____ , and _____.
l	The first syllable, *lav,* consists of the onset _____ and the
av	rime _____.
en	The second syllable, *en,* consists of the rime _____.
d, er	The third syllable, *der,* consists of the onset _____ and the rime _____.
	20. You have studied the relationship of letters and letter
sounds (phonemes)	combinations to the _____ they represent and have built a
phonics	depth of understanding in the content of _____. You will use that content to help those learning to read to develop skill in the recognition and identification of words. It must be pointed out that the use of phonics is the basis of <u>one</u> of the word-attack skills (skills needed to attain independence in reading) and that the mastery of
reading	the total _____ process requires the development of still other sets of skills, including the understanding of the material read. Reading is a complicated process!
	21. You are now ready for the posttest. Show your mastery of the content of phonics! Best wishes.

Part V and VI Answers to the Reviews

Review 21

1. *wr, c, sh, h, st, s, b, sch, st, g*   **2.** *ask, ouch, am, old, if*   **3.** vowel,
consonant(s)   **4.** *ain, ent, ice, amp, our, ild, ought, ince, ouse, ip*   **5.** *rain, flour,
bought, since, house*

Scores:

Review 22

1. syllable   **2.** phoneme   **3.** yes   **4.** no   **5.** accented
6. a. The accent usually falls on or within the root word.   *in ter change'a ble*
  b. In compound words, the accent usually falls on the first word.   *cow' boy*
  c. One-syllable words are accented.   *fast'* or *fast*
  d. When a word functions as different parts of speech, the accent is usually
     on the first syllable of the noun.   *ex'port* (noun)
  e. The primary accent is usually on the syllable preceding the *tion* ending.
     na' tion
  f. The accent usually falls on the syllable that closes with the first letter of a
     double consonant.   *dol' lar*
  g. When two vowel letters are within the last syllable of a two-syllable word,
     that last syllable is most often accented.   *con ceal'*
  h. When there is no other clue, the accent most often falls on the first syllable
     of a two-syllable word.   *pa'per*

Scores:

Review 23

1. a. CV/CVCC   The syllable division is between the single vowel and the
        single consonant.
  b. CVC/CVC   The syllable division is between the two consonants when
        there is a single vowel on both sides of the two consonants.

    c. CVC/CV   The syllable division is between the two consonants when there is a single vowel on both sides of the two consonants.

    d. CCV/CVCC   The syllable division is between the single vowel and the single consonant.

2. a. *play ful*   Suffixes and prefixes generally make separate syllables. This root word has one syllable.

    b. *ca pa ble*   The syllable division is between the single vowel and single consonant. If the last syllable of a word ends in *le* preceded by a consonant, that consonant usually begins the last syllable.

    c. *fa ther*   You cannot divide between letters of a digraph; treat the digraph as though it were one consonant. The division is between the single vowel and the digraph.

Scores:

Self-Evaluation II:
A Posttest

This test is designed to help you evaluate your growth in the field of phonics. Read each item, including all choices. Indicate the answer you consider best by circling the appropriate letter (a, b, c, d, or e) or by marking the appropriate letter on an answer sheet. Please respond to every item. Time: 30 minutes.

I. Multiple Choice. Select the best answer.

1. Which of the following most adequately completes the sentence? The consonant phonemes in the English language are represented by
   a. the consonant-vowel combinations.
   b. the distinctive speech sounds we associate with each of the 21 consonant letters of the alphabet.
   c. 18 of the consonant letters of the alphabet plus seven digraphs.
   d. the single-letter consonants plus their two- and three-letter blends.
   e. the English language is too irregular to represent the consonant phonemes with any degree of accuracy.

2. The second syllable of the nonsense word *omethbin* would be expected to rhyme with
   a. see.   b. pet.   c. wreath.   d. breath.   e. kin.

3. The open syllable in the nonsense word *phattoe* would be expected to rhyme with
   a. *fa* of fatal.   b. day.   c. fat.   d. dough.   e. a and b.

4. How many phonemes are represented in the nonsense word *ghight*?
   a. one   b. two   c. three   d. four   e. six

5. The sound of the *schwa* is represented by
   a. the *a* in *carry*.
   b. the *e* in *lemon*.
   c. the *i* in *lighted*.
   d. the *o* in *falcon*.
   e. the *u* in *rule*.

6. A diphthong is best illustrated by the vowels representing the sound of
   a. *oo* in *foot*.
   b. *oy* in *employ*.
   c. *ow* in *low*.
   d. *ai* in *said*.
   e. All of the above.

7. Generally, when two like-consonants appear together in a word
   a. one is sounded with the first syllable and the other with the second.
   b. both are sounded when the preceding vowel is *e*.
   c. both are sounded when the following vowel is *i*.
   d. only one is sounded.
   e. neither is sounded.

8. A requirement of a syllable is that
   a. it contains no more than one vowel letter.
   b. it contains no more than one vowel phoneme.
   c. it contains at least one consonant phoneme.
   d. it contains no more than one phoneme.
   e. None of the above.

9. An example of a closed syllable is found in the word
   a. *low*.
   b. *sofa*.
   c. *doubt*.
   d. All of these.
   e. None of these.

10. The letter *y* is most likely to be a consonant when
    a. it follows *o* in a syllable.
    b. it has the sound of *i* as in *light*.
    c. it is the first letter in a word or syllable.
    d. it is the last letter in a word or syllable.
    e. None of the above.

11. The letter *q* could be removed from the alphabet because it could adequately and without conflict be represented by
    a. *ch* as in *chair*.
    b. *k* as in *kite*.
    c. *cu* as in *cubic*.
    d. All of the above.
    e. The idea is foolish; *qu* represents a distinctive consonant phoneme.

12. An example of an open syllable is found in the word
    a. *be*.
    b. *replay*.

   c. *tree.*
   d. All of these.
   e. None of these.

13. Which of the following has the incorrect diacritical mark?

   a. băll   **b.** fĕll   **c.** wĭsh   **d.** drŏp   **e.** cŭt

14. Which of the following has an incorrect diacritical mark?

   a. spāde   **b.** rēady   **c.** insīde   **d.** lōne   **e.** fūse

15. When *o* and *a* appear together in a syllable, they usually represent the same sound as

   a. the *a* in *bacon.*
   b. the *o* in *done.*
   c. the *o* in *force.*
   d. the *o* in *ghostly.*
   e. the *a* in *camel.*

16. The symbol *s* is used in the dictionary to show the pronunciation of the sound heard in

   a. *should.*
   b. *has.*
   c. *sure.*
   d. *zoo.*
   e. *waltz.*

17. If *e* were the only vowel in an open syllable, that *e* would most likely represent the same sound as

   a. the *y* in *by.*
   b. the *ea* in *seat.*
   c. the *e* in *get.*
   d. the *e* in *fine.*
   e. None of these.

18. The consonant cluster is illustrated by

   a. the *ch* in *chin.*
   b. the *ng* in *sing.*
   c. the *bl* in *black.*
   d. the *ph* in *graph.*
   e. a, c, and d.

19. When the single vowel *i* in an accented syllable is followed by a single consonant and a final *e*, the *i* would most likely have the sound of

   a. the *i* in *readily.*
   b. the *i* in *active.*
   c. the *y* in *cry.*
   d. the *e* in *sea.*
   e. the *y* in *happy.*

20. If *a* were the single vowel in an accented syllable ending with a consonant, that *a* would most likely represent the same sound as

    a. the *ay* in *daylight*.
    b. the *a* in *mad*.
    c. the *a* in *many*.
    d. the *a* in *wall*.
    e. the *a* in *car*.

21. When *c* is followed by *i*, it is most likely to represent the same sound as

    a. the *c* in *cube*.
    b. the *c* in *chime*.
    c. the *c* in *cello*.
    d. *c* followed by *o*.
    e. None of these.

22. The word *if* ends with the same sound as

    a. the *ph* of *phrase*.
    b. the *f* in *of*.
    c. the *gh* in *cough*.
    d. All of the above.
    e. a and c.

23. The symbol *w* is used in the dictionary to show the pronunciation of the sound heard in

    a. *want*.   **b.** *now*.   **c.** *who*.   **d.** *two*.   **e.** a, b, and c.

24. When the letter *g* is followed by *a*, it most likely will represent the same sound as

    a. the *j* in *jam*.
    b. the *g* in *go*.
    c. the *g* in *gnat*.
    d. the *g* in *bring*.
    e. the *g* in *giant*.

II. Complete each sentence by selecting the word for which the correct pronunciation is indicated.

25. When I picked my vegetables, I dropped a

    a. *răd′ĭsh*.   **b.** *kăr′ŏt*.   **c.** *kŭ kŭm′bĕr*.   **d.** *pë*.   **e.** *kăb′ĭg*.

26. I went to the park for a

    a. *kŏn′cûrt*.   **b.** *rās*.   **c.** *wôlk*.   **d.** *pĭk′nək*.   **e.** *păr′tē*.

27. The wall is

    a. *thĭn*   **b.** *stŭck′ o͞od*.   **c.** *pĭngk*.   **d.** *lōu*.   **e.** *krăk′əd*.

28. The tree we planted was a

    a. *fĭr*.   **b.** *ăzh*.   **c.** *spro͞os*.   **d.** *bərtch*.   **e.** *cē kwoi′ə*.

29. I went to the grocery store for

    a. *ôr′ĭng əz*.   **b.** *brēd*.   **c.** *jăm*.   **d.** *ko͞ok′ēz*.   **e.** *kăn′dÿ*.

30. I washed the

    a. *wôls.*   **b.** *wĭnd'ōs.*   **c.** *kown'tər.*   **d.** *nīvz.*   **e.** *sĭnk.*

III. Multiple Choice. There are three words in each item (a, b, c). Select the word in which you would hear the same sound as that represented by the underlined part of the word at the left. You may find that the sound is heard in all three words; if so, mark d. If none of the words contain the sound, mark e.

31. tent	**a.** missed	**b.** listen	**c.** catch	**d.** All	**e.** None
32. pleasure	**a.** vision	**b.** sabotage	**c.** rouge	**d.** All	**e.** None
33. tanker	**a.** banner	**b.** singer	**c.** nose	**d.** All	**e.** None
34. gem	**a.** edge	**b.** soldier	**c.** jelly	**d.** All	**e.** None
35. that	**a.** bath	**b.** theory	**c.** this	**d.** All	**e.** None
36. chill	**a.** chute	**b.** chord	**c.** question	**d.** All	**e.** None
37. hook	**a.** pool	**b.** moose	**c.** tooth	**d.** All	**e.** None
38. ace	**a.** bead	**b.** said	**c.** lab	**d.** All	**e.** None
39. now	**a.** snow	**b.** joyous	**c.** cow	**d.** All	**e.** None
40. sock	**a.** sure	**b.** sugar	**c.** city	**d.** All	**e.** None

IV. Multiple Choice. Select the letter(s) at the right that represents the onset in the one-syllable words.

41. might	**a.** mi	**b.** ight	**c.** m	**d.** migh	**e.** igh
42. scratch	**a.** scr	**b.** ch	**c.** sc	**d.** scra	**e.** atch
43. choice	**a.** oi	**b.** ce	**c.** oice	**d.** ch	**e.** choi
44. ghost	**a.** st	**b.** gh	**c.** hos	**d.** ost	**e.** gho
45. blank	**a.** ank	**b.** la	**c.** lan	**d.** bla	**e.** bl

V. Multiple Choice. Select the letter(s) at the right that represents the rime in the one-syllable words.

46. climb	**a.** cl	**b.** imb	**c.** mb	**d.** limb	**e.** cli
47. juice	**a.** ui	**b.** jui	**c.** ce	**d.** uice	**e.** j
48. shoal	**a.** oal	**b.** oa	**c.** hoa	**d.** sh	**e.** al
49. spill	**a.** ll	**b.** sp	**c.** pill	**d.** spi	**e.** ill
50. prince	**a.** nce	**b.** rince	**c.** ince	**d.** ce	**e.** pr

VI. Multiple Choice. Where does the accent fall in the words or nonsense words given at the left? Indicate your answer by selecting the last two letters of the accented syllable found in the same row as the word.

Look at the example: *showboat.* The first "word" in a compound word is generally accented: *show'boat.* Look for the last two letters of *show, ow,* in the row to the right.

You would circle b or mark b on your answer sheet.

Example:

showboat   **a.** ho   (**b.**) ow   **c.** bo   **d.** at

51. tenlaim   **a.** te   **b.** en   **c.** nl   **d.** la   **e.** im
52. grottome   **a.** ro   **b.** ot   **c.** to   **d.** om   **e.** me
53. religherly   **a.** re   **b.** nl   **c.** gh   **d.** er   **e.** ly
54. pnight   **a.** pn   **b.** ni   **c.** ig   **d.** gh   **e.** ht
55. damapantion   **a.** am   **b.** ma   **c.** pa   **d.** an   **e.** on
56. present (verb) **a.** re   **b.** es   **c.** se   **d.** nt   **e.** pr

VII. Multiple Choice. Select the word in each row which is *incorrectly* syllabicated.

57. a. li ly   **b.** li lac   **c.** fa tal   **d.** ma trix   **e.** lu rid
58. a. fin ger   **b.** cot ton   **c.** gamb ol   **d.** for get   **e.** pas tel
59. a. par don a ble **b.** re sist i ble **c.** in dent ion **d.** in fu sion **e.** ex hale
60. a. saw dust   **b.** to get her   **c.** side walk   **d.** shark skin **e.** loop hole

(See p. 227 for answers to Self-Evaluation II.)

Self-Evaluation II: Number correct _____

Self-Evaluation I: Number correct _____

Answers to the Pretest and Posttest

Answers to Self-Evaluation

I. Pretest

1. c	13. d	25. b	37. e	49. c
2. b	14. b	26. e	38. b	50. a
3. a	15. d	27. d	39. b	51. b
4. a	16. c	28. d	40. c	52. a
5. c	17. a	29. d	41. d	53. c
6. d	18. e	30. d	42. a	54. d
7. b	19. d	31. b	43. a	55. b
8. c	20. b	32. b	44. d	56. e
9. c	21. a	33. c	45. e	57. e
10. d	22. e	34. c	46. b	58. b
11. d	23. b	35. c	47. b	59. a
12. a	24. b	36. d	48. a	60. c

Answers to Self-Evaluation

II. Posttest

1. c	13. a	25. a	37. e	49. e
2. d	14. b	26. b	38. e	50. c
3. d	15. d	27. c	39. c	51. e
4. c	16. e	28. c	40. c	52. b
5. d	17. b	29. c	41. c	53. c
6. b	18. c	30. d	42. a	54. e
7. d	19. c	31. a	43. d	55. d
8. b	20. b	32. d	44. b	56. d
9. c	21. e	33. b	45. e	57. a
10. c	22. e	34. d	46. b	58. c
11. b	23. a	35. c	47. d	59. c
12. d	24. b	36. c	48. a	60. b

Glossary*

Accented syllable   A syllable that receives greater stress than the other syllables in a word. *188*

Allophone   A variant form of the same phoneme (as the /p/ in *pin* and the /p/ in *spin*). *13*

Blending   The ability to combine individual phonemes together so as to pronounce a meaningful word (/m/ + /a/ + /n/ = /man/). *19, 20*

Breve   A diacritical mark (˘) used to indicate the short (unglided) sound of a vowel, as the /ĕ/ in *red*. *105*

Closed syllable   A syllable that ends in a consonant phoneme (*trip*). *109*

Compound word   A word made up of two or more shorter words (*cowboy* and *rainbow*). *191*

Consonant   One of the two classifications of speech sounds. There are 21 consonant letters and 25 consonant sounds. *28, 31*

Consonant blend   A combination of two or more adjacent consonant phonemes pronounced rapidly, as the /bl/ in *blue*, the /st/ in *still*, and the /spl/ in *splash*. The term refers to the sounds that the consonant clusters represent. *89*

Consonant cluster   Two or more consonant letters appearing together in a syllable that, when sounded, form a consonant blend. Consonant clusters are taught as units rather than as single graphemes (e.g., *st* as representing two blended phonemes rather than an isolated /s/ and an isolated /t/. *89*

Consonant digraph   Two-letter consonant combinations that represent phonemes not represented by the single letters, such as the *sh* in *shoe*. *74*

Decoding   Translating graphemes into the sounds of spoken language so as to pronounce a visually unfamiliar word. Teachers may refer to this process of word identification as "sounding out" words. *10*

Digraph   A grapheme composed of two letters that represent one speech sound (phoneme). *28*

Diphthong   A single vowel phoneme resembling a "glide" from one sound to another, represented by the graphemes *oi* (/noise/), *oy* (/toy/), *ou* (/found/), and *ow* (*now*): key symbols *oi* and *ou*; key words *oil* and *house*. *139*

---

* The number following each entry refers to the page on which the word is introduced.

Grapheme   The written symbol used to represent the phoneme. It may be composed of one or more letters, and the same grapheme may represent more than one phoneme. *13*

Graphophonic cues   The 26 letters (graphemes), the 44 sounds (phonemes), and the system of relationships among graphemes and phonemes. These cues are used to translate the written code into the sounds of spoken language. *21*

Key symbol   Forty-four specific graphemes representing the 44 phonemes of the American-English language (as presented in this text), thus achieving a one-to-one correspondence between key symbol and phoneme: one symbol for each phoneme; one phoneme for each symbol. *29*

Key word   One word selected for each of the 44 phonemes, identifying the specific phoneme. *32*

Long vowel   The five vowels represented by *a, e, i, o,* and *u* that, in the context of the teaching of phonics, are indicated by a macron (-) and "say their names." Key words: *apron, eraser, ice, overalls,* and *unicorn.* These vowels are also referred to as glided vowels. *114*

Macron   A diacritical mark (-) used to indicate the long (glided) sound of a vowel. *114*

Onset   One or more consonant letters that precede the vowel phoneme in a syllable (the *c* in *cat*, the *ch* in *chat*, the *chr* in *chrome*). *27*

Open syllable   A syllable that ends in a vowel phoneme (*play, blue*). *17*

Phoneme   The smallest unit of sound that distinguishes one word from another. This program identifies 44 phonemes. *10, 22*

Phoneme addition   Attaching one or more phonemes to a word or word part (adding /t/ to /able/ to pronounce /table/). *18*

Phoneme deletion   Removing one or more phonemes from a word or word part (removing /s/ from /stop/ to pronounce /top/). *18*

Phoneme substitution   Deleting one or more phonemes from a word or word part, and then replacing the deleted phoneme(s) with one or more different phonemes (deleting the /t/ from /sat/ and replacing it with a /d/ to pronounce /sad/). *19*

Phonics   The study of the relationships of the letter and letter combinations (the graphemes of the English language) in written words to the sounds they represent in spoken words. The study of phonics provides the content for developing skill in the decoding of visually unfamiliar words. *8*

Phonogram   Another term for the rime in a syllable. *180*

Phonemic awareness   The ability to conceptualize speech as a sequence of phonemes (sounds), combined with the ability to consciously manipulate the phonemes of the English language. Children who are phonologically aware can separate words into their individual phonemes, add, subtract, substitute, and re-arrange the phonemes in words, and blend phonemes together to pronounce words. *31*

Rime   The vowel and consonant letter(s) that follows it in a syllable. There is only one vowel phoneme in a rime (the /ă/ in *at*, the /ō/ in *oat*). *117*

Schwa   A vowel phoneme in an unaccented syllable that represents a soft "uh," and is indicated by the key symbol, ə, which resembles an inverted *e*. Key words: comm<u>a</u>, chick<u>e</u>n, fam<u>i</u>ly, butt<u>o</u>n, circ<u>u</u>s. *128*

Segmentation   The process of separating spoken words or syllables into their individual phonemes. *17*

Semantic cues   The general meaning of a passage that gives the reader useful information for word identification. *22*

Short vowel   The vowel letters *ă, ĕ, ĭ, ŏ,* and *ŭ* that, in the context of the teaching of phonics, are indicated with a breve (˘), and are heard in the key words, *apple, elephant, igloo, ox,* and *umbrella*. *105*

Silent letter   A name given to a letter that appears in a written word but is not heard in the spoken word: *knight* has six letters, but only three are sounded, *k, g,* and *h* are "silent." *38, 40*

Slash marks   Slanting lines / / enclosing a grapheme indicating that the reference is to its sound, not to the letters. *11*

Syllable   The unit of pronunciation. The English syllable has only one vowel phoneme. There are as many syllables in a word as there are vowel phonemes; there is only one vowel phoneme in a syllable. *187*

Syntactic cues   Information from the order of words in phrases, clauses, and sentences that also gives the reader useful information for the identification of visually unfamiliar words. *22*

Voiced th   The initial phoneme heard in the key word *that* in which the vocal cords vibrate during the production of the phoneme. *80*

Voiceless th   The initial phoneme heard in the key word *thumb*, in which the vocal cords do not vibrate during the production of the phoneme. *80*

Vowel digraph   A two-letter vowel grapheme that represents one sound. In this text, the vowel digraphs are the o͞o in *food* and the o͝o in *hook*. *142*

Vowel pair   Two adjacent vowel letters that represent a phoneme associated with one of the letters, such as the /ā/ in *rain* that is represented by the *ai* grapheme. In this text, we use the term *vowel pair* to distinguish two-letter vowel graphemes that do not represent a distinct sound, that is, a sound that is not already represented by one of the vowel letters individually. *145*

Vowels   One of the two classifications of speech sounds. The vowels are *a, e, i, o, u,* and sometimes *w* and *y*. (*See* Consonant.) *101*

Word family   Words with the same rime (*at*) and rhyming sound (*cat, fat, hat*). *180*

Appendix A:

Phonics Generalizations

Consonant Generalizations

1. Consonant letters are fairly reliable: There is a high relationship between the letter and the sound (/ /) we expect it to represent. p. 29. However, there are irregularities:

   a. A letter may represent more than one phoneme. p. 52,71. Some common patterns are:

c: /k/, /s/	n: /n/, /ng/
d: /d/, /t/	s: /s/, /sh/, /z/, /zh/
g: /g/, /j/	z: /z/, /s/, /zh/

   b. A phoneme may be represented by more than one letter. p. 43,44,52,71. Some common patterns are:

/f/: f, gh, ph	/s/: s, z
/j/: j, g, dg, d	/w/: w, u
/k/: k, ch, q	/z/: z, s

   c. A letter may represent no phoneme, that is, it may be silent. When two like-consonants appear together, the second usually is silent. p. 38, 43, 52, 71. Some common silent letter patterns occurring in the same syllable are:

b following m	k followed by n
b followed by t	l followed by m, k, d
c following s	p followed by s, t, n
c followed by k	t following f; followed by ch
g followed by n	
h following k, g, r, following a vowel and as the initial letter in certain words	

2. When the letter c or g is followed by e, i, or y, it usually represents its soft sound as in *city* or *gem;* when c or g is followed by any other letter or appears at the end of a word, it usually represents its hard sound as in *cup* or *go.* p. 71.

3. The suffix *ed* usually forms a separate syllable when it is preceded by *t* or *d*. When *ed* does not form a separate syllable, the *d* may represent /*t*/ or /*d*/. p. 48, 52.

4. The letter *q* always represents /*k*/. p. 35, 43.

5. The letters *c, q,* and *x* have no distinctive phonemes of their own. p. 31.

6. The consonants *w* and *y* are positioned before the vowel in a syllable. The consonant *y* is never silent. p. 62, 71.

7. We use two-letter combinations (digraphs) to represent the seven consonant phonemes not represented by single letters (*ch, sh, th, th, wh, zh, ng*). p. 74, 87.

Vowel Generalizations

1. A letter may represent more than one phoneme. p. 103.

2. A phoneme may be represented by more than one vowel letter. p. 103.

3. A single vowel in a closed accented syllable usually represents its short sound. p. 110, 112.

4. A letter may represent no phoneme; that is, it may be silent. p. 111, 116, 146.

5. When a one-syllable word or accented syllable contains two vowels, one of which is a final *e,* the first vowel usually represents its long sound and the final *e* is silent. p. 116, 126.

6. A single vowel in an open accented syllable often represents its long sound. p. 121, 126.

7. When *i* is followed by *gh* or when *i* or *o* is followed by *ld,* the vowel usually represents its long sound. p. 123, 126.

8. If the only vowel letter in a word or syllable is followed by *r,* the vowel sound will be affected by that *r.* p. 137, 138.

9. If the only vowel in a word or syllable is an *a* followed by *l* or *w,* the sound of the *a* is usually that heard in *ball.* p. 137, 138.

10. When two vowel letters appear together in a one-syllable word or in an accented syllable, the first vowel often represents its long sound and the second is silent. This holds true most often for *ai, oa, ee, ey, ay* combinations. p. 146, 147, 149.

11. The vowel *y* always follows the vowel or is the only vowel in a syllable and is silent or represents the phonemes we associate with *i* or *e.* p. 124, 126.

12. Although a syllable may have more than one vowel letter, there is only one vowel phoneme in a syllable. p. 146, 197.

13. Vowels behave differently in accented and unaccented syllables. The vowel is most clearly heard in the accented syllable. p. 123, 189, 197.
14. The vowel in most unaccented syllables represents the ə or ĭ. p. 128, 131.

Accent Clues

1. The vowel phoneme is the most prominent part of the syllable. p. 189.
2. When a word contains a prefix and/or a suffix, the accent usually falls on or within the root word. p. 190, 197.
3. The accent usually falls on or within the first word of a compound word. p. 191, 197.
4. In a two-syllable word that functions as either a noun or a verb, the accent is usually on the first syllable when the word functions as a noun and on the second syllable when the word functions as a verb. p. 191, 197.
5. When there is a double consonant within a word, the accent usually falls on the syllable that ends with the first letter of the double consonant. p. 191, 197.
6. In multisyllabic words ending in *tion* or *ic,* the primary accent falls on the syllable preceding the *tion* ending. p. 192, 197.
7. When the vowel phoneme within the last syllable of a two-syllable word is composed of two vowel letters, that syllable is usually accented. p. 193, 197.
8. When there is no other clue in a two-syllable word, the accent most often falls on the first syllable. p. 194, 197.

Syllabic Division

1. In a compound word, the syllabic division usually comes between the words of which it is composed. p. 204, 211.
2. Prefixes and suffixes usually form separate syllables from the root word. p. 207, 211.
3. If the last syllable of a word ends in *le* preceded by a consonant, that consonant usually begins the last syllable. p. 208, 211.
4. If the first vowel in a two-syllable word is followed by a single consonant, that consonant often begins the second syllable. p. 199, 202, 211.
5. When two vowel letters are separated by two consonants, the syllabic division usually occurs between the consonants. p. 200, 211.
6. In syllabication, digraphs are treated as representing single phonemes. p. 205, 211.

Appendix B:

Graphemes, Key Symbols, and Key Words

Grapheme	Key Symbol	Key Word	Grapheme	Key Symbol	Key Word
Single Consonants			**Long Vowels**		
b	b	*boat*	a	ā	*apron*
c	no key symbol	no key word	e	ē	*eraser*
d	d	*dog*	i	ī	*ice*
f	f	*fish*	o	ō	*overalls*
g	g	*goat*	u	ū	*unicorn*
h	h	*hat*			
j	j	*jeep*			
k	k	*kite*			
l	l	*lion*			
m	m	*moon*	**Schwa** (Vowels in Unaccented Syllables)		
n	n	*nut*	a	ə	*comma*
p	p	*pig*	e	ə	*chicken*
q	no key symbol	no key word	i	ə	*family*
r	r	*ring*	o	ə	*button*
s	s	*sun*	u	ə	*circus*
t	t	*table*			
v	v	*van*	**Other Single Vowels**		
w	w	*wagon*	a	â	*care*
x	no key symbol	no key word	u	û	*fur*
y	y	*yo-yo*	a	ä	*father*
z	z	*zipper*	a	ô	*ball*

Grapheme	Key Symbol	Key Word	Grapheme	Key Symbol	Key Word
Consonant Digraphs			**Diphthongs**		
ch	ch	*chair*	oi, oy	oi	*oil*
sh	sh	*ship*	ou, ow	ou	*house*
th	th	*thumb*			
th	t͟h	*that*	**Digraphs**		
wh	wh	*whale*	oo	$\overline{oo}$	*food*
	zh	*treasure*	oo	$\overset{\smile}{oo}$	*hook*
ng	*ng*	*king*			
Short Vowels			**Vowel Pairs**		
a	ă	*apple*	ai (rain)	ā	*apron*
e	ĕ	*edge*	ay (play)	ā	*apron*
i	ĭ	*igloo*	ea (each)	ē	*eraser*
o	ŏ	*ox*	ee (keep)	ē	*eraser*
u	ŭ	*umbrella*	oa (boat)	ō	*overalls*